STUDIES IN HONOR OF
ROBERT TER HORST

STUDIES IN HONOR OF ROBERT TER HORST

Edited by

Eleanor ter Horst, Edward H. Friedman
&
Ali Shehzad Zaidi

TSI Press

Transformative Studies Institute Press
39-09 Berdan Avenue
Fair Lawn, NJ 07410 USA.

Names: Ter Horst, Eleanor E., 1965- editor. | Friedman, Edward H., editor. | Zaidi, Ali Shehzad, 1959- editor. | Ter Horst, Robert, 1929- honouree.

Title: Studies in honor of Robert ter Horst / edited by Eleanor ter Horst, Edward H. Friedman & Ali Shehzad Zaidi.

Description: Fair Lawn, NJ: Transformative Studies Institute Press, [2017] Includes bibliographical references.

Identifiers: ISBN: 978-0-9832982-2-9 | LCCN: 2016958967

Subjects: LCSH: Ter Horst, Robert, 1929- | Spanish literature--History and criticism. | Spanish fiction--Classical period, 1500-1700--History and criticism. | Comparative literature --Spanish and English. | Comparative literature--English and Spanish. | American literature—Spanish influences. | English literature--Spanish influences. | LCGFT: Festschriften. | BISAC: LITERARY CRITICISM / Comparative Literature. | LITERARY CRITICISM / European / Spanish & Portuguese. | LITERARY CRITICISM / Modern / 17th Century.

Classification: LCC: PQ6132 .S88 2017 | DDC: 860.9--dc23

Copyeditor: Norman Ware
Cover Design: Carlos Ramirez Ruiz
Print Compilation: John Asimakopoulos
Technical Processing: Sviatoslav Voloshin

Contents

Introduction

"Ce vice impuni, la lecture":
A Double Life in Reading and Writing

Eleanor ter Horst

The lure of reading and a temptation to disturb the writing process drew me into my father's study on summer mornings, when the heat of the Arizona sun seemed to melt the streets and I sought the cooler recesses of the house. I knew that I should leave him alone to concentrate on his book, or the article that he was trying to finish, but I also knew that my intrusion would remain unpunished. Though my father did his best to sequester himself while he wrote, his study became a crossroads of sorts: its sliding glass door opening to the back yard provided a quick passageway for me and my sister, our dogs would sometimes trot up and press their noses to the glass from the outside, and a cat would occasionally venture in to sleep in the sun. Irresistibly drawn inside to search out a book, ask him a question, or show him some object that I had found or made, I would find him perched at the desk, surrounded by books stacked on the desk itself, on the floor, and of course filling the shelves that covered almost every inch of available wall space. In front of him on the desk resided a neat stack of legal-sized yellow pages filled with careful, precise, but not always decipherable handwriting, exceeding the marked margins of the page. If I ventured to take a peek at the writing on the yellow pads, I could find little evidence of changes or corrections, no apparent eraser dust or words crossed out, at most an addition inserted between two lines. Later, he told me that he composed in his head before committing words to paper. Over pre-dinner cocktails, he would sometimes read aloud to my mother what he had written during the day and, though I understood little of what he read, I liked to listen to the rise and fall of his voice, followed by my mother's softer and more concise reply.

My parents were both devoted to the literary vices, having met as graduate students at Johns Hopkins. They traded books back and forth, discussed the merits and flaws of various authors, and spent much of their available free time reading novels, biographies, magazines, and newspapers. After dinner every night, my father would read aloud to me and my sister, starting with children's books when we were young and progressing through classic authors such as Dickens. At times, he may have regretted these more sophisticated choices, as when he found himself compelled to explain as best he could to a literate but inexperienced preteen the illogic of a debtors' prison or the work of a prostitute. Reading was my solitary entertainment too; my parents never had a television when my sister and I were growing up, and I had only a vague familiarity with the popular shows that I watched occasionally at the houses of friends who thought me deprived. I preferred an absorbing book to most television, though, and was unmoved by my friends' favorite vices: soap operas or superheroes. My parents both helped guide my choice of reading while giving me full freedom to peruse even the lowest of genres (science fiction, according to my father). My mother often took me and my sister to the public library and let us loose among the reading selections. My father bought us books, starting with the Little Golden Books series, of which we acquired a large collection, and, as I grew older, made suggestions of books that I might enjoy from the collection in his study, or from my parents' combined library.

My father has always been a patient and insightful reader of my writings, beginning with the poems and short stories that filled my notebooks as a child and continuing with the papers that I wrote as an undergraduate, and my first articles as an assistant professor. He took particular delight in reading the comments of my college professors—he did not see the papers until after they had been turned in and graded—some of whom wrote lengthy exhortations that I consider a different approach or method of organization. My father was amused by the exchanges, although he took a dim view of the prescriptive approach to writing. As I began to read his scholarly work, I understood why, since he prefers to approach a topic via a circuitous route that accumulates many fascinating, sometimes seemingly arbitrary connections along the way, only to shape all the disparate pieces of the journey into a meaningful pattern at the end: not your standard academic prose. He has always been a discerning reader of my scholarly work; I believe that he has read all of my articles either before or after publication, and though I sometimes fear that his critical eye will pick out a hidden flaw in the argument, I know he will also find a facet that lends itself to further exploration or connects with something else that he has read. I am glad that we can now read and write in closer proximity, since he and his library moved to Mobile, Alabama, shortly after I made the move here to take a job at the University of South Alabama.

Although I work in French and German rather than Spanish and fill computer screens rather than yellow pads with prose, my father's devotion to the twin vices of reading and writing helped me to see the scholarly life as not only possible but intrinsically rewarding. My contribution to this volume is meant as a continuation of the dialogue that we have held over the years, as well as a tribute to his influence as my first teacher and guide.

Introduction

A Guide in the Desert

Edward H. Friedman

When I started a new position at Arizona State University in Tempe in the fall of 1977, I was fortunate to find a colleague in early modern Spanish literature and a soon-to-be friend at the University of Arizona in Tucson. I was familiar with the publications of Professor Robert ter Horst, and I had met him at a conference and had seen him at others, but it was a privilege and a learning experience to have him a two-hour drive away. As all who know him realize, Bob ter Horst is exceptionally erudite, and his routine conversation is as elegant and allusion filled as his writing. Over the years, I invited him to speak at ASU, and he invited me to speak at the U of A. I appreciated and profited from the encounters, and I considered him to be a model and a mentor. His expertise in poetry, narrative, and drama impressed me tremendously, as did his skills in comparative studies and his equally admirable background in the plastic arts. We spoke, with good memories and high regard, of our graduate programs at Johns Hopkins. Even after we both left Arizona for different positions—Bob's was at the University of Rochester—we stayed in touch and saw each other at meetings, and, of course, I continued reading his always brilliant work with great interest. I regularly assign his books and essays to my graduate students, who praise his broad knowledge and his eloquent style. They also note, most respectfully, that it takes some effort to absorb the wealth of ideas contained in every essay or chapter. It may not be coincidental that Bob has chosen to write primarily on the baroque period. He has an indisputably baroque sensibility and, arguably, and in the best sense of the term, a baroque mind. He is a unique, fascinating, and decisive presence. I am grateful for his friendship. I congratulate Robert ter Horst on his distinguished career and on his accomplishments in the profession. I wish him the best in his retirement. I am delighted to collaborate here with his scholar/daughter Nell, whom I have known since she was a young girl, and with Ali Zaidi, one of his more recent doctoral students.

Introduction

High Tea

Ali Shehzad Zaidi

Scholars are best honored through scholarship, and this volume, comprising contributions from former colleagues and students, friends, and a daughter, is meant to honor Professor Robert ter Horst and a lifetime of scholarly absorption and patient mentoring. Over the years, I have reminisced about Professor ter Horst with former classmates at the University of Rochester (UR), including Micaela Heigl, Arleen Chiclana, and Joseph Oliveira. His lectures would unfold in marvelously complex sentences with richly expressive subordinate clauses, displaying a prodigious understanding of classical mythology and of the artistic, literary, historical, and religious contexts of the Spanish Golden Age.

I took two graduate courses with Professor ter Horst during my first year of doctoral study in comparative literature at UR: Colonial Latin American Literature in fall 1993 and Parallel Lives in spring 1994. From the latter course, in which we examined paired Shakespearean and Calderonian plays, I finally emerged as a scholar. Professor ter Horst never failed to recognize the occasional flash of insight or flight of poetry, and he gently steered me away from purple prose. Once, when I described a character in the process of spiritual awakening as having an "enlarged heart," Professor ter Horst observed that it sounded like a medical condition.

Around this time I became acquainted with Professor ter Horst's magnificent book, *Calderón: The Secular Plays*, which I used for my doctoral dissertation. Even before reading it, I already knew that Professor ter Horst was a great scholar. Professor Ottavio Di Camillo, my graduate advisor at Queens College, where I had completed a master of arts in Spanish, had urged me to attend UR in order to study under Professor ter Horst. Although my first year at UR proved fulfilling, the idyll did not last long.

In November 1995, barely a year and a half after I had entered the doctoral program in comparative literature, the UR administration, as part of its Renaissance Plan, suspended that program along with the master's programs in French, Spanish, and German. In the wake of those devastating cuts, two professors on my thesis committee promptly departed UR for greener academic pastures. Several fellow graduate students left UR in order to complete their doctoral study elsewhere.

During this period, in which the Department of Modern Languages and Cultures felt like a sinking ship, Professor ter Horst remained a constant source of support for his remaining graduate students, without which we could never have completed our doctorates.

I still recall the discussions that I had with Professor ter Horst regarding the corporate greed that was destroying the humanities. Professor ter Horst once remarked to me that our universities were beyond redemption and that we would have to begin anew. He envisioned small colleges in which faculty would take turns serving as administrators. Although he expressed his concern to me that we were losing our sense of the past, Professor ter Horst reassured me: "There is still something that they cannot take." In the years that followed those conversations, the corporatization of universities continued apace with the advent of automated virtual learning, the growing impoverishment of adjunct instructors, and steep increases in student debt that now surpasses $1.3 trillion in the United States. Even so, Professor ter Horst's words continue to resonate and ground me in a reality that even our corporate overlords, who seem to want it all, still cannot take.

Prior to his recent move to Mobile, Alabama, Professor ter Horst lived on Milton Street in the Nineteenth Ward, Rochester's only integrated neighborhood. His bookshelves overflowed with the complete works of Balzac, Zola, Dickens, and a great many other writers. A few years ago, accompanied by my wife Yasmeen, I visited Professor ter Horst in his Rochester home. Yasmeen, who is from Pakistan, was delighted by our reception, which unexpectedly included high tea complete with the fine fruit, pastries, hospitality, and decorum that it entails. There was something eminently civilized about the experience.

Looking back, I realize now that the same could be said about Professor ter Horst's classes. For those of us who were about to be initiated into a profession now under siege, those classes were nothing less than High Tea. Although, as Max Leon Forman avers, "teachers are people who start things they never see finished and for which they never get thanks until it is too late," we trust that this volume will appear in time to pay homage to a dedicated scholar and express gratitude to a venerated teacher.

1

On the Road: Traveling in the *Comedia*

William R. Blue

Pennsylvania State University

As part of the introduction to his topically arranged anthology of selections from the writings of foreign visitors to the Iberian peninsula in the seventeenth century, José María Díez Borque signals the role of the journey in a number of Spanish texts: *Poema de Mío Cid*, *Libro de Apolonio*, *Lazarillo de Tormes*, *Don Quijote*, *Naufragios*, *Historia de la Conquista de Méjico*, and others (12–17). The picaresque novel's episodic, discontinuous form lends itself to considerations of the spaces and places through which the peripatetic characters move, and Don Quijote's late-life odyssey is displayed through three cotangent circular voyages (see Steven Hutchinson's *Cervantine Journeys*). Literature, historical narrative, and travelers' memoirs converge on the adventure and adversity of the journey and on its potentially transformative powers.

The *Comedia*, too, presents characters traveling from one place to another, and most often Madrid is their destination. All or parts of the following works, among others, take place on the road: *Desde Toledo a Madrid*, *La villana de Vallecas*, *La huerta de Juan Fernández*, and *La villana de la Sagra* by Tirso de Molina; *La moza de cántaro*, *La villana de Getafe*, and *La dama boba* by Lope de Vega Carpio; *Las paredes oyen* by Juan Ruiz de Alarcón; *Entre bobos anda el juego* by Francisco de Rojas Zorrilla; and *Famoso Entremés Getafe* by Juan Hurtado de Mendoza. While the *Comedia* does not have the novel's extension to show how characters can slowly change over time due to their travel experiences, the dramatized road adventure nonetheless produces modulations, and sometimes transformations, in characters' actions and attitudes. In this essay, I will examine several aspects of travel and of space and place as observed by travelers and officials in seventeenth-century Spain. Then I will show how some of the plays mentioned take up these elements. Finally, I will focus on the effects of being on the road on the character Baltasar in *Desde Toledo a Madrid*.

The role of place and space in life and literature has recently been reconsidered as much more than a neutral background against which actions are played out.[1] A number of years ago, Henri Lefebvre, in *The*

Production of Space (1974), offered three separate but always interrelated definitions of space. The first is perceptible, sensible space, open to measurement and description. This space is materially as well as socially produced, both the medium and outcome of human activity, behavior, and experience. The second space is conceptual and thus involves the words, ideas, and abstractions used to try to make sense of spaces; therefore, it includes the realm of signs, codes, and discourse about space. It also engages with propositional knowledge of city planners, urbanists, and subdividers as well as the space of power, control, semiotic production, and ideology. This second space is a world of representations. Third is the lived space of inhabitants and users, the space of actual life and interchange among humans. It encompasses material and conceptual space simultaneously and depends on both. None of the three types of space exist in pure form independent of, or discrete from, the others, but rather all are forms or aspects of space that come fully into being by means of their complex interrelationships. All of these spaces come into play in the *Comedia* in general and the road plays in particular.

There was a lot of traffic on the roads in sixteenth- and seventeenth-century Spain, and the majority was commercial (see Ringrose 20–31). Providing for the needs and wants of citizens was the mainstay of commercial traffic, since, according to the Cortes de Castilla in 1579–1582, "not more than one household in thirty ... could get by with what it grew for itself" (Casey 55). In Philip II's survey, *Relaciones topográficas*, respondents from many towns are asked to report to "las cosas de las que tienen más falta, y de dónde se proveen de ellas" (4:206). To cite but one example, Getafe, a town that appears in several plays, the local officials state:

Las cosas de que hay más falta es de leña, aunque de muchas cosas tienen falta, que todas vienen de acarreo, que es de fruta y de aceite, hierro y herrajes y jabón y hortaliza, el hierro y herraje provéese de Vizcaya, y jabón de Valencia y de Ocaña, fruta verde y seca de la Vera de la Plascencia y de Almorox y de Illescas, leña donde tenemos dicho. [In answer to another question, the officials report that] ... es muy falto de leña, y los labradores que tienen carros y mulas van por ello al Real de Manzanares, que está siete u ocho leguas de este pueblo, y algunos van por ellos a Guadarrama que son a nueve leguas, y los serranos lo traen a vender con sus bueyes y carretas, y carbón se provee de Yébenes, que está diez y seis leguas de aquí ... y hortalizas de invierno y verano de Leganés, que está media legua de este pueblo. (1:392)

Other towns tell of their own shortages and relate from where they get their necessities, which accounts for some of the substantial cartage (*de acarreo*) traffic on the roads and in the inns in this period.

For a traveler, however, a journey in Spain in the early modern period was not a light undertaking because of the logistical difficulties, inconveniences, and real dangers of travel.[2] Reports from travelers who went to and through the peninsula on pilgrimages, on ambassadorial missions, as escorts to the high-born, or as part of a job are often vivid testaments to such hardships. In 1623, going south from Santander to Madrid, Richard Wynne found "the most wicked ways and country that ever Christian passed"; the mountains and woods were "very full of wild bears and wolves that divers times kill men" (qtd. in Hillgarth 44). In 1616, when the wife of John Digby (he was the English ambassador to Spain during the time of the "Spanish Match") "was traveling home in the spring through Asturias, 'divers of the mules that carried her stuff fell from the high rock of a great height into a river'" (44). According to a group of French Cistercians, along the way, "horses were treated better than human beings. ... In one village the Cistercians were 'lodged like pigs'; in another place they were without even bread, fire or water" (41). In addition, "[i]n the early sixteenth century robbers haunted the road over the Pyrenees and also that along the coast south of Barcelona. ... While the danger from bandits in Catalonia diminished after 1640 it continued to be felt in the rest of Spain, and especially in Andalusia and the Kingdom of Valencia" (45, 46).

But not just foreigners complain. The Count of Gondomar, Spain's ambassador to England (1613–1618), "got to know the roads well between Madrid, then capital of a world empire, and the Cantabrian ports. His verdict was that 'traveling through (Spain) is more painful and uncomfortable than through any deserted region anywhere in Europe, for there are no beds to be had, no inns, no food'" (Casey 12). Saint Teresa writes of her journey to Andalusia:

> Por priesa que nos dimos, llegamos a Sevilla el jueves antes de la Santísima Trinidad, habiendo pasado grandísimo calor en el camino; porque, aunque no se caminaba las siestas, yo os digo, hermanas, que como había dado todo el sol a los carros, que era entrar en ellos como en un purgatorio. (Teresa de Jesús 1:49)

Traveling often involved the use of coaches, litters, and carts, and the animals that provided the power for these conveyances most frequently in Spain were mules. "Spain could boast of fine Andalusian thoroughbreds," James Casey writes, "but they were scarce. ... Spain was, above all, the land of the mule" (12; see also Ringrose 43–44). A good day's travel, then, depended upon the animals' speed and the weight they were transporting, so one could expect about eight to ten leagues (a league is 5.5 kilometers, or 3.42 miles) on average.[3] A trip from Barcelona to Madrid would take about two weeks, and then from Madrid to Seville, ten days. In total, and if all went well, it took twenty-four to twenty-five days of steady trekking from the principal Mediterranean port to reach the departure point to the New World (Casey 14).

In 1593, Philip II set the price and average day's journey for "el alquiler de bestias." He estimated that "las tales bestias andan ocho leguas por día de promedio" (Menéndez Pidal 89). The price was to be

> dos reales por día y cincuenta reales por mes, ... [y] por el mozo que acompañe, se pagarán cuatro reales diarios. Pero solo siete años después, los precios habían subido bastante, ya que los siete reales que ... se habían de pagar diariamente por acémila y mozo, en 1600 se han convertido en once reales." (Menéndez Pidal 89)

To get to their destinations and ease the burdens of the journey, travelers sometimes depended on professional drivers. As Antoine de Brunel recounts,

> Muy pronto nos fue preciso aprender a viajar a la moda del país, que es ir a comprar en diversos lugares lo que se quiere comer. Habíamos hecho alto en San Sebastián en parte para proveernos de un *mozo de mulas*, es decir, de un criado de cochero que nos sirviese de guía hasta Madrid, y que cuidara de comprar nuestros víveros y de llevar nuestras provisiones. (qtd. in Díez Borque 219; emphasis mine)

Jean Muret, who was an aide to the French ambassador, recalls:

> Ordinariamente no encontraréis más que una [posada] o dos en cada legua, y notáis que no os proporcionan allí más que la cama y los utensilios, de suerte que necesitáis ir a buscar vosotros mismos la vianda, el pan, el vino y hasta la sal. Por suerte, yo tenía un *mozo de mulas* muy inteligente, que me libraba de ese trabajo. (qtd. in Díez Borque 222; emphasis mine)

The *Comedia* also dramatizes that reality. When the Indiano in Lope's *La moza de cántaro* mentions that the party is near Adamuz, his *mozo de mulas* assents and adds: "Mas mira que desde aquí / comienza Sierra Morena"; the Indiano responds by delegating travel planning responsibility to his guide: "Tú las jornadas ordena; / eso no corre por mí" (Vega Carpio 129–30). In *Desde Toledo a Madrid*, Baltasar, disguised as Lucas Berrio, not only is in charge of the trip, even to the point of telling the travelers how they will ride, but he gives them a description of the various jobs of those who work in the companies that take travelers from one place to another.

All along the route, finding food and adequate lodging was often a problem for travelers. In 1560, Philip II lifts a ban against inns selling food to travelers:

> Para evitar los daños e inconvenientes que los caminantes se siguen de no hallar, en los mesones donde vienen a posar, los mantenimientos necesarios, y los ir a buscar fuera de ello, viniendo como vienen cansados, por razón de las ordenanzas que hay en los pueblos para que en los dichos mesones no se vendan ni tengan, Ordenamos … que en los mesones de estos reinos … puedan tener y vender, para la provision y mantenimiento de los caminantes …, y que los dichos caminantes puedan tomar y comprar, así de los mantenimientos que en los dichos mesones hobiere como de otras partes como quisieran. (Menéndez Pidal 87)

Antoine de Brunel wrote the following less generous account about the provisions on the road and advice for preparations:

> En cuanto se ha llegado a la posada, se pregunta si hay camas, y después de haberse provisto de ellas, es preciso o dar la carne cruda que se lleva a cocer, o bien ir a comprarla a la carnicería. Si se encuentra algún capón, gallina o perdiz, se trata de acomodarse con ello. Nos decían que de estos últimos animales, comeríamos gran cantidad y mucho más gruesos y grandes y de mejor gusto que los de Francia; pero jamás encontramos más que uno, que además no tenía todas estas ventajas. Lo mejor es llevar la carne en sus alforjas, y comprar y aprovisionarse de lo que se encuentra en el lugar donde se esté. (qtd. in Díez Borque 219)

Madame D'Aulnoy, on the other hand, presents a mixed review:

> These ceremonies over, you are asked if you will eat anything, and though at midnight, you must send to the butchery, the market, the tavern, the bakers, in fine, to all parts of town, to gather wherewith to make a sorry meal. For though the mutton here be very tender, their way of frying it with oil is not to everybody's relish. Here are a great

store of partridges, and those very large; they are not very fat, but dry, and to make'em drier they roast them to a coal. The pigeons here are excellent. … The bread is white enough, and sweet that one would think it made up with sugar; but it is ill-wrought and so little baked that it is as heavy as lead in the stomach; it has the shape of a flat cake and is not much thicker than one's finger. The wine is good and fruits in their season, especially grapes, which are very large and of delicate taste. You may reckon yourself certain of a good dessert. You have salads here of such good lettuce as the world cannot afford better. (71–72)

One can find in the plays even more information about speed of travel, expenses, contractual terms, and towns, while others reference the material aspects of roads, towns, inns, and conveyances as well as some of the semiotic, conceptual aspects of the inconveniences, the dirtiness, and the bother of travel.

Yet despite hardships and scarcities, travel could lead to conviviality. In *La villana de Vallecas*, Don Pedro de Mendoza and his servant, Agudo, arrive around midnight to the rather well-appointed inn in Aranda, described above, some four leagues from Madrid on the road between the capital and Valencia. They have come from Mexico via San Lúcar and most recently Cuenca, where Pedro had family business that required his attention. They plan to have dinner and briefly rest before pushing on to Madrid. When Pedro asks what they have for dinner, Agudo lists some items the inn will provide and others he has brought along:

> Puesto está un conejo a asar,
> y una perdiz, a quien coca
> una bota yepesina,
> mezclada con hipocraz … (Molina, *La villana de Vallecas* 419–22)
> Hay una gallina,
> fiambre y medio pernil … (424–25)
> Hay medio barril
> de aceitunas … (429–30)
> Y si en postres asegundas,
> en conserva hay piña indiana,
> y en tres o cuatro pipotes
> mamayes, cipizapotes;
> y si de la castellana
> gustas, hay melocotón
> y perada; y al fin saco
> un tubano de tabaco
> para echar la bendición. (432–40)

Pedro, content with what his servant has to offer for dinner, also wants to know if there might be someone of his rank to dine with. At that moment, Don Gabriel arrives with his servant, Cornejo. Pedro immediately seeks his company and invites Gabriel to share his room and food:

Cornejo:	Huésped, venga un aposento.
Pedro:	En el nuestro puede estar,
	Que luego hemos de picar,
	Y recibiré contento
	Que favorezcáis mi mesa. (461–65)

The two men then combine their provisions as Pedro adds another rabbit and partridges to the meal and Gabriel, a capon (470–72). Brief pleasantries precede friendly conversation about goings-on in Madrid.

The conditions in many inns, however, were less agreeable. In 1616, the Count of Gondomar complains that the rascals who run the inns are making commerce and travel impossible because one cannot find "en España mesones en que pueda posar un caballero que camina, cosa que la desacredita mucho con las demás naciones, y dicen que es menester caminar en España con bota y alforja, y dormir en el suelo como por los desiertos de Armenia" (Menéndez Pidal 87–88). Saint Teresa recalls her experiences, while ill, in an inn near Córdoba in 1575:

No os dejaré de decir la mala posada que hubo para esta necesidad: fue darnos una camarilla a teja vana; ella no tenía ventana, y si se abría la puerta, toda se henchía de sol. … Hiciéronme echar una cama, que yo tuviera por mejor echarme en el suelo; porque era de unas partes tan alta y de otras tan baja que no sabía cómo poder estar, porque parecía de piedras agudas. (50–51)

María de San José, remembering the same inn, adds:

Teníamos … un aposentillo—que creo habían estado en él puercos— tan bajo el techo que apenas podíamos andar derechas y que por mil partes entraba el sol, que con mantos y velos separábamos. La cama era tal que nuestra madre significa en el "Libro de las fundaciones"; solo esto echaba de ver, y no la multitud de telarañas y sabandijas que había. Y esto, que estuvo en nuestra mano remediar, se hizo. Mas fue lo que pasó por el espacio que allí estuvimos con los gritos y juramentos de la gente que había en la venta y el tormento de los bailes y pandero, sin bastar ruegos ni dádivas para los hacer quitar de sobre la cabeza de nuestra santa madre. (qtd. in Teresa de Jesús 51n82)[4]

As late as 1679, Madame D'Aulnoy writes: "I am told I must furnish myself with good stores of provisions to prevent starving in some places through which we must pass; and gammons of bacon, dried tongues, being much esteemed in this country. I have taken up a good quantity; and as to the rest we have been sufficiently provided" (29). She offers the following descriptions and observations:

> [Near Huesca] you are shown a chamber whose walls are white enough. ... The beds are without curtains, the covertures of cotton, the sheets as large as napkins, and the napkins like pocket handkerchiefs. ... They have only a cup in the house; and if the muleteers get first hold of it, you must stay patiently till they have done with it or drink out of an earthen pitcher. It is impossible to warm one at the kitchen-fire without being choked, for they have no chimneys. ... There is a hole in the top of the ceiling and the smoke goes out there. (69)
>
> ... We can easily perceive that we are not far from Madrid ... but it seems very strange to us that in the inns which are nearest to the great town you are worse used than in those which are a hundred leagues distant. ... [M]y chamber stands even with the stable; it is a hole that needs a light at noon. (157)

Travelers write that it is advisable to bring along bedding as well as food (as did Juan Pérez de Viedma, *el oidor*, in *Don Quijote* 1:42), and yet others complain of small but constant annoyances and inconveniences, such as the Italian priest who says he could rarely find privies and thus was forced to use the stable or look for a nearby bush (Hillgarth 41; for more, see 38–51). Travel required people to adapt.

Characters, too, describe and comment on the inns where they stay, mentioning, for example, the *puerta principal*, *postigo*, *patio*, and distribution of rooms (see Rojas Zorrilla 950, 1160, 1317, 1322). Cabellera, a servant in *Entre bobos*, talks about the conditions and accommodations when rudely awakened one morning and having to leave "mi media con limpio" (946), a half of a bed that the innkeeper rents out guaranteeing that the occupant of the other half was "limpio" or disease free. But the definition of clean was relative, since Cabellera does grumble about fleas, "que hay muchas en este mesón" (1450). Alonso, a noble in Tirso's *Desde Toledo*, has an aversion to beds in any inn: "me recato / de camas que a tantos son / comunes" (2158–60). Don Felipe, a fellow traveler, adds that he always brings along his own bedding: "yo siempre me prevengo / de sábanas y almohadas / caseras, por las posadas" (2163–65). Don Alonso agrees that "el mismo cuidado tengo; / y de ordinario las llevo / en baúl como agora" (2166–68). Another character in *Entre bobos*, complaining about being up well past bedtime to help his master seek out the noble woman he loves, advises him that his search is ill timed: "Durmiendo todos agora / ... / De verla no es ocasión, / y ésta en que la vas a hablar / solo es hora de buscar / a la moza del mesón" (1351, 1355–58), perhaps bringing to mind Maritornes's late-night adventure in Juan Palomeque's inn (*Don Quijote* 1:16). In *Desde Toledo*, Don Felipe puts the two topics plus the seasonal difficulties of travel together with the following indelicate comparison: "Camas y lodos / déjanse pisar de todos, / como mozas de mesón" (2160–62).

Miserable though some inns may have been,[5] others, perhaps a rare few to judge by travelers' accounts, are well kept and well appointed. To Don Pedro's question about the accommodations in Arganda del Ray in *La villana de Vallecas*, his servant Agudo offers a glowing description of the fine sheets and pillowcases, of paintings and decorations.[6]

The dramatists seem to be quite familiar with the towns and inns, especially those near Madrid, and some of the plays present a virtual travel map and guidebook. Places such as Getafe, Arganda del Rey, Torrejón, Illescas, Cabañas, Olías, Magán, and Leganés regularly appear. The dramatists were also knowledgeable about the roads and distances. For example, Doña Mayor in *Desde Toledo a Madrid* accurately states that "hemos andado / legua y media" since leaving Toledo and arriving in Olias. Doña Petronila in Tirso's *La huerta de Juan Fernández* remarks that the distance the disguised Tomasa has covered between Ocaña and the Venta del Promultor where the first scene of the play occurs is far enough to justify giving more feed to her mule than Tomasa had planned: "Si tres leguas caminó, / no me parece, mancebo, / que es el pienso suficiente / de un cuartillo (11–14). In the *Repertorio*, we discover that, in fact, the distance from Ocaña to Toledo was two leagues (40), and from Toledo to the Venta, another league (39).[7]

Characters in the plays talk about and offer their opinions of the towns and inns they pass through:

Cabañas: No son las posadas frescas;
            pero todo carro o coche
            en Cabañas da cebada.
            Venteros leí que fueron
            sus fundadores; sacad

destos principios qué tales
serán los más principales
desta insigne vecindad.
(Molina, *Desde Toledo* 1471–73, 1474–80)

Arganda: No es Arganda mala villa
tiene un soto que sustenta con su
caza, y entretiene
a sus vecinos y dueños.
Corren toros jarameños
que a gozar la corte viene
por pasar por el Jarama,
de quien sus vecinos beben
las fuerzas con que se atreven,
que son bravos de la fama.
(Molina, *La villana de Vallecas* 299–305)

Road conditions were often difficult, and delays and accidents happened. Saint Teresa, about one of her journeys, says: "Pues las posadas, como no se podían andar jornadas a causa de los malos caminos, que era muy ordinario anegarse los carros en el cieno, habían de pasar de unas bestias a el otro para sacarles" (Teresa de Jesús 2:188). In the very first scene of Tirso's *Por el sótano y el torno*, near the Venta de Viveros on the road from Alcalá to Madrid, the audience might not be too surprised to hear off-stage voices narrate a similar accident:

Rincón: ¿Atascóse en el barro?
¡Ahí mil diablos con el coche y el carro! …
desunce aquesas mulas, picarillo …
prestadme las reatas …
Polonia: ¡Ay, que se vuelca!
Ramos: Pónganse de patas;
Apéense señores …
Muchas voces: ¡Jesús, Jesús!
Ramos: Desunce. ¿Qué reculas,
Perico, que se ahorcan esas mulas?
Rincón: Corta camellos, puto.
¡Que se te vuelque el coche en lo enjuto!
Date prisa, desata.
Una mujer: ¡San Diego, que me ahoga, que me mata! (1–18)

There were other kinds of problems on the road, for example, breakdowns: "¡Para, cochero" Cabellera shouts in *Entre bobos*, "el coche se ha volcado! / El cibión del coche se ha quebrado" (Rojas Zorrilla 2015–16). Baltasar (disguised as Lucas Berrío in *Desde Toledo*) reports that "Hase quebrado la rueda, / y es fuerza arrancar más tarde" (2511–12). More personal accidents may occur as well: "Parad el coche, hermano," warns Doña Mayor (*Desde Toledo*), "¿Quieran que eche las entrañas?" Let's keep going, says another traveler, "Poco hay desde aquí a Cabañas," to which Mayor responds, "Menos hay de la boca a las entrañas" (984, 988, 1053–54). And in *La villana de Vallecas*, in an inn, two groups of travelers take the wrong luggage: "Las maletas troqué, señor, por yerro. / Era de noche y mucha la bebida" (702–3). Characters, like real travelers, must learn to adjust to unpredictable circumstances.

In the plays, the road can become a kind of liminal space where, for example, class or even gender can be questioned, exchanged, or reversed.[8] It can promote the quick establishment of friendships and may reduce the standard formalities that would be required if the same people were in their hometowns. When the Indiano sees Doña María (*La moza de cántaro*) dressed as a lower-class "mujer brava," he approaches her, saying:

> Como suelen los caminos
> Dar licencia a los que pasan
> Para entretener las horas
> Que por ellos son tan largas,
> A preguntaros me atrevo. (Vega Carpio 825–29)

In *La huerta de Juan Fernández*, Doña Petronila, disguised as a man (Don Gómez), meets Tomasa, also in male dress (Bargas), in an inn between Toledo and Madrid, and the two strike up a conversation: "Mientras guisan la comida / en esa venta, y mi mesa / alegráis, a que os convido ..." (116–18). When another group arrives later on, Petronilla/Gómez becomes fast friends with the most important of the travelers, Conde Galeazo, such that, as she later states: "Hame cobrado amistad / de suerte, que no me permite / que de su lado me quite" (1202–4).

The plays also show how lived or experienced liminal space affects some characters. As *Desde Toledo a Madrid* opens, Tirso takes the chance encounter and love-at-first-sight motifs in the *Comedia* to nearly absurd extremes, given that Baltasar meets Mayor when he breaks into her house and room running from the law after killing a man on the street. She is to leave for Madrid the next morning with her father, other family members, and her fiancé and will be married upon arrival. Baltasar has abandoned a woman in Madrid, and one of her relatives is looking for him. Nonetheless, the two "fall in love" and at the end of the play, marry. Act 1 takes place in Toledo, while Acts 2 and 3 are on the road. In order to accompany

Mayor and not arouse suspicion, Baltasar rents an entire team of mules and conveyances, adopts the guise of Lucas Berrío, *sobrestante de ganado*, and hires himself out to Alonso, Mayor's father. Baltasar adopts a blunt, rough language, as well as a defiant attitude, and manages to fool everyone so thoroughly that even Mayor questions what she sees: "¿Ansí se desautoriza / valor y sangre que ilustra / persona de tantas partes? / ¿No pudiera hallar la industria / artificio más decente?" (1161–65). She expresses her doubts to him:

> Prométoos que cuando os vi
> concertar cabalgaduras
> con mi padre esta mañana,
> diestro en la desenvoltura
> interesable en el precio,
> malicioso en las preguntas
> y grosero en el lenguaje,
> que hizo el alma conjeturas
> sobre si érades de versa
> lo que parecéis de burla. (1331–40)

However, for the trick to work, Baltasar must be Lucas Berío. He must know how to act, talk, walk, eat, and treat everyone. He must absorb "the road" and make it his. By means of his transformation, the advantage he gains is that the traveling noblemen must deal with this person in ways that they would not have to deal with such people in the city. And, they believe, he is of no lasting consequence to their lives, since their contact is temporary. Thus, when Mayor devises a game in which she will pretend to be in love with and offer her hand to Lucas Berío, both her father and her fiancé think that it will be a grand joke. Alonso, Mayor's father, is delighted, "Por Dios que es el mejor rato / que nunca pensé tener" (2671–72), and when Don Luis, Mayor's fiancé, at first objects, Alonso says: "Pues hácenos merced Dios / de darnos con qué alegrar / molestias del esperar, / ¿y alborotáisnosla vos?" (2683–86). Luis relents and dismisses Lucas, "¡Hay más simple mentecato!" (2538). The atmosphere, the lived space he briefly shares with the *sobrestante de ganado*, is too fleeting for Luis to worry. Lucas and those of his ilk are simply dismissed as "grosero" (1453), "bárbaro" (1456), "mentecato" (2673), "bruto" (2692), and even as "animal" (2644).

When we first meet Baltasar, however, he speaks not like Lucas Berío but like the enamored *galán*. When he sees Mayor with a lighted candle in his hand, he exclaims:

¡Qué divina perfección!
Poco a poco resplandece
la mañana que enriquece
flores que su afeite son;
pero tanta agregación
junta, al mismo sol cegara.
Luz los ojos, luz la cara,
luz en las manos también.
Pródiga de luces, ten,
que más te quisiera avara. (445–54)

Later in Act 2, when he speaks to Mayor as himself and not as Lucas
Berrío, he still employs metaphors, but they are now more direct and
physical and thus show how his experiences on the road and as "Lucas"
influence Baltasar. So that they can be alone for a few minutes to talk,
Baltasar places thorns under the saddle of the mule on which Mayor is
riding:

valíme de las tinieblas
y del ramo de un espino,
plumaje de unos cambrones
que al bruto sin culpa aplico
debajo de la grupera,
el cual [al] instante mismo,
que sin ser enamorado,
lo escoció lo pungitivo
de los celos, y en tal parte
a puras coces y brincos
procuró librarse dellos,
de puro correr, corrido;
porque celos y cambrones
son deudos muy parecidos. (1813–26)

While on the road in Act 2, both Mayor and Baltasar speak very plainly,
leaving behind the courtly images and metaphors that they used in Act 1
(Blue 77–80). Equally interesting is that they employ *romances* in Act 2,
whereas in Act 1, before the journey and in Toledo, they spoke in
redondillas and *décimas*. In Act 2, while on the road, they use a more
popular form. In Act 3 as they approach Madrid and at the play's
conclusion, they return to *redondillas* and *décimas*; nonetheless, of the
play's last 423 lines, all but 59 are *romances*. Thus, when Baltasar
reappears dressed as himself ("Sale Don Baltasar muy bizarro ...") (3102),

he uses the same verse form as did Lucas Berrío in Act 2 and even declares: "No se altere / ninguno: Lucas Berrío / está aquí, si ya no quieren / que sea don Baltasar / de Córdoba" (3110–14). The road experience has produced a "new" character that speaks like and combines qualities of both Lucas and Baltasar.

In these plays, characters sometimes find themselves in the company of others on the road who regale them with songs, crude jokes, and *vayas*, which are a kind of insulting, name-calling banter between people from different towns or villages (see Salomon, esp. 566–71). In these exchanges, insults range from *mariones* to *berenjeneros* (people from Toledo), *ballenatos* (people from Madrid), *zupia* and *vinorres* or drunkards, *carnero* or cuckolds, *ninfa* or prostitutes, *puto*, *patán* (louts), and so on.

In *Desde Toledo a Madrid* and in the other plays, we can observe how the represented experience of the road affects the characters and changes their language, their perceptions of themselves and others, and their possibilities of action. On the road, the characters abandon not only their geographical space but at least partly their social place. They enter into a world on the move, a world of other travelers, of merchants, muleteers, innkeepers, peddlers, transporters, soldiers, thieves, migrant laborers, vagabonds, and *pícaros* (*communitas*, using Victor Turner's term).

In that sense, traveling in the *Comedia* in the "road environment" entails entertaining a broader view of others and a loosening of identity. Characters come unfixed from the familiar, safe, and secure social order where they and others "know their place." Being on the road may suggest that if this space—the road—can produce a more fluid self, then the place, the "safe space" the people must abandon to embark on a journey, may have produced a brittle personal and social construct that was "the cause" of their problems, and that is now subject to change by the constant movement and friction of the people and goods going from one place to another. But it may also be that the characters' experiences in the road plays are simply an interlude that catches them in flux between one station and another such that when they arrive at the new place or return to the old place, they will revert to who and what they were rather quickly. But for others, a return to the original place and state will not be easy because they have changed as a result of their encounters and adventures on the road. Planned marriages have fallen apart, new alliances have been created, and characters have developed new ways of seeing and being. Space has had an effect because the road is not neutral, not just an arbitrarily chosen and meaningless backdrop against which a set of actions have been displayed. The "road plays" portray the characters in transition, "betwixt and between," and allow them to explore their options, their identity, and their values as they move through a dynamic space.

Notes

[1] For example, see Sullivan, McMorran, Padrón, and García Santo-Tomás.

[2] Traveling anywhere in Europe in this period was an adventure. See Maczac.

[3] Average distances traveled depended, of course, on road conditions, season, and so on. While a league is officially 5.5 kilometers, people's perception of distance varied. In volume 3 of the *Relaciones*, we read: "[R]ecordemos que la legua equivale a unos 20.000 pies, es decir, 5.5 kms., en definitiva aproximadamente una hora andando a un ritmo normal, sin apretar el paso ni descansarlo—, nos hablarán de una legua 'grande,' 'pequeña,' o 'no grandes ni pequeñas' …, en donde más que la exactitud … regía la costumbre o la práctica: la legua grande sería algo más de una hora, la pequeña, unos tres cuartos de hora" (64).

[4] See also González Tascón 102.

[5] Some inns were often proverbially bad. See the Venta de Viveros in Fradejas Lebrero 142–46.

[6]   De Holanda
    prometen sábanas
    colcha y rodapiés también
    de red, con su flueco y randa;
    dos almohadas que alistan
    lazos de azul y amarillo
    debajo de un acerillo;
    y porque sus faldas vistan
    las manchas de la pared,
    tres sábanas …
    ya de lienzo, ya de red.
    Un cielo encima colgado,
    con fluecos del mismo modo,
    que, viéndole blanco todo,
    Dije, "el cielo esta mudado,"
    y los doseles, que son
    adorno del aposento;
    un prolijo paramento

pintada en él la Pasión,
y la historia de Susana
con los dos viejos y el baño,
y al otro lado del paño
un San Joaquín y Santa Ana,
y un ángel sobre la puerta
que con las alas los junta;
al otro un sayón que apunta
a un San Sebastián, que acierta,
luego un San Antón muy viejo
con su vestido de estera,
y debajo de la escalera,
junto a el, un San Alejo.
Remátase la labor
con la espigadera de Rud. (261–94)

[7] For distances, see *Repertorio de caminos ordenado por Alonso de Meneses Correo*, 1576. See also the commentary on Meneses's *Repertorio* and an earlier one by Pero Juan Villuga in González Tascón 91–92 and Menéndez Pidal 84–87. For more examples of literature and the towns, see Fradejas Lebrero.

[8] Parts of this section and others refer to Victor Turner's *The Ritual Process: Structure and Anti-Structure* wherein he introduced his ideas of "liminality" and "communitas." Among other pertinent observations are the following: "Liminal entities are neither here nor there; they are betwixt and between the positions assigned by law, custom, convention. … [A]s liminal beings they have no status. … It is as though there are two major 'models' for human interrelatedness, juxtaposed and alternating. The first is a society as a structural, differentiated … hierarchical system of politico-legal-economic positions with many types of evaluations separating men in terms of 'more' and 'less.' The second, which emerges recognizably in the liminal period, is of society as unstructured or rudimentarily structured and relatively undifferentiated comitatus." (95–96). While Turner confined his study to rituals and rites, as Simon Coleman and John Eade note, Turner's paradigm ran "the risk of … [the] implication that such travel [as pilgrimage] could somehow … be divorced from more everyday social, political, and cultural processes" (3), and they argue for broadening his notion to the point where the borders between travel, tourism, and pilgrimage blur, thus my adoption of some of Turner's ideas.

Works Cited

Blue, William R. *Spanish Comedias and Historical Contexts in the 1620s*. University Park: Pennsylvania State UP, 1996.

Casey, James. *Early Modern Spain: A Social History*. London: Routledge, 1999. http://dx.doi.org/10.4324/9780203255148

Coleman, Simon, and John Eade, eds. *Reframing Pilgrimage: Cultures in Motion*. London: Routledge, 2004.

D'Aulnoy, Marie Catherine Jumelle de Berneville. *Travels into Spain*. Ed. Sir E. Denison Ross and Ellen Power. London: George Routledge and Sons, 1930.

Díez Borque, José María. *La sociedad española y los viajeros del siglo XVII*. Madrid: S.G.E.L., 1975.

Fradejas Lebrero, José. *Geografía literaria de la provincia de Madrid*. Madrid: Instituto de Estudios Madrileños, Consejo Superior de Investigaciones Científicas, 1992.

Frye, Northrop. *Anatomy of Criticism*. Princeton: Princeton UP, 1957.

García Santo-Tomás, Enrique. *Espacio urbano y percepción literaria en el Madrid de Felipe IV*. Madrid: Iberoamericana Vervuert, 2004.

González Tascón, Ignacio. *Felipe II: Los ingenios y las máquinas; Ingeniería y obras públicas en la época de Felipe II*. Madrid: Sociedad Estatal para la Conmemoración de los Centenarios de Felipe II y Carlos V, 1998.

Hillgarth, J. N. *The Mirror of Spain, 1500–1700: The Formation of a Myth*. Ann Arbor: U of Michigan P, 2000. http://dx.doi.org/10.3998/mpub.16832

Hutchinson, Steven. *Cervantine Journeys*. Madison: University of Wisconsin Press, 1992.

Maczac, Antoni. *Travel in Early Modern Europe*. Tr. Ursula Phillips. Oxford: Polity Press, 1995.

McMorran, Will. *The Inn and the Traveler: Digressive Topographies in the Early Modern European Novel*. Oxford: Legenda, 2002.

Menéndez Pidal, Gonzalo. *Los caminos en la historia de España*. Madrid: Ediciones Cultura Hispánica, 1951.

Molina, Tirso de. *Desde Toledo a Madrid*. Ed. Berta Pallares. Madrid: Castalia, 1999.

———. *Don Gil de las calzas verdes*. Ed. Alonso Zamora Vicente. Madrid: Castalia, 1990.

———. *La huerta de Juan Fernández*. Ed. Berta Pallares. Madrid: Castalia, 1982.

———. *Por el sótano y el torno*. Ed. Alonso Zamora Vicente. Madrid: Castalia, 1994.

———. *La villana de la Sagra / El colmenero divino*. Ed. Berta Pallares. Madrid: Castalia, 1984.

———. *La villana de Vallecas*. Ed. Sofía Eiroa. Pamplona: GRISO, 2001.

Padrón, Ricardo. *The Spacious World: Cartography, Literature, and Empire in Early Modern Spain*. U of Chicago P, 2004.

Relaciones topográficas de Felipe II, Madrid. Vols. 1–2. *Transcripción de los manuscritos*. Ed. Alfredo Alvar Ezquerra, María Elena García Guerra, and María de los Angeles Vicioso Rodríguez. Madrid: Comunidad de Madrid / Consejo Superior de Estudios Científicos, 1993.

———. Vol. 3. *Estudio introductorio*. Ed. Alfredo Alvar Ezquerra. Madrid: Comunidad de Madrid / Consejo Superior de Estudios Científicos, 1993.

———. Vol. 4. *Apéndices y mapas*. Ed. Alfredo Alvar Ezquerra et al. Madrid: Comunidad de Madrid / Consejo Superior de Estudios Científicos, 1993.

Repertorio de caminos ordenado por Alfonso de Meneses Coreo (1576). Madrid: La Arcadia, 1946.

Ringrose, David R. *Transportation and Economic Stagnation in Spain, 1750–1850*. Durham: Duke UP, 1970.

Rojas Zorrilla, Francisco de. *Entre bobos anda el juego: Spanish Drama of the Golden Age*. Ed. Raymond R. MacCurdy. New York: Appleton-Century-Crofts, 1971. 521–72.

Salomon, Noël. *Lo villano en el teatro del Siglo de Oro*. Madrid: Castalia, 1985.

Sanford, Rhonda Lemke. *Maps and Memory in Early Modern England*. New York: Palgrave, 2002.

Sullivan, Garrett A., Jr. *The Drama of Landscape: Land, Property, and Social Relations on the Early Modern Stage*. Stanford: Stanford UP, 1998.

Teresa de Jesús. *Libro de las fundaciones*. 2 vols. Ed. José María Aguado. Madrid: Espasa Calpe, 1940.

Turner, Victor. *The Ritual Process: Structure and Anti-Structure*. Chicago: Aldine, 1969.

Vega Carpio, Lope de. *La moza de cántaro*. Ed. José María Díez Borque. Madrid: Espasa Calpe, 1970, 1990.

West, Russell. *Spatial Representations and the Jacobean Stage: From Shakespeare to Webster*. New York: Palgrave, 2002. http://dx.doi.org/10.1057/9781403913692

2

Self-Examination and Re-Creation in Early Modern Spanish Poetry

Edward H. Friedman

Vanderbilt University

My favorite sequel—as I suspect is the case for a corps of Hispanists—is the Alonso Fernández de Avellaneda *Quijote* of 1614, not so much because of an obvious brilliance as because of its timing. Avellaneda assuredly tortured Cervantes, but he also inspired and engaged him, and, as a result, the "legitimate" part 2 of *Don Quijote* is, as unions are sometimes called, "more perfect." Analogously, the Juan Martí sequel to *Guzmán de Alfarache*—published in 1602, between Mateo Alemán's two parts—allows the reader to see how the original writer processes the shock to his system and, significantly, to that of the eponymous protagonist. Alemán cannot bring about the tour de force of the *Quijote*—who can?— but he exposes new strings, new allegiances, and new creative powers, along with old resentments. *Don Quijote* and the picaresque have provided a rich legacy: a rich set of offspring that continue popping out, so to speak, to the present. The genre of poetry demonstrates a range of variations on themes *and* unlimited takes on what Harold Bloom famously has denominated as "the anxiety of influence." Poetic creation is a combination of re-creation and a struggle for innovation, or, as T. S. Eliot puts it, "tradition and the individual talent." The early modern Spanish sonnet lends itself beautifully to the dialectics of the stable and the unstable, a rigid form and a history of artistic achievement versus a search for novelty of expression and content. The sonnet originated in late medieval Italy, but its roots lay in classical antiquity, and such conventions as carpe diem and memento mori—not to mention mythological figures and topoi—belong to the ancient periods of poetic composition. And, of course, one does not want to forget the Bible. In Spain, the trajectory of Italianate verse and of the sonnet can be said to begin in the fifteenth century with Juan Boscán, or, earlier, with Íñigo López de Mendoza, the Marqués de Santillana. The calculated elegance, symmetry, and moderation of the Renaissance cede to baroque flourishes, conceits, relaxation of restraint, and excesses *sin límites*. The paths are often wondrous to behold, given that one can, in a sense, track changes in the development and evolution of motifs, subjects, and subject positions.

As a rule, then, the Renaissance poet blends into the scenery, as it were, while the baroque poet is patently, even egregiously, self-conscious. It would be a mistake, however, to suggest that Renaissance poets were other than strikingly inventive and resourceful, although they certainly were more controlled and less flagrantly competitive than their baroque counterparts. Conveyed broadly, all poets must bear in mind the burden and the provocation of the intertext. The writers must strive to be highly resourceful within structured patterns and long histories and to seek unique signatures as they both respect and confront precedent.

In preparing a recent essay, I looked at how early modern poets—from Juan Boscán to Sor Juana Inés de la Cruz—represent dreams in sonnets. In this context, dreams take numerous shapes. They may give the lover a respite from the pain of rejection by supplying happy endings. Some poets stress the idea of poetic justice: if one suffers in the real world, let him (or her) enjoy success in the realm of dreams; that is simply how it should be. To make the point, poets may emphasize the life-death dichotomy through antithesis, hyperbole, and other figures. One is *dying* in life, so let him (or her) *live* in dreams. Dreams may even take the lover all the way, as in the case of Francisco de Quevedo's admirer of the lady Floralba: "¿Dirélo? / Sí, pues que sueño fue: que te gozaba" (Rivers, *Renaissance* 280). The poetic speakers who find in the dream a salvation from the catastrophes of life beg not to wake up, although the return to reality is unavoidable. Still, the dream can be a welcome relief. The speaker may await the next slumber with optimism or may resent the inescapable return to "normalcy." The sonnets treat the theme of *engaño* negatively (as is to be expected) and positively (a paradoxical addendum to tradition). What if the dream *is* pure illusion, fantasy? If that is where one is to find satisfaction, so be it. Let *desengaño* be deferred, or eliminated; invert the premises. As more credence is conferred on the dream, the dream content is taken more seriously, to the extent that poets connect the love object to the soul, and the sonnets thus take on a spiritual aspect. On one end of the spectrum is the dream as unadulterated deception, while on the other extreme is a defense of the deception as redemptive, egalitarian, and part of a corrective mission. The feminine presence in the dream, in exceptional instances, can be linked to the soul. An intense departure from the saving grace of dreams is the approach in which the dream is merely an extension of hell on earth. The lover's humiliation is repeated in the dream, and the agony never subsides. Taken even further, the dream can be worse than a reality that is bad enough. The figurative death of unrequited love turns into dreams about death, on occasion administered by the lady herself. Dreams are corrective and dreams are nightmarish, and dreams can lie between the two. Luis de Góngora and Sor Juana Inés de la Cruz, among the writers of early modern Spain in general (and of Spanish inflection in the New World), glorify the imagination—also a locus of the best and the worst human instincts—and they transform the dream into a metonym for artistic creation and its countless orientations.

The sonnets are less about the interpretation of dreams than about the dialectics of dreams and love and about the creative process per se. What can be achieved in the fixed space of the sonnet is remarkable and demanding. Here, I would like to concentrate on the matter of continuity through repeated emphasis on the idea of introspection: "Cuando me paro a contemplar mi estado" (Rivers, *Renaissance* 34), the opening verse of Garcilaso de la Vega's Sonnet 1. This brand of self-examination forms part of a tradition that has been traced as far back as Ovid and that has been studied by eminent scholars including, among others, Rafael Lapesa, Elias Rivers, Edward Glaser, Arthur Terry, Bruce Wardropper, Antonio Prieto, Ignacio Navarrete, José Rico Verdú, Maria Rosso Gallo, Darci L. Strother, José Montero Reguera, Álvaro Alonso, and Nadine Ly, the last in a superb 1998 essay published in *Criticón*. Ly—and we—owe a debt of gratitude to Edward Glaser, a first-rate *recopilador*. My approach uses Garcilaso's sonnet as a center and as an exemplary site of "the anxiety of influence." In order not to make poetry analysis more suspenseful than it has to be, let me reveal that I will point to a type of disconnect between the borrowed elements and the ultimate direction of the poem, and I then will look at how Lope de Vega and Miguel Colodrero de Villalobos, in variations, handle the aspect of coordination among the parts. The focus will be on sonnets by Garcilaso, Lope, and Colodrero, and the reference to Colodrero (a seventeenth-century *culteranista* from Andalucía whose commentators include Glaser and Jesús Ponce Cárdenas) will lead to a brief consideration of the motif in a spiritual context.

Garcilaso de la Vega is known as the Spanish Renaissance poet par excellence for a reason. To argue that he had a way with words is an understatement. He juxtaposes linguistic subtlety and refinement with sincerity of feeling, and evocation of the glories of nature with a mixture of head and heart. His Sonnet 23, "En tanto que de rosa y azucena" (Rivers, *Renaissance* 37–38), defines a paradigm of his poetry: a paradoxical addendum that serves to place the rest of the poem in perspective. To the carpe diem message, he appends a commentary on *mudanza*: Everything changes but change itself. This is more than a signatory gesture; it is philosophy, pragmatism in verse. The second tercet is a sharp, sophisticated, and—notably—*chaste* complement to the seduction stratagem. In short, it has style and class, and it would seem to want to improve upon the old while respecting the customs of the past.

Garcilaso de la Vega, Soneto 1

Cuando me paro a contemplar mi estado,
y a ver los pasos por do me ha traído,
hallo, según por do anduve perdido,
que a mayor mal pudiera haber llegado;

mas cuando del camino estó olvidado,
a tanto mal no sé por dó he venido:
sé que me acabo, y más he yo sentido
ver acabar conmigo mi cuidado.

Yo acabaré, que me entregué sin arte
a quien sabrá perderme y acabarme,
si ella quisiere, y aun sabrá querello:

que pues mi voluntad puede matarme,
la suya, que no es tanto de mi parte,
pudiendo, ¿qué hará sino hacello? (Rivers, *Renaissance* 34–35)

In his reworking of Petrarch's model in Sonnet 1, Garcilaso starts with a degree of optimism. On the road of life, the poetic speaker observes, essentially, that, with digressions and misjudgments, things could have been worse. The first quatrain sets the stage—or sets a tone—for what follows, but what follows takes a different path. The speaker has acknowledged that he has been lost—"anduve perdido"—but that he has somehow recovered, helped by *a dose of serendipity*. Now, a series of missteps has caused him to lose his sense of orientation; he has strayed from the straight and narrow, he is directionless, and the threat of death is all around him. Love is a tragic route, and the reigning verb becomes *acabar*. There is no clear transition from a satisfied attitude toward a looming and seemingly inevitable death from unrequited love. The description of the downfall is deftly rendered. The tercets set up and complete the paradox. The cold woman is the culprit—the agent of devastation—but the victim accepts a good portion of the blame for pursuing an impossible goal. He has sought love without understanding the art of amorous engagement, the rules of the game. He has brought this on himself, and the outlook is not promising. His inexperience and ignorance likely will lead to his demise.

And what about the lady? She wants nothing to do with him, so that if he is self-destructive despite being his own strongest advocate, what can be expected of her, when she has no inclination whatsoever to protect him?

The rhetorical question at the conclusion of the sonnet brings closure to what may be termed the poem's rhetorical strategy. Life is a journey, filled with wrong turns. If one analyzes the good and bad decisions, the fact that the process continues can be taken as an encouraging sign. But, from there, the poem's semiotics shifts to another tenor, far more fatalistic. The disjunction, or rupture, between the first stanza and the rest of the sonnet appears to revise the direction in mid-stream, or, more appropriately, in the middle of the road. Complacency is replaced by doubt, fear, and despair. The end is near, thanks to the gentleman's ineptitude and the lady's ill will. He has proceeded "without art"—uneducated in the recourses of love and courtship—yet the sonnet transfers the lack of artistry on one plane to full compensation on another, since the poem is laden with displays of finesse and ingenuity.

Does Garcilaso get "off-track" in Sonnet 1? Sonnet 298 of Petrarch's *Canzionere* ("Quand'io mi volgo in dietro a miarar gli anni") is about remembrance, which sustains and torments—every day is "dolce e crudo"—but primarily the latter, more bitter than sweet. For Petrarch, sentiment and lamentation are in the foreground, as the speaker cries out, in his lowly state ("in basso stato") to fate and fortune.[1] In Garcilaso's sonnet, which has been studied by scholars such as Hayward Keniston, Luis Avilés, and Gareth Walters (to name but a few), the reflection is on life, but mainly on love, or on love as inseparable from life. It is as if the speaker had wished to communicate an "all things considered" note of acquiescence and quickly had changed his mind, for after the "mas" that initiates the second quatrain, the "landscape" of the journey moves from a studied complacency to distraction, hopelessness, and thoughts of death (and not in the "muero porque no muero" vein).

An echo of courtly love—love equated with dire consequences—is heard. Love is about to kill the ardent but hapless suitor, and he can do nothing about it. And, as if that were not enough, the image of a scornful love object intensifies the pain and the imminence of the end. Art encompasses cause and effect. The man in love cannot master the art of persuasion, so he resorts to another branch of rhetoric, verbal dexterity. He fuses despondence with figurative language. Sonnet 1 is symbolic, even emblematic: Garcilaso embarks on a poetic excursion that heralds its distinctiveness, its newness, and its dependence on paradox. It targets passion and the intellect, thereby—simultaneously—appealing to the emotions and establishing an ironic distance. Garcilaso's "detour" may not reflect indecision, but instead—whether consciously or unconsciously inscribed—the deviation could be viewed as the announcement of a new poetic itinerary. Part of this—as it may be labeled, declaration of dependence—is to recognize, if somewhat paradoxically, the permanence of tradition within all creation. *Breaking away* always presupposes links, however tenuous, to what is being overwritten, which makes the palimpsest not only an attractive but an accurate marker of the phenomenon. Within this reading, *what may be perceived* as an inconsistency or flaw in Sonnet 1 becomes the indicator of an alternate code, *un arte nuevo de hacer poemas*, in which classical antiquity, Renaissance Italy, and points in between interact, rival each other, and foreshadow future rivalries. After all, the Renaissance cannot be conceived in isolation; it is—literally, uncompromisingly—a meeting of minds, and Garcilaso is a follower as well as a leader. His sonnets exhibit the push-and-pull of the poetic imagination.

Lope de Vega, *Rimas sacras*, 1

Cuando me paro a contemplar mi estado
y a ver los pasos por donde he venido,
me espanto de que un hombre tan perdido
a conocer su error haya llegado.

Cuando miro los años que he pasado,
la divina razón puesta en olvido,
conozco que piedad del cielo ha sido
no haberme en tanto mal precipitado.

Entré por laberinto tan extraño,
fiando al débil hilo de la vida
el tarde conocido desengaño;

mas, de tu luz mi escuridad vencida,
el monstro muerto de mi ciego engaño,
vuelve a la patria, la razón perdida. (Rivers, *Renaissance* 219–20)

If Garcilaso's inconsolable lover is mired in darkness, the speaker of Lope de Vega's Sonnet 1 of the *Rimas sacras* praises the light. Lope commonly is classified as a baroque poet, although he is, overall, less a *culteranista* than Góngora and less a *conceptista* than Quevedo. Lope is, brilliantly, all over the map: prolific, unpredictable, and indisputably flexible. He can be as subtle and understated and as over-the-top and attention-grabbing as any of his comrades in poetic arms, and rarely in literary history have verses poured so freely from a single author's pen. How does Lope deal with "Cuando me paro a contemplar mi estado"? And how does he give the line a baroque thrust? For two verses, Lope follows

Garcilaso, and then he veers in a different direction and, in due course, in multiple directions. Lope's speaker has strayed horribly, and it astonishes him that he has been able to comprehend the enormity of his errors. A fundamental phrase in the sonnet is "la divina razón puesta en olvido" (verse 5). Belatedly aware of his lapses in judgment, he realizes that heaven has taken pity on him and that his survival has depended on forgiveness from above. By combining divinity with reason, Lope places the dialectics of "self and circumstance" in the dual spheres of heaven and earth. If anachronistically I have invoked José Ortega y Gasset, let me summon Miguel de Unamuno to propose that Lope employs reason to justify faith.[2] Reason has permitted the speaker not only to see the error of his ways but to appreciate the source of this knowledge. Something has stopped him from hurling himself headlong into disaster, and it is important to grasp how *engaño* becomes *desengaño*, words that conclude verses 11 and 13.

The tercets contain the baroque impetus of Lope's sonnet, and the road converges, fittingly, into the labyrinth. Although the message is the same—*perdido* at the end of verse 3 becomes *perdida*, the final word of the poem, in verse 14—the associative fields revisit the realm of pre-Christian mythology. The speaker is grateful to have been liberated from life's illusions, symbolized by the labyrinth, which houses the Minotaur ("el monstruo" of verse 13) in a situation not unlike like of Theseus, aided by Ariadne's thread (the "débil hilo" of verse 10). The thread is a manner of addressing the "light" that constitutes the crux of the poem, an anagnorisis that leads to crucial insights.

Every poem is, in some measure, a metapoem, a commentary that is linguistically and conceptually self-referential, self-reflexive, whereby the reader can witness the creative act in motion and contemplate the decisions made as the compositional process advances. Lope builds upon a familiar trope as he stakes out new territory. It could be said that he converts the metaphor of the labyrinth into metonymy. He seems to want to synthesize philosophy and theology—in order to show their interdependence and compatibility—and the language and imagery reinforce the connection. "Seeing the light" relates to reason and to spirituality. In the latter category, one can think of the light that guides the soul (*la amada*) toward a union with God (*el amado*) in San Juan de la Cruz's "Noche oscura" (Rivers, *Renaissance* 138–39). Lope recasts the argument and the scope of enlightenment by going backward, but ironically so, to pagan mythology. He recasts, as well, the paradox as envisioned and captured by Garcilaso in the lover's plaint of his Sonnet 1. The themes of *engaño* and *desengaño* are strongly identified with—and identifiable with—early modern Spanish literature, but the topic is, unquestionably, universal, and Lope accentuates both domains, the immediate and the permanent. He enhances the indistinct geography by inserting the rather enigmatic "patria" of the last verse. Lope's speaker talks of a load that has been lifted. He is a Theseus of his age, bearing the brunt of responsibility: cognizance of his transgressions, the imperatives of repentance and atonement, and the hope of salvation. Lope underscores the notion of reciprocity through indetermination, by joining the threads of existence in the broadest sense. The mythological allusions let the subject—the poetic speaker and the reader—step out of time and give them the opportunity to construct an all-inclusive path.

The labyrinth evokes the traps into which humanity can fall and the exit strategies that are available, albeit quite elusive. To bring together this world and the next, Lope chooses a backward glance and a pre-Christian mystique. His amalgamation and accumulation of motifs is a baroque touch, as is the blurring of lines and the conscious mixing of metaphors (and other figures, including a decisive example of metonymy). The word "fiando" in verse 10 unites emotion with faith and Catholicism with the religions of antiquity. From darkness comes the light, from monsters come—though not necessarily in Goyesque fashion—reason and its allies, and, in its perfect state, an anticipated divine realism. Elaborately encoded, the sonnet puts forth an assessment and a lesson.

Miguel Colodrero de Villalobos, "Gran dicha es llegar un hombre a estar desengañado"

Cuando me paro a contemplar mi estado
y a ver los pasos por do me ha traído,
hallo, según por do anduve perdido,
que a mayor mal pudiera haber llegado,

Aquel ingenio dijo celebrado,
a quien jamás se atreverá el olvido,
y yo del desengaño así advertido,
todo el cuarteto le tomé prestado.

En tanto que de mí la muerte cobra
la deuda que le debo por humano,
donde voy caminando como río,

tenedme, inmenso Dios, de vuestra mano
aunque para salvarme, Señor mío,
de vuestro pie que me tengáis me sobra.
(qtd. in Ly 16; from Glaser, "El cobre convertido en oro" 400)

The sonnet "Gran dicha es llegar un hombre a estar desengañado" by Colodrero de Villalobos is a touching and unusual double tribute: to Garcilaso de la Vega and to God. Colodrero repeats the first quatrain of Garcilaso's Sonnet 1 and devotes the second quatrain reverently to explain the attribution: the celebrated poet, never to be forgotten, has led him to a fruitful *dis-illusionment* and to a faith in salvation. With a trace of Jorge Manrique's "Coplas por la muerte de su padre"—our lives as rivers that move toward the sea of death—Colodrero's speaker ends the sonnet with an apostrophe to God. He asks the Lord to redeem him, to give him a hand, and then finishes the plea by saying that it will suffice if God can offer a foot to hang onto. In this pure, humble, and movingly simple sonnet, Colodrero unites poetry and spirituality. One may not want to spend the time to question whether Garcilaso's poem is an exemplar—as is Lope's Sonnet 1—of *desengaño* in a religious context. Garcilaso has been a source of inspiration, and it may be the continuity and expansion of the theme of self-contemplation that Colodrero has borne in mind. Through its self-referentiality, Colodrero's poem covers a lot of ground, and it reflects an intimate—personal—view of the individual's relationship with God that may hint of an Erasmian influence. With nods to Garcilaso and, less explicitly, to Lope, the sonnet evinces the two strains of self-analysis and of *desengaño*: the here-and-now of love's tribulations and the bigger picture of inexorable death.

I would like to end my commentary with sonnets that demonstrate the dualism: one of 1646 by Miguel Botelho de Carvalho and one of 1675 by Fray Paulino de la Estrella. Botelho de Carvalho presents love as a maritime journey that leads nowhere:

Quando me paro a contemplar mi llanto,
testigo de mi amor, claro testigo,
tanto sufrir me pone mal conmigo,
pasmo de ver que puedo sufrir tanto.

Causando mi dolor al mundo espanto,
la mayor confusión abrazo y sigo,
viviendo en este encanto por castigo,
si es que puedo vivir en este encanto.

Sin alcanzar del tiempo la mudanza,
falto de luz, camino sin sosiego.
Lleno de amor, navego sin bonanza.

En el mar de mis lágrimas navego,
llevando en el bajel de mi esperanza,
por guía un niño, y por piloto un ciego.
(qtd. in Ly 17; from Glaser, "Cuando me paro a contemplar mi
estado" 76)

His tercets, painfully yet cleverly, transmit the misery that faces and will keep facing him. Love makes him suffer, and love makes him blind. This perpetual voyage is in the here and now.

Fray Paulino's speaker, in contrast, is cognizant of his past sins and his imminent death, and he is overcome with remorse. In "De una alma contrita," he understands, if a bit late, that love lasts but a minute and that it is no match with eternity:

Cuando me paro a considerar mi estado,
y a ver la mala vida que he vivido,
reparo en que el gran Dios me haya sufrido
pudiendo haberme a tanto condenado.

Atónito, confuso y admirado,
estoy en ver el tiempo que he vivido
en vicios, y pecados consumido,
y en vanos pensamientos mal gastado.

¿Qué resta, pues, ahora, o alma mía?
Aprovechar del tiempo lo restante,
y pensar en la muerte cada día,

con una contrición perseverante.
que locura fatal cierto sería
trocar lo eterno por un breve instante.
(qtd. in Ly 17–18; from Glaser, "El cobre convertido en oro" 401–2)

The poems prompted by the sonnet of Petrarch join poetry to life. They also may motivate the reader to contemplate the artistic process in itself, as part of a movement of intertextuality and of individual confrontation with a poetic text. Self-consciousness on one level extends to another: self-reflection to poetic assessment. The sonnets based on the motif of contemplation invite one to think about correlations and independence. The sonnet form is fixed, uniform; a poetic determinism is in place. As in matters of faith, aspiring writers may envision a space for free will, and, analogically speaking, this would be the space in which artists can insert, and assert, themselves. Respectfulness can go only so far for the fledgling poet in search of distinction (as difference and recognition). Poets must be, at the very least, gentle adversaries. Like Cervantes, Garcilaso depends on the past for inspiration, but he reinvents the past. And, as in the case of Cervantes, his reinventions serve as models for future creation. In the great dialectic of similitude and difference that characterizes literary history, the contemplation of one's status in the world can be instructive, and, it might be argued, a step in the right direction.

Notes

[1] The sonnet is number 298 of Petrarch's *Il Canzoniere* (see Ly 10), from Luis Rosales, *Estudios sobre el Barroco* (Madrid: Trotta, 1997), 59:

> Quand'io mi volgo indietro a miarar gli anni
> ch'anno fuggendo i miei penseri sparsi,
> et spento 'l foco ove agghiacciando io arsi,
> et finito il riposo pien d'affanni,
> rotta la fe' degli amorosi inganni,
> et sol due parti d'ogni mio ben farsi,
> l'una nel cielo et l'altra in terra starsi,
> et perduto il guadagno de' miei damni,
>
> i' mi riscuto, et trovomi sí nudo,
> ch'i' porto invidia ad ogni extrema sorte:
> tal cordoglio et paura ò di me stesso.
> O mia stella, o Fortuna, o Fato, o Morte,
> o per me sempre dolce giorno et crudo,
> come m'avete in basso stato messo!

[2] Ortega y Gasset's "Yo soy yo y mi circunstancia" is from *Meditaciones del Quijote* (1:757). In various passages of *Del sentimiento trágico de la vida*, in narratives such as *San Manuel Bueno, mártir,* and elsewhere, Unamuno endorses the paradox of using reason to demonstrate the superiority of faith over reason.

Works Cited

Alemán, Mateo. *Guzmán de Alfarache.* Ed. José María Micó. 2 vols. Madrid: Cátedra, 2006.

Alonso, Álvaro. *La poesía italianista.* Madrid: Ediciones del Laberinto, 2002.

Avilés, Luis F. "'Contemplar mi stado': Las posibilidades del yo en el soneto I de Garcilaso." *Calíope* 2.1 (1996): 58–78.

Bloom, Harold. *The Anxiety of Influence: A Theory of Poetry.* New York: Oxford UP, 1973.

Cervantes, Miguel de. *Don Quijote.* Ed. Tom Lathrop. Newark, DE: Juan de la Cuesta, 2012.

Eliot, T. S. "Tradition and the Individual Talent." *The Critical Tradition.* Ed. David H. Richter. New York: St. Martin's, 1989. 466–71.

Fernández de Avellaneda, Alonso [pseud.]. *El ingenioso hidalgo don Quijote de la Mancha, que contiene su tercera salida y es la quinta parte de sus aventuras.* Ed. Fernando García Salinero. Madrid: Castalia, 1987.

Glaser, Edward. "'El cobre convertido en oro': 'Rifacimentos' cristianos en la poesía de Garcilaso en los siglos XVI y XVII." *La poesía de Garcilaso: Ensayos críticos.* Ed. Elias L. Rivers. Barcelona: Ariel, 1974. 381–403.

———. "'Cuando me paro a contemplar mi estado': Trayectoria de un *Rechenschafts-Sonett.*" *Estudios hispano-portugueses: Relaciones literarias del Siglo de Oro.* Madrid: Castalia, 1957. 59–95.

Lapesa, Rafael. *La trayectoria poética de Garcilaso.* Madrid: Revista de Occidente, 1948.

Ly, Nadine. "La rescritura del soneto primero de Garcilaso." *Criticón* 74 (1998): 9–29.

Manrique, Jorge. *Poesía.* Ed. Jesús-Manuel Alda Tesán. Madrid: Cátedra, 2004.

Martí, Juan [pseud. Mateo Luján de Sayavedra]. *Segunda parte de la vida del pícaro Guzmán de Alfarache.* Ed. David Mañero Lozano. Madrid: Cátedra, 2007.

Montero Reguera, José. "En torno a un soneto garcilasiano de Lope de Vega." *Actas del XIII Congreso Internacional de Hispanistas.* Madrid: Castalia, 2000. 1:616–22.

Navarrete, Ignacio. *Orphans of Petrarch: Poetry and Theory in the Spanish Renaissance.* Berkeley: U of California P, 1994.

Ortega y Gasset, José. *Obras completas.* Vol. 1. Madrid: Taurus / Fundación José Ortega y Gasset, 2004.

Petrarca, Francesco. *Il Canzoniere.* Turin: Einaudi, 1964.

Ponce Cárdenas, Jesús. "En torno a algunos sonetos 'ejemplares' de Miguel Colodrero de Villalobos." *Península: Revista de Estudos Ibéricos* 3 (2006): 151–64.

Prieto, Antonio. *Garcilaso de la Vega*. Madrid: Sociedad General Española de Librería, 1975.

Rico Verdú, José. *La innovación literaria del Renacimiento: Garcilaso de la Vega*. Madrid: Cincel, 1985.

Rivers, Elias L. *Garcilaso de la Vega: Poems*. London: Grant and Cutler, 1980.

———, ed. *La poesía de Garcilaso: Ensayos críticos*. Barcelona: Ariel, 1974.

———, ed. *Renaissance and Baroque Poetry of Spain, with English Prose Translations*. Long Grove, IL: Waveland, 1988.

Rosso Gallo, Maria. *La poesía de Garcilaso de la Vega: Análisis filológico y texto crítico*. Madrid: Real Academia Española, 1990.

Strother, Darci L. "'Cuando me paro a contemplar mi estado': El concepto de género en tres sonetos del Siglo de Oro español." *Romance Notes* 34.1 (1993): 61–69.

Terry, Arthur. *Seventeenth-Century Spanish Poetry: The Power of Artifice*. Cambridge: Cambridge UP, 1993. http://dx.doi.org/10.1017/CBO9780511553851

Unamuno, Miguel de. *Del sentimiento trágico de la vida: La agonía del cristianismo*. Madrid: Akal, 1983.

———. *San Manuel Bueno, mártir*. Ed. Víctor García de la Concha. Madrid: Espasa Calpe, 2007.

Vega, Garcilaso de la. *Poesías castellanas completas*. Ed. Elias L. Rivers. Madrid: Castalia, 1972.

———. *Works: A Critical Text with Bibliography*. Ed. Hayward Keniston. New York: Hispanic Society of America, 1925.

Walters, D. Gareth. *The Cambridge Introduction to Spanish Poetry*. Cambridge: Cambridge UP, 2002.

Wardropper, Bruce W., ed. *Spanish Poetry of the Golden Age*. New York: Appleton-Century-Crofts, 1971.

3

The Captive as Ethnographer:
Antonio de Sosa's *Topography of Algiers* (1612)

María Antonia Garcés

Cornell University

In the mid-1570s, a young Spanish soldier and a slightly older Portuguese ecclesiastic arrived in Algiers as captives of Turkish-Algerian corsairs. Captivity in North Africa would transform the lives of both personages. The first one, Miguel de Cervantes, would eventually view the Iberian Empire and the Mediterranean from "the other shore," the side excluded and rejected by Spain (Goytisolo 60–61). The second prisoner, Antonio de Sosa, would turn the city of Algiers into the protagonist of his great chronicle on daily life in a Muslim metropolis, a monumental work titled *Topographia e Historia general de Argel* (1612).

Significantly, both Cervantes and Sosa became writers during their enslavement in Barbary. The soldier of Lepanto composed various long poems in the course of his confinement, such as the rediscovered *Epístola a Mateo Vázquez* (Epistle to Mateo Vázquez), written to Philip II's famous secretary in 1577.[1] In addition, Cervantes produced an extensive testimonial document written in Algiers after his liberation, known as *Información de Argel* (1580).[2] Sosa, on the other hand, would deal with his imprisonment in Barbary by becoming a meticulous historian and ethnographer, who wrote continuously about the Turkish-Algerian society. His friendship and "close conversations" with Cervantes led him to write the first biography of the future author of *Don Quijote*, included in Sosa's *Diálogo de los mártires de Argel* (178–81).[3]

In this essay, I propose to present a panoramic vision of Sosa's magisterial treatise, particularly highlighting the contents of the first of these works, the *Topography of Algiers*. This book was recently published in an annotated English translation titled: *An Early Modern Dialogue with Islam: Antonio de Sosa's* Topography of Algiers *(1612)*. Because the extant (1927–1930) Spanish version of this chronicle is both inaccessible and deficient, our English version of the *Topography* is the first critical edition of this fascinating account of daily life in Algiers during the last third of the sixteenth century.[4] As in the case of Cervantes, Sosa's captivity can be seen as a form of testimony that transformed the captive (*malgré lui*) into an acute observer of a different culture. Certainly, during his Algerian imprisonment between 1577 and 1581, Sosa turned into a meticulous ethnographer keen on documenting each of the customs of the inhabitants of Algiers. In the following pages, then, I explore the author's ethnographic description of Algerian inhabitants, mores, and religious rituals. Finally, I present a summary of my findings in regard to the fraud that ascribed Antonio de Sosa's work to Archbishop Diego de Haedo from Palermo, Sicily.[5] Returning the *Topography of Algiers* to its true author is crucial because Sosa was deprived of the authorship of most important ethnographic and historiographic treatises on the first seventy years of Algiers under Ottoman rule.[6]

Ecclesiastical Life in Sicily and Captivity in Algiers

As a writer and ethnographer, Antonio de Sosa (Portuguese Sousa), or "el doctor Sosa" as he signed himself, documents a critical juncture in the history of the relations between Spain and North Africa during the last years of the sixteenth century. I mentioned above that the Portuguese cleric Sosa wrote his riveting chronicle of European and North African cultural contacts while he was held captive in Algiers near the end of the 1570s. A fascinating eyewitness account, this five-book treatise is also the most sophisticated and original of the histories and descriptions of a North African city drawn by a European observer at the time. Thanks to its nineteenth-century French translations, both the *Topography of Algiers* and its historical sequel, *Epítome de los reyes de Argel*, became the primary source of information on early modern Algerian history and customs.[7] More recently, the English translation of the first book of Sosa's chronicle, the *Topography of Algiers*, has allowed English-speaking readers to access a fundamental treatise that illustrates the porosity of cultural, political, and religious frontiers in the sixteenth-century Mediterranean (Garcés, "Introduction" 8–10).

Born in Portugal around 1538, Sosa obtained a doctorate in theology and a degree in canon and civil law at an unknown Iberian university, possibly Coimbra. Around 1557, he professed in the Augustinian Order in Portugal. Soon after, he was promoted to the presbytery. Although he professed as an Augustinian, he nevertheless later presented himself in Sicily in the habit of a lay priest. In December 1562, Doctor Sosa joined Bishop Juan Orozco de Arce at his bishopric in Syracuse, Sicily, and was appointed vicar of this diocese.[8] When Orozco de Arce was elevated to the bishopric of Catania in 1574, Sosa followed him as vicar general (Garcés, "Introduction" 58–60).

Orozco de Arce's untimely death in 1576 forced Sosa to look for another ecclesiastical position. In September of that same year, he wrote Philip II from Rome, requesting the post of dean and vicar general of the cathedral of Agrigento, Sicily, vacant because of the death of the prior dean. A month later, the king nominated Sosa for the deanship and demanded a papal appointment for his protégé, an appointment that was soon confirmed (Garcés, "Introduction" 58–61). In the last days of March 1577, then, Sosa sailed from Barcelona to Valetta, Malta, aboard the galley *San Pablo* of the Order of Malta, on his way to Sicily. A few days later, a violent storm swept the *San Pablo* across the Mediterranean, separating it from the group of galleys from the Order of Malta that escorted it. The semidestroyed *San Pablo* took refuge on the island of San Pedro, near Sardinia, where it was attacked on April 1, 1577, by a squadron of twelve Algerian galliots. During the battle that ensued, the captain and numerous crew members were killed. The surviving 290 passengers, including Doctor Sosa, his widowed sister, a nephew, and three servants, were taken as captives to Algiers. Sosa would remain a captive in this North African city for four and a half years (Garcés, "Introduction" 41–42).

In Algiers, Sosa was purchased by the Jewish renegade Muhammad, a municipal official who was in charge of the city's mint. Sosa's captivity is documented through his own testimony included in *Topographia*. His two dialogues on captivity (*Diálogo de los mártires de Argel* and *Diálogo de la captividad*) and his theological debate between Christianity and Islam (*Diálogo de los morabutos*) (Dialogue of the Marabouts) are rich sources of information about his incarceration and the way that he occupied his time reading and writing, as well as composing his ethnographic and historical works on Algiers (Garcés, "Introduction" 42–45).

As a high-ranking ecclesiastic, Sosa elicited an enormous ransom (2,400 gold escudos), almost five times larger than the sum fetched by the captive soldier Miguel de Cervantes (Garcés, "Introduction" 64–65). In fact, as mentioned earlier, Sosa was not only Cervantes's friend in Algiers but also his first biographer. In addition, Sosa's testimony regarding Cervantes's captivity, included among the twelve affidavits collected by Cervantes in the so-called *Información de Argel* (1580), sheds light on the soldier's four escape attempts and his literary conversations with Sosa (Garcés, "Introduction" 38–41). More importantly, Sosa's biography of Cervantes included in his *Diálogo de los mártires de Argel* helped various scholars in the eighteenth century discover the Spanish author's baptismal records in Alcaná de Henares (Astrana Marín 1:179, 190, 219–21).

Sosa testifies to his vicissitudes during his captivity, when he was frequently weighted with fetters and chained in his cell. He also recounts his experiences with hard labor in 1578, when he was forced to haul rocks and sand and to mix lime, while chained (Sosa, *Diálogo de los mártires* 190). In the course of these difficult years, he wrote continuously to Philip II, begging for money to pay for his ransom. Nevertheless, Sosa also composed other texts, such as detailed reports on the forts and ramparts of Algiers, which he sent to the Spanish court. This was a common practice: state archives in Spain and Italy, among other European countries, are full of spies' reports often sent by merchants and Christian captives incarcerated in Muslim countries.[9] Sosa's meticulous information on the defensive fortifications of Algiers is included in his *Topography* (Garcés, "Introduction" 19–20, 37–38, 44–46).

Testimony and Intercultural Dialogue

For the duration of his ordeal as a captive, likewise, Sosa wrote constantly, annotating the events that marked daily life in the Muslim city (Garcés, "Introduction" 20, 49–50). Significantly, his experiences as a captive allowed him to offer new perceptions on Islamic customs from the viewpoint of a Western observer. Throughout his dialogues, moreover, Sosa describes his writing habits and the titles of the books he was reading, such as Leo Africanus's *Description of Africa* (1550), which he had in his prison cell in 1579. The book had been loaned to Sosa by a Muslim émigré from Granada brought up in Fez (Haedo, *Diálogo tercero*; Haedo, *Topografía* 3:201; Garcés, "Introduction" 50). This may be one of the most significant allusions to the circulation of Leo Africanus's book in Algiers and the Maghreb among exiled Moriscos and other learned Moors.

Sosa's insatiable curiosity about Algerian customs and his keen eye for ethnographic observation stand out in his *Topography of Algiers*. Among his informers, he mentions Christian captives and galley slaves, janissaries, Turks, Jews, and renegades or converts to Islam. In spite of his cultural distance as a Catholic theologian who opposed the religious beliefs of Islam, he gives prominence to detailed descriptions of Muslim and Jewish religious ceremonies in his work. He also reports on his religious discussions with Muslim, Jewish, and renegade interlocutors. For instance, speaking of the ceremonies and of the religious obstinacy of Jews in Algiers, he states: "I can attest to this, having debated with some of them not infrequently" (Sosa, *An Early Modern Dialogue* 181); and in relation to the intransigence of Algerian Muslims regarding their law: "One can hardly find somebody who wishes to listen to reason, let alone obey" (234). In addition, his dialogues with Algerian women stand out in his work; he reports that they enlightened him about their mores (Garcés, "Introduction" 4–5, 7, 47–48).

Sosa's Ethnographic and Historical Treatises on Algiers

Sosa's *Topographia* is a riveting work about European and North African cultural contacts that highlights relations between Christians and Muslims in North Africa. As suggested earlier, the first book of this monumental treatise is a notable eyewitness account of cultural life in Algiers toward the end of the sixteenth century. No other European work takes us so deeply into the quotidian life of an Islamic city during the early modern period, a time of expansion and glory for the Ottoman Empire and its territories, especially the Turkish-Algerian Regency. Captured in 1516 by Arudj Barbarossa, Algiers soon became under the rule of his brother Khayr al-Din Barbarossa the farthest Ottoman province in the Maghreb. During the next fifty years, the influx of Turks, renegades, and corsairs from all over the world, as well as the arrival of thousands of Christian slaves and booty seized in attacks on the coasts of Spain and Italy and their islands, transformed Algiers into the corsair capital of the Mediterranean (Braudel 2:870; Garcés, *Cervantes in Algiers* 31–32).

Sosa's treatise is divided into five books, which number 236 folios in the Princeps edition (1612). The first, the *Topography of Algiers* proper, offers a meticulous description of the city of Algiers, its inhabitants, and their customs in the last years of the 1570s. The second book of the *Topographia*, titled *Epítome de los reyes de Argel* (Epitome of the kings of Algiers), recounts the history of its rulers from the foundation of the State of Algiers to the last decades of the sixteenth century.[10] Certainly, *Epítome* is one of the great historical works of its time, described by a French historian as "the most complete and exact of the documents" on the first seventy years of Algiers under Turkish rule (Grammont, "Foreword" 15). Like his *Topography*, Sosa's history of Algiers is based on eyewitness accounts furnished by Turks and elderly renegades in the city. The historian, states Grammont, "rarely recounts an event of certain importance without invoking the authority of eye-witnesses" (15–16).

The third part of the *Topographia* contains two dialogues on captivity and a debate between Christianity and Islam. The first two dialogues are titled *Diálogo de la captividad en Argel* (On Captivity in Algiers) and *Diálogo de los mártires de Argel* (On the Martyrs of Algiers). *De la captividad* embodies a historical-philosophical study on captivity, which probes into the juridical aspects of slavery. In turn, *De los mártires* selects a few exemplary biographies among many cases that illustrate faith and courage in the face of Turkish-Algerian brutality. Both dialogues present a denunciation of Muslim religion and culture as well as a scathing critique of the cruelties perpetrated by Turks against Christian captives in Barbary.[11] The third dialogue, titled *Diálogo de los morabutos*, contains a dispute between Christianity and Islam, which follows sixteenth-century religious polemics. Organized by way of a dialogue between an autobiographical character named Antonio de Sosa and a historical renegade called Amud, the son-in-law of Sosa's master Muhammad, this piece contains rich autobiographical references regarding Sosa's life as a captive in Algiers.[12]

Live Tableau of Algerian Society

The *Topography of Algiers* paints a lively portrait of daily life in this Muslim city between 1577 and 1581. Algiers was then a prosperous urban center inhabited by a multicultural society consisting of Turks, Arabs, Berbers, Christian captives, Jews, exiled Moriscos, and converts to Islam from different parts of the world. The detailed description of every echelon and métier of Algerian society, including women, illuminates the social, cultural, religious, military, and commercial activities of this North African seaport. This ethnographic treatise stands out for its complexity, its vitality, and the sharpness of the author's ethnographic vision. According to historian Jocelyne Dakhlia, no other account of captivity in this period "offers such a complete, animated, and live tableau of Algerian society at the end of the sixteenth century" ("Une ethnographie" 7).

From an ethnographic perspective, moreover, the *Topography* offers valuable information on Algerian history and mores in premodern times. Along these lines, Sosa often presents himself as an eyewitness who testifies about a custom he has personally observed. As underlined above, the *Topography* often alludes to the author's dialogue with Muslim, Jewish, and renegade interlocutors. Among them, we can mention the inhabitants of his master Muhammad's household, including his wife and various visitors to this home (Haedo, *Diálogo tercero* 210). His references to lively debates with Jews and Muslims evoke a sophisticated social arena that allowed conversations and even religious discussions among the ethnic groups that inhabited the city (Garcés, "Introduction" 7, 47–48).

The very title of the *Topography of Algiers* highlights the urban scope of this enterprise, centered on the description of a Muslim city with its principal landmarks, gates, walls, buildings, and streets. Sosa's work depicts, first, the systems of defense and ramparts of the city; second, its streets, monuments, and houses; third, its political regime and administration, including its military and judicial organization; and fourth, the customs of the population, especially its leaders. In his introductory historical presentation, the author relates the ancient history and the founding of Algiers, including how it came under the Turks. He closes the *Topography* with an illustration of the fertility and richness of the countryside around the capital (Garcés, "Introduction" 17–20).

Beyond the physical descriptions of the city, Sosa directs his keen eye to its inhabitants, beginning with the Moors and *baldis* (urban dwellers), Berbers, Kabyles, Turks, renegades, Ka'ids, and Sipahis, among others. One of the most important chapters of the *Topography* deals with renegades (converts to Islam, called "Turks by profession") (chapter 13). Sosa's constant mention of renegades, in the *Topography*, the *Epítome de los reyes de Argel*, and his three dialogues, speaks to both his preoccupation and his fascination with these men and women who lived on the frontiers between cultures (Garcés, "Introduction" 43–44, 228). His descriptions highlight not only the particular mobility of Algerian society at this time but also a certain fluidity of identities that speaks to the multiple passages and circulation of individuals in the early modern Mediterranean.

In addition, five chapters of the *Topography* describe the Turkish-Algerian janissary organization, the different ranks of janissaries, and their customs during war and peace. The author's detailed knowledge of the Ottoman military can be attributed to the presence in his master's household of a Greek renegade named Boluk-Bashi Farat. This name, *boluk-bashi*, alludes to his rank as captain of an infantry division. Most likely, Sosa interviewed him about various janissary practices, such as the salaries earned by different military ranks (Garcés, "Introduction" 48–49).

Three chapters of the *Topography*, moreover, are dedicated to the Algerian corsairs, primarily their habits and religious ceremonies. Likewise, the catalog of corsair captains living in Algiers in 1580, including the list of those who owned frigates, sheds light on the constitution of the *taifa* or corsair corporation during this time (chapters 22, 23). Paradoxically, 76 percent of the thirty-five corsair captains listed in Sosa's "Catalogue of Corsairs" were Spanish, Italian, Sicilian, Albanian, and Greek renegades, among others (Sosa, *An Early Modern Dialogue* 160–61).

Another chapter of the *Topography* focuses on Algerian merchants and their commercial enterprises in diverse seaports such as London, Marseille, Genoa, Naples, Venice, and Valencia, as well as Constantinople and various Maghrebi urban centers. Additional sections of this ethnographic treatise portray laborers and artisans, the Marabouts of Algiers, and the Jews who inhabited the city. Again, the information offered on Algerian Jews is highly detailed. In this context, let us recall that Sosa's master Muhammad was a renegade Jew with close connections to the city's Jewish community (Garcés, "Introduction" 42–45, 47–49).

One of the most valuable sections of the *Topography*, moreover, is the chapter on the languages spoken in Algiers and the types of currency used around 1580 in North Africa (chapter 29). The author confirms that many Jews, former Muslim captives, and children of renegades spoke Spanish, French, and Italian "very prettily." In addition, numerous Christian captives and Moors learned Turkish and spoke it well (Sosa, *An Early Modern Dialogue* 184–85). In spite of his complete ignorance of Arabic, Turkish, and other languages spoken by Muslims in North Africa, Sosa's meticulous depiction of the lingua franca of Algiers has been central to scholars who study this Mediterranean phenomenon, such as Dakhlia in her magisterial work *Lingua franca*.

In turn, the author's research about Algerian women covers four long chapters of the *Topography*. Women's lifestyles—their quotidian activities, religious rites, marriage customs, celebrations, and fashions—attracted much of the author's attention. He also focuses on childbirth and child rearing, as well as on makeup and female footwear (chapter 32). According to the author, many renegade women overtly practiced their Christian devotions. Nevertheless, the Portuguese cleric criticizes Algerian wives for living a leisurely life, dedicated to continuous parties (chapter 33). The influence of Algerian women, both Jewish and Muslim, also stands out in the *Topography*: in the *Diálogo de los morabutos*, an autobiographical character named Antonio de Sosa recounts to his interlocutor, the renegade Amud, various stories that had been related to Sosa by the mistress of the house. Such stories reappear in the *Topography* (Garcés, "Introduction" 46–47).

In sum, three topics in his *Topography* elicited most of the author's attention: the corsairs of Algiers and their practices, the Ottoman-Algerian janissary organization, and the lives and customs of women. Yet Sosa's ethnographic treatise similarly includes a very complete report on Islamic feast days, religious ceremonies, and festivals celebrated in Algiers toward the end of the sixteenth century. Other sections contain a miscellany of Algerian customs, a catalog of Algerian vices and virtues, and a detailed account of death and burial in the city, including Jewish funerals. Along these lines, anthropologists and historians have noted the great similarity between the domestic rituals described by Sosa, such as circumcision, marriage, and childbirth rituals, and the same rituals as practiced today, for instance, in Tunisia (Dakhlia, "Une ethnographie" 12).

Alternative Subject Positions

Algerian customs in this work are colored by mixed perspectives. As a Portuguese theologian brought up and educated in sixteenth-century Iberia, Sosa was influenced by contemporary polemical treatises that argued for the superiority of Christianity over Islam. Above all, his experience as a captive in Algiers under very difficult conditions led him to try to prove the errors of Islam, and to depict the tortures inflicted by Algerian corsairs on their Christian slaves. The author's vicissitudes as a captive would explain in part the radical distance that separates his world view from the practices and religious traditions of the Algerians. Yet most Western travelers in the early modern period adopted militant political and religious outlooks in regard to unknown cultures, especially vis-à-vis the customs and political organization of Muslim countries (Garcés, "Introduction" 3–7).

Nevertheless, the Portuguese captive produced a thoroughly comprehensive and methodical work that offers a wide range of information about the cultures of Algiers. Conversely, the *Topography* is often characterized by alternatively antagonistic positions. For instance, while the text voices a drastic criticism of the Qur'an, some passages reveal the author's respect for the qualities of devout Muslims, such as their observance of the law, their piety, their fasts, and their abstention from wine and gambling, virtues that would shame most Christians (chapter 37). Moreover, while the author views Turkish immigrants as "the vilest of all people, stupid and villainous," he acknowledges that some turn out to be "men of worth and valor" (chapter 12). Such contrasts extend to the writer's vision of the city of Algiers, first viewed as an impugnable fortress, surrounded by ramparts and the sea. Yet Sosa also praises its lovely houses, "all with elegant and open patios," including some beautiful edifices (chapters 9, 10). His treatise also includes many passages with descriptions of the fertile Algerian countryside, with its "infinite number of farms, orchards, and vineyards" (chapter 40). In this sense, one could suggest that, in spite of Sosa's afflictions as a captive, the real protagonist of the *Topography* is the city of Algiers (Garcés, "Introduction" 20).

As mentioned earlier, captivity, "understood as a physical detention or a subjective intellectual fascination," is an essential condition of opportunity for ethnography (Staden, lxxxix). Sosa's experience as a captive in close contact with the enemy forced him to engage actively in the lives of others. Along these lines, the *Topography* is constructed like a contemporary ethnographic study with descriptions of the material culture, kinship, marriage and death rituals, and religious beliefs in Algiers at the end of the sixteenth century. We must inquire, however, whether the political and religious ideology that distinguished Sosa and a majority of Iberian writers at the time invalidated the Portuguese cleric's ethnographic observations of Algerian mores. I propose that, beyond his religious proclivities, Sosa's ethnographic account effectively offers a variety of riches for the reader interested in early modern cultural contacts with Islam.

Scandals in Madrid and Rome

Sosa was finally liberated in July 1581 in a mysterious way that involved a daring escape from Algiers (Garcés, "Introduction" 63–65). He resided in Madrid between July 1581 and August 1582, as attested by various documents, such as a letter to Philip II written on August 26 of that year that confirms Sosa's connections to the Spanish Court (Garcés, "Introduction" 65–66). A terrible scandal surrounding Sosa's name erupted, however, in November 1582. As a result, the former captive was incarcerated at the Augustinian Convent of San Felipe in Madrid. He was then tried and convicted for apostasy—specifically, for leaving the Augustinian Order and taking the habit of a lay priest without a papal dispensation. His accusations involved other sins, such as living with a woman who passed as his widowed sister. As mentioned earlier, this mysterious woman had been captured with Sosa aboard the galley *San Pablo* along with a "nephew" and three servants. Although not much is known about her, she was also imprisoned in Algiers, perhaps even in Muhammad's house. Before escaping from his Algerian prison, however, Sosa took care to ransom his "sister," as detailed by his letters to the Spanish Court and other archival documents. His trial in Madrid and the succeeding events turned into an international saga involving Philip II, the prior of the Augustinians in Portugal, the Count of Olivares in Rome, Pope Gregory XIII, and the viceroy of Sicily, among other personages. After incessant endeavors at the Roman Curia on Sosa's part, the pope finally pardoned him through a Papal Bull issued on November 11, 1583, for his apostasy and desertion of his Order (Garcés, "Introduction" 67–70).[13] Despite Philip II's immense wrath, reiterated in continuous letters to the pope, his ambassador in Rome, and the viceroy of Sicily, Gregory XIII maintained Sosa in the position of dean and vicar general of the Cathedral of Agrigento. Most importantly, the pope authorized Sosa to abandon the Augustinian Order and continue his work as a lay priest, even as he admonished both Church officials and Spanish authorities not to bother him again.

In July 1584, Doctor Antonio de Sosa formally took possession of his post as dean and vicar of the Agrigento Cathedral according to the tenets of the Council of Trent. His capture by Barbary corsairs and ensuing incarceration in Algiers, as well as his imprisonment in Madrid and his endeavors in Rome to recuperate his post, had separated him from Sicily for seven years (Garcés, "Introduction" 70–71). While exercising his church functions in Agrigento, Sosa probably edited and refined the five books of his *Topographia e Historia general de Argel*, in particular his *Diálogo de la captividad*, which has countless references to classical Greek and Roman authors. This work allowed Sosa to flaunt his knowledge of scholarly historical, literary, and juridical discourses even as he cited the classical authorities respected in his epoch.[14] Various archival documents, in fact, attest to Sosa's work as dean of the Cathedral of Agrigento during these years and his close collaboration with Bishop Diego de Haedo. Yet the scandal that surrounded Sosa's name, as well as his conflicts with Philip II, who insisted on removing him from office well into 1585, made it impossible for Antonio de Sosa to author a book with his name on it, at least until Philip II died. In spite of these problems, Sosa remained active in his position until death surprised him in 1587 (Garcés, "Introduction" 72–75). His *Topographia e Historia general de Argel* appeared in 1612, thirty years after his death, ascribed to Archbishop Diego de Haedo, who had been Sosa's bishop and collaborator in Agrigento.

The True Author of the *Topographia*

Since the 1970s, Antonio de Sosa has been identified as the true author of the *Topographia e Historia general de Argel*, attributed for centuries to Diego de Haedo. As illustrated by my earlier comments on Sosa's biography, the reasons for the fraud that ascribed his work to another man were of a scandalous and political nature. The *Topographia* was edited and published in Valladolid (1612) by the Benedictine abbot Diego de Haedo, who credited the work to his uncle, Archbishop Diego de Haedo of Palermo—uncle and nephew had the same name. Fra Diego de Haedo affirms that he obtained these papers from his uncle (Haedo the elder) while he was in Palermo at his service between 1593 and 1599. Presumably, Archbishop Haedo, "informed by Christian captives who were many years in Algiers, especially about what is contained in the *Dialogues*," composed these materials and delivered them in a draft to his nephew. Fra Diego claimed that he polished the drafts and gave them their "final form" ("Dedicatory Letter to Archbishop Haedo"; see Sosa, *An*

Early Modern Dialogue 89). Nevertheless, the mention of the Dialogues, where Sosa appears both as an author and an autobiographical character, should alert us in regard to the real author of these manuscripts.

Certainly, Archbishop Haedo could not have composed this monumental treatise from accounts provided by former captives who arrived in Sicily. First, the *Topography* covers hundreds of pages with details about life in Algiers in the late 1570s, while the author speaks on numerous occasions as an eyewitness who offers his personal views (Camamis 124–36). Second, between 1577 and 1581, when Sosa was a captive in North Africa, Haedo was an inquisitor in Palermo, where he remained until 1585, when he took possession of the bishopric of Agrigento in Sicily. There he met Dr. Sosa, who had finally acceded in 1584 to the deanship of the Cathedral of Agrigento, offered to him in 1576 by Philip II. For a few years, then, Bishop Haedo shared his episcopal duties with Sosa. Haedo, in fact, never set foot in Algiers (Garcés, "Introduction" 57–78).

Cervantes definitely had access to Sosa's work when it appeared in 1612 under the name of Diego de Haedo. The author of *Don Quijote* used parts of the *Topographia* as a source of information for his posthumous novel *Persiles* (Garcés, *Cervantes en Argel* 400–402). In addition, Cervantes had lived in Valladolid between 1604 and 1606, and he still had personal connections with the Fernández de Córdoba family, who owned various printing shops in the city, such as the press that published the *Topographia*.[15] The former captive surely knew that Sosa was the true author of the *Topographia*, because he must have seen him writing his manuscripts in Muhammad's prison in Algiers between 1577 and 1581. Furthermore, Cervantes had been in Madrid in November 1582, when the scandalous trial of Philip II's protégé Sosa took place at the Convent of San Felipe. Thirty years later, however, Cervantes was obliged to remain silent in regard to the authorship of the *Topographia*, first in order to avoid resurrecting the scandal that had tarnished Sosa's reputation as an ecclesiastic, and second because his posthumous book had been ascribed to Archbishop Haedo of Palermo. Although Archbishop Haedo had died in 1608, his prestige both as a saintly man and a powerful ally of Philip II's government in Sicily still abided in both Spain and Sicily (Garcés, "Introduction" 77).

The suggestion that the true author of the *Topographia Historia general de Argel* was Antonio de Sosa is not new. In 1902, the renowned bibliographer Cristóbal Pérez Pastor clearly stated that Sosa was the author of "the summaries that helped Archbishop Haedo write the *Historia general de Argel*" (*Documentos* 1:235n1). Luis Astrana Marín also confirmed in 1949 that the three Dialogues that constitute the third part of

Haedo's *Topographia* were composed by Sosa (2:468). Moreover, George Camamis definitively demonstrated in 1977 that Sosa composed his monumental work between 1577 and 1581, while he was a captive in Algiers (132–43, 234–45). Likewise, historian Emilio Sola has corroborated that the *Topographia* was written by Sosa during his captivity (Sola, "Antonio de Sosa"; Sola and Peña 277–91). In turn, José María Parreño summarizes the discussions in favor of Sosa's authorship (9–12). I also offered further evidence to prove that the *Topographia* was written by Sosa while he was incarcerated in Algiers: multiple cross-references between the five books of this treatise also confirm the existence of a single author for these works (*Cervantes in Algiers* 70–77).

Lastly, through intensive research in various Spanish and Italian archives, including Church archives in Sicily, I was able to determine Sosa's identity, which was unknown until 2011. I uncovered numerous archival documents that provide proof of Sosa's ecclesiastical career in the Kingdom of Sicily and of his captivity in Algiers, including his relations with Philip II and Pope Gregory XIII. In addition, I discovered the motives for the fraud that saw his work attributed to Haedo (Garcés, "Introduction" 67–78). To conclude, after four hundred years, through the work of various scholars, the *Topography of Algiers* has been finally restored to its true author, Antonio de Sosa.

In sum, the *Topography of Algiers* constitutes a unique source of information on daily life in Algiers at the end of the sixteenth century. Its richness and density enhance the clarity of the author's vision. Sosa's fine narrative gift and keen talent for ethnographic observation turn this work into an essential resource on early modern European contacts with Muslim cultures in North Africa. Perhaps the most important information derived from his work regards the particular mobility of Algerian society toward the end of the sixteenth century, a mobility that also permeated the Mediterranean basin and its islands. Significantly, Sosa's life as a Hispano-Italian ecclesiastic with a clandestine existence, his vicissitudes as a captive in Barbary and a prisoner of the Augustinians in Madrid, and his frantic efforts displayed in Rome to recover his post in Agrigento, turn his saga into one of the most extraordinary "cases" buried in the Vatican Secret Archives and other Italian and Spanish documentation. Most importantly, the captive turned ethnographer transformed Algiers into the protagonist of his magisterial work. Indeed, the North African city where the Portuguese cleric spent four and a half years as a captive also captivated Antonio de Sosa in body and spirit.

Notes

[1] *Epístola a Mateo Vázquez* represents one of the few biographical testimonies written in captivity by Cervantes. See Gonzalo Sánchez-Molero.

[2] For a reading of the *Información de Argel*, see Garcés, *Cervantes in Algiers* 99–106; and Sola and Peña 242–59.

[3] See Sosa's testimony on behalf of Cervantes, "Declaración del doctor Antonio de Sosa," in *Información de Miguel de Cervantes*.

[4] Our critical edition and translation of two of the five books composed by Antonio de Sosa during his captivity in Algiers was funded by a National Endowment for the Humanities Collaborative Research Grant (2007–2012). The project was conceived with the collaboration of Professor Diana de Armas Wilson (translator; Emerita, University of Denver) while I am the general editor of the project.

[5] Citations of the *Topographia* in Spanish refer to the three-volume edition attributed to Haedo, *Topografía e Historia general de Argel*, a work that includes Sosa's three dialogues on captivity and Marabouts.

[6] See Sosa, *An Early Modern Dialogue*; and Garcés, "Introduction," 1–78.

[7] After the French invasion of Algeria in 1830, scholars and historians began a systematic translation into French of the most important sources on the Maghreb, such as the *Topographia* and *Epítome de los reyes de Argel*. Since Sosa's works were attributed to Diego de Haedo, they appear under the latter's name. See Haedo, *Topographie et histoire générale d'Alger*. *Epítome de los reyes de Argel* was translated as Haedo, *Histoire des rois d'Alger*. Both the *Topographie* and *Histoire des rois d'Alger* have been reissued continuously in France and Algeria (1998, 2004, 2007).

[8] Pirri, *Sicilia Sacra*, Notitia II, Lib. III, XC, 641.

[9] On the so-called *literatura de avisos* (spies' reports), see Emilio Sola's *Los que van y vienen* and *Uchalí*.

[10] Professor Diana de Armas Wilson and I currently are preparing the publication of our critical edition and English translation of this work, entitled *Of Caliphs and Corsairs: Antonio de Sosa's History of Algiers in the Sixteenth Century* (forthcoming from the University of Notre Dame Press).

[11] Sosa, *Diálogo de los mártires de Argel*, ed. Sola and Parreño (1990), with a foreword from each of the editors.

[12] Sosa's first two dialogues on captivity were translated into French (attributed to Diego de Haëdo) as *De la captivité à Alger* (1911). This book includes *De la captivité à Alger* and *Des martyrs d'Alger*.

[13] Most of the information on Sosa's endeavors in Rome in 1583 is contained in the Archivo del Ministerio de Asuntos Exteriores, "Embajada de España ante la Santa Sede," Legajo 35, now housed at the Archivo Historico Nacional, Madrid. The letters from Don Silvestre Mauroli, a noble from Messina, Sicily, named by Philip II as dean of the Cathedral of Agrigento in replacement of Antonio de Sosa, corroborate the latter's access to cardinals and other officials at the Roman Curia. In May and June 1584, Mauroli wrote various hysterical letters to Phillip II from Genoa attesting to Sosa's influence at the Holy See (Legajo 35, fols. 129–129A, 130–130A, 131–131A) (Garcés, "Introduction" 60, 70, 301n209).

[14] One may presume that the bishop's palace in Agrigento had a good library with classical books that Sosa could consult at his leisure. The Biblioteca Lucchesiana, donated to Agrigento in 1765 by Bishop Andrea Lucchese Palli, probably absorbed many of the books originally held at Bishop Haedo's library in Agrigento. Today it is one of the richest libraries in Italy, housing precious manuscripts in Greek and Latin as well as Arabic codices in parchment.

[15] A new edition of Cervantes's *La Galatea* came out in 1617 in Valladolid by Francisco Fernández de Córdoba's press. Francisco was a brother to Diego Fernández de Córdoba, who had published the *Topographia* in 1612. Most probably, through his connections in Valladolid, Cervantes managed to organize the reprinting of *La Galatea* before his own death in 1616 (Canavaggio 191–220; Delgado Casado 1:219–31).

Works Cited

Archivo del Ministerio de Asuntos Exteriores. "Embajada de España ante la Santa Sede." Legajo 35, Archivo Historico Nacional, Madrid.

Astrana Marín, Luis. *Vida ejemplar y heroica de Miguel de Cervantes Saavedra.* 7 vols. Madrid: Editorial Instituto Reus, 1948–1958.

Braudel, Fernand. *The Mediterranean and the Mediterranean World in the Age of Philip II.* Trans. Siân Reynolds. 2 vols. New York: Harper and Row, 1972.

Camamis, George. *Estudios sobre el cautiverio en el Siglo de Oro.* Madrid: Gredos, 1977.

Canavaggio, Jean. *Cervantes.* New York: W. W. Norton, 1990.

Cervantes, Miguel de. "Epístola a Mateo Vázquez." *Cervantes* 23.1 (2003): 215–22.

———. *Información de Miguel de Cervantes de lo que ha servido á S. M. y de lo que ha hecho estando captivo en Argel ... (Documentos)* [1580]. Ed. Pedro Torres Lanzas. Madrid: El Árbol, 1981.

Dakhlia, Jocelyne. *Lingua franca: Histoire d'une langue métisse en Méditerranée.* Arles: Actes Sud, 2008.

———. "Une ethnographie du mélange." Foreword to *Topographie et Historie générale d'Alger*, by Diego de Haëdo. Saint-Denis, France: Bouchène, 1998. 7–16.

Delgado Casado, Juan. *Diccionario de impresores, siglos XV a XVII.* Madrid: Arco Libros, 1996.

Garcés, María Antonia. *Cervantes en Argel: Historia de un cautivo.* Madrid: Gredos, 2005.

———. *Cervantes in Algiers: A Captive's Tale.* Nashville: Vanderbilt UP, 2002.

———. Introduction to *An Early Modern Dialogue with Islam: Antonio de Sosa's* Topography of Algiers *(1612)*, by Antonio de Sosa. Trans. Diana de Armas Wilson. Notre Dame: U of Notre Dame P, 2011. 1–78.

Gonzalo Sánchez-Molero, José Luis. *La Epístola a Mateo Vázquez: Historia de una polémica literaria en torno a Cervantes.* Alcalá de Henares: Centro de Estudios Cervantinos, 2010.

Goytisolo, Juan. *Crónicas sarracinas.* Barcelona: Ibérica, 1982.

Grammont, Henri-Delmàs de. Foreword to *Histoire des rois d'Alger*, by Diego de Haedo. Saint-Denis, France: Bouchène, 1998. 15–16.

Haedo, Diego de. *De la captivité à Alger.* Trans. Michel F. A. Moliner-Violle. Algiers: A. Jourdan, 1911.

————. *Diálogo primero: De la captividad en Argel. Topografía e Historia general de Argel.* Ed. Ignacio Bauer y Landauer. Madrid: Imp. de Ramona Velasco, Vda. de Prudencio Pérez, 1927–1929. 2:1–217.

————. *Diálogo segundo: De los mártires de Argel. Topografía e Historia general de Argel.* Ed. Ignacio Bauer y Landauer. Madrid: Imp. de Ramona Velasco, Vda. de Prudencio Pérez, 1927–1929. 3:1–192.

————. *Diálogo tercero: De los morabutos de turcos y moros. Topografía e historia general de Argel.* Ed. Ignacio Bauer y Landauer. Madrid: Imp. de Ramona Velasco, Vda. de Prudencio Pérez, 1927-1929. 3:193–274.

————. *Epítome de los reyes de Argel: Topografía e historia general de Argel.* Ed. Ignacio Bauer y Landauer. Vol. 1. Madrid: Sociedad de Bibliófilos Españoles, 1927. 213–426.

————. *Histoire des rois d'Alger.* Trans. Henri-Delmàs de Grammont. Algiers: Adolphe Jourdan, 1881.

————. *Histoire des rois d'Alger.* Trans. Henri-Delmàs de Grammont. Saint-Denis, France: Bouchène, 1998.

————. *Topographia, e historia general de Argel, repartida en cinco tratados do se verán casos extraños, muertes espantosas y tormentos exquisitos ...* Valladolid: Diego Fernandez de Córdoba y Oviedo, 1612.

————. *Topografía e Historia general de Argel.* Ed. Ignacio Bauer y Landauer. 3 vols. Madrid: Imp. de Ramona Velasco, Vda. de Prudencio Pérez, 1927–1929.

————. *Topographie et Histoire générale d'Alger.* Trans. Dr. Monnereau and Adrien Berbrugger. Saint-Denis, France: Bouchène, 1998.

————. *Topographie et Histoire générale d'Alger.* Trans. Dr. Monnereau and Adrien Berbrugger. Algiers: Éditions Grand-Alger Livres, 2004.

Leo, Joanne Africanus. *Volume delle navigationi et viaggi 1, nel qvale si contengono la descrittione dell'Africa (per Giouan Lioni Africano) ...* Ed. G. B. Ramusio. Venice: Giunta, 1563.

Parreño, José María. "Experiencia y literatura en la obra de Antonio de Sosa." *Diálogo de los mártires de Argel,* by Antonio de Sosa. Ed. Emilio Sola and José María Parreño. Madrid: Hiperión, 1990. 7–23.

Pérez Pastor, Cristóbal. *Documentos cervantinos hasta ahora inéditos.* 2 vols. Madrid: Establecimiento Topográfico de Fontanet, 1897–1902.

Pirri, Rocco. *Sicilia sacra disquisitionibus et notitijs illustrata: ubi libris quatuor postquam de illius patriarchia, et metropolita disquisitum est, à christiane religionis exordio ad nostra usque tempora cuiusque praesulatus, maiorumque beneficiorum institutio, archiepiscopi, episcopi, abbates, priores, singulorum iura, priuilegia, praeclara monumenta, ciuitates dioeceseon cum praecipuis earum templis, religiosisq[ue] familijs, atque viri siculi vel sanctitate, vel doctrina illustres continentur, explicantur.* Palermo: Petri Coppulae, 1633.

Sola, Emilio. "Antonio de Sosa: Un clásico inédito amigo de Cervantes." *Actas del Primer Coloquio Internacional de la Asociación de Cervantistas, Alcalá de Henares 29/30 nov.-1/2 dic.1988*. Barcelona: Anthropos, 1990. 409–12.

———. *Los que van y vienen: Información y fronteras en el Mediterráneo clásico del siglo XVI*. Alcalá de Henares: U de Alcalá, 2005.

———. "Miguel de Cervantes, Antonio de Sosa y África." *Actas del primer encuentro de historiadores del Valle de Henares*. Guadalajara/Alcalá de Henares: Institución de Estudios Complutenses, 1988. 617–23.

———. "Renacimiento, Contrarreforma y problema morisco en la obra de Antonio de Sosa." *Diálogo de los mártires de Argel*, by Antonio de Sosa. Ed. Emilio Sola and José María Parreño. Madrid: Hiperión, 1990. 25–52.

———. *Uchalí: El calabrés tiñoso, o el mito del corsario muladí en la frontera*. Barcelona: Bellaterra, 2010.

Sola, Emilio, and José F. de la Peña, *Cervantes y la Berbería: Cervantes, mundo turco-berberisco y servicios secretos en la época de Felipe II*. Mexico City: Fondo de Cultura Económica, 1995.

Sosa, Antonio. "Declaración del doctor Antonio de Sosa." *Información de Miguel de Cervantes de lo que ha servido a S. M. y de lo que ha hecho estando captivo en Argel ... (Documentos)* [1580], by Miguel de Cervantes. Madrid: El Árbol, 1981. 155–66.

———. *Diálogo de los mártires de Argel*. Ed. Emilio Sola and José M. Parreño. Madrid: Hiperión, 1990.

———. *An Early Modern Dialogue with Islam: Antonio de Sosa's Topography of Algiers (1612)*. Ed. María Antonia Garcés. Trans. Diana de Armas Wilson. Notre Dame: U of Notre Dame P, 2011.

Staden, Hans. *Hans Staden's True History: An Account of Cannibal Captivity in Brazil*. Ed. and trans. Neil L. Whitehead and Michael Harbsmeier. Durham: Duke UP, 2008. http://dx.doi.org/10.1215/9780822389293

4

La dama duende and the "Reversible" *Corral* Stage

Patricia Kenworthy

Emerita, Vassar College

In 1975, when he was directing my doctoral dissertation, Professor Robert ter Horst published "The Ruling Temper of Calderón's *La dama duende*." With heartfelt thanks to Bob for having ignited my interest in the *Comedia* and for decades of guidance and friendship, I offer another look at this wonderful play. His analysis addressed questions of timing, governance, and genre; mine will deal with space and staging.

The comic confusions of Pedro Calderón de la Barca's *La dama duende* (The Phantom Lady) hinge on a piece of stage décor: the *alacena*, a glassware cupboard that conceals, yet functions as, a door. Until the final scene, only two characters, Don Manuel and his servant Cosme, are ignorant of the fact that this disguised door leads from Manuel's guest suite to the interior of the house in which the honor-conscious Toledo brothers, Juan and Luis, are attempting, unsuccessfully, to sequester their debt-laden, spritely, widowed sister, Ángela. In the first scene of Act 2, Ángela's cousin Beatriz expresses doubts about Manuel's intelligence, citing his inability to figure out how the "dama duende" has entered to leave love letters on his bed. Ángela replies with an anecdote: the riddle of "el huevo de Juanelo" (Juanelo's egg).[1] In this traditional story, the wisest men in the land are stumped about how to stand an egg on end until the clever Juanelo solves the puzzle by cracking the egg on the marble table. In contrast to the quick—if destructive—solution to the riddle of the egg, the process of piecing together the staging puzzle has been evolutionary.

Scholars interested in recovering the original *corral* (public playhouse) staging have focused on three key topics: the (fictional) architecture of the house, the placement of the *alacena* and the furniture, and the setting of each scene. With regard to the architecture, Marc Vitse was the first to recognize that Calderón's text makes clear that the rooms of Ángela and Manuel are not contiguous, separated only by the disguised door, but rather located at opposite ends of an interior garden. Manuel's guest suite, which has its own exterior door to the street, contains four areas separated by doors: a vestibule (*portal*), a main room (where the *alacena* is), and a bedroom with an adjoining small room (*retrete*). Agustín de la Granja's illustration of the floor plan (232) demonstrates that Calderón placed his characters in a conventional seventeenth-century Madrid house.

Essential elements of this fictional floor plan are represented by the real features of the *corral* stage. To perform the play's twelve scenes (three in Act 1, five in Act 2, and four in Act 3), the actors need only the thrust stage with its three curtained partitions at the rear plus the first balcony for the 1636 version printed in Madrid (M); the text printed in 1636 in Valencia and Zaragoza (V/Z), with its alternate version of the third act, does not require the balcony. In the five scenes that take place in Manuel's suite, the audience must see the *alacena* plus the basic furniture required for the action: a chair and a table (alternately referred to as *bufete* and *mesa*)[2] with a candelabra and writing kit on top and charcoal-filled brazier beneath. Critics concur that these elements of stage decor are revealed by opening curtains at the rear of the stage. John E. Varey (171) and Marc Vitse (23) place the *alacena* in the central discovery space, but neither discusses the furniture.[3] J. M. Ruano de la Haza and John Allen's proposed staging for Manuel's room requires that all three rear curtains be open. He places the *alacena* in one lateral space and a wooden door—"una puerta practicable que puede ser cerrada con llave" (a workable door that can be locked with a key)—to the vestibule in the other lateral space. Into the central discovery space that serves as Manuel's bedroom, Ruano puts the *bufete* (small table with drawers) and the *mesa* (table), which he believes are two separate pieces of furniture, along with the chair (401–3). In their editions of the play, Fausta Antonucci (36n780) and Jesús Pérez Magallón (148n214) accept Ruano's solution. Agustín de la Granja places both the *alacena* and the furniture in the central discovery space (236–38). To support his position, he cites the manuscript of an *entremés* (one-act farce), *Los figurones*, which specifies that "*habrá una alacena en la puerta de enmedio*" (*there is a cupboard in the middle door*) and argues that Calderón's stage directions do not specify "the middle door" because, for the dramatist, it was "algo tan obvio que no necesitaba ser comentado" (something so obvious that it didn't need to be mentioned) (236).

While Ruano's option is certainly possible, I favor de la Granja's more "economical" staging and would have only the central rear curtain open to reveal both the furniture and the *alacena*. The central discovery space is routinely the locus of *admiratio*, whether horrific (a garroted captain, a bloody Mencía) or farcical (secret passageways, hidden doors). Calderón wrote a cluster of four urban comedies that feature concealed doors; the other three plays all contain references to *La dama duende*. In *Casa con dos puertas mala es de guardar*, the door between Marcela's and her brother Felix's room is disguised on his side by an *antepuerta* (curtain hanging from the door lintel). In *El escondido y la tapada*, a staircase is hidden behind a door painted to look like a whitewashed wall: *"Quitan las colgaduras, y queda debajo una pared blanca con dos puertas a los lados, y en medio una blanqueada disimulada"* (*The curtains are removed to reveal a white wall with two lateral doors and, in the middle, a whitewashed, concealed door*) (952). In *El galán fantasma*, a tunnel connects the gardens of neighboring houses. The staging of Act 2, scene 3, of this play requires a *bufete* (small table), a *tapete* (throw rug), and an *almohada* (cushion); the cushion is used to conceal the *escotillón* (trapdoor) that represents the mouth of the tunnel. To judge by the evidence of Calderón's *Fineza contra fineza*, trapdoors were cut in the floor of the central discovery space—*"Éntranse los dos por una parte, y abriéndose un escotillón en medio del tablado, salen todos por otra"* (*The two* [characters] *exit through one side door and, a trapdoor having opened in the middle of the stage, all the others enter from the other side*) (562). These texts indicate a pattern of placing the *alacena* and its cousins behind the central rear curtain.

De la Granja makes two additional suggestions regarding Manuel's suite: (1) that, when not needed for the action, the furniture was lowered by elevator from the stage level to the space beneath; and (2) that the *alacena* was merely a painted flat (237–38). Since the furniture is required in all but the fourth of the five scenes, the elevator—if it existed—strikes me as cumbersome and unnecessary. Painted glassware would have the advantage of never falling and breaking when the actors open and close the disguised door. However, in Act 3, an offstage noise alerts Luis, who dashes, light in hand, from Ángela's to Manuel's room: *"Hacen ruido en la alacena Isabel y Cosme"* (*Isabel and Cosme make noise in the cupboard*) (2698 in M).[4] Although the corresponding stage direction in V/Z suggests that the sound effect is that of doors slamming—*"Ruido de puertas dentro"* (*Offstage, the sound of doors*) (2591 in V/Z)—the dialogue clearly indicates that the noise is made by clinking glass.[5] In M, Ángela does not respond to Luis's question, "Y aquel ruido, ¿qué es?" (And that noise, what is it?) (2699), but in V/Z she fibs that some maid must be in "el camarín"(the china closet) (2593), and Manuel, having passed through the *alacena* into his unlit room, reasons that he and Cosme must be in a "camarín, porque al ir / entrando por una breve / puerta, topé con la espada / en unos vidrios que tiene / al entrar" (china closet, because when I came in through a narrow door, my sword bumped into some glassware near the entrance) (2634–38). Breaking glass is also the characteristic sound of two men hiding in an *alacena* in Calderón's *No hay burlas con el amor*: *"Éntranse en una alacena, quiébranse vidrios"* (*As they exit into a cupboard, glasses are broken*) (*Love Is No Laughing*

Matter 1944). While the *alacena* in *No hay burlas* is imagined—created by the dialogue and the sound effect—rather than seen by the audience, the stage direction in *La dama duende* does seem to call for real glasses on the shelves of a three-dimensional cupboard: "*una alacena que estará hecha con anaqueles y vidrios en ella*" (*a glassware cupboard that is made with shelves and glasses in it*) (780).

Blocking the movements of the characters in Manuel's suite demonstrates one of the basic staging conventions of the *Comedia*: that entry/exit point identity is fixed within a scene and in subsequent scenes set in the same locale. That is, in Act 1, scene 3, when Juan and Manuel first enter the suite, the curtain they use will be "the door to and from the street" every time the action takes place in the suite. There is critical agreement that, in Manuel's suite, one of the rear niches gives access to the bedroom, one to the *alacena*, and the third to the vestibule leading to the exterior door. When all three accesses are blocked, in order to stage Cosme's plea to be released from the *retrete* adjoining the bedroom, the actor must be either offstage (as in V/Z 2851) or, in violation of normal spatial relations, on the balcony: "*Asómase Cosme en lo alto*" (*Cosme leans out from the balcony*) (M 2868). (The balcony option is visually funnier.) In Ángela's room, all exits to, and entrances from, the route to the *alacena* must be through the curtains of one lateral niche, while the opposite one is used by the brothers when they are keeping tabs on her; the third is the "cuadra" (room) (M 2441) where Beatriz hides.

The biggest puzzle for modern critics and performances of *La dama duende* is the location of the first scene of Act 2 (1103–530). The scene begins with the entrance of Ángela, Beatriz, and Isabel. Since they are not wearing *mantos* (shawls), they are indoors in Ángela's quarters.[6] All the other characters—Juan, Luis, his servant Rodrigo, Manuel, and Cosme—subsequently appear in this scene. If Manuel is not to know that Ángela lives in the house, how could Juan and Luis—and Calderón (!)—allow the two of them to occupy the same space? John Varey (175), Antonio Serrano (62), and Pérez Magallón (124) all identify the space as Ángela's room. Ruano (60) and Vitse (31n5), noting all the traffic through this scene, place it in an unspecified but public room of the house. Modern productions that use stage sets to represent the interior rooms of the house and set this scene in Ángela's room solve the problem by eliminating the final third of the scene—the section in which Manuel and Cosme appear. The 1980 performance by the Pequeño Teatro de Madrid cut verses 1381–1530, and the 1991 staging by the Compañía Nacional de Teatro Clásico cut verses 1401–1530.[7] Matthew Stroud's English translation, *The Phantom Lady*, performed at Trinity University in San Antonio, Texas, in 2000, retains the full text but divides the sequence into two scenes to permit a change of place. The split occurs after the equivalent of verse 1380: "*Luis leaves the room and enters a patio, where he runs into Rodrigo.*" In contrast, the undecorated *corral* stage offers a marvelous malleability within the confines of a single scene.

These modern performances point to the spot in the scene where the dialogue seems to be at odds with the stage directions. Beatriz brushes off Luis's declaration of love and exits after line 1364, to be followed by Ángela and Isabel five lines later, leaving Luis alone on stage to lament. At the conclusion of Luis's ten-line soliloquy, the text reads:

> *Sale* RODRIGO.
> RODRIGO   ¿De dónde vienes?
> DON LUIS   No sé.

> (*Enter* RODRIGO.
> RODRIGO   Where are you coming from?
> DON LUIS   I don't know.) (1381)

While Luis's reply surely generates a laugh at his befuddlement, it also contains an important clue for the *corral* audience. As Pérez Magallón notes, the text makes more sense if the speakers are reversed: "Puesto que es Rodrigo quien llega, la pregunta '¿De dónde vienes?' debería hacérsela su amo, y no a la inversa" (Since it is Rodrigo who arrives, the question, "Where are you coming from?," should be posed by his master and not the reverse) (184n372). The situation has indeed turned inside out at this very moment.

The critics differ on the fictional location of this scene because they assume that each scene takes place in a single locale. Midscene location changes from inside to outside and vice versa are a standard, if somewhat infrequent, feature of the *Comedia*.[8] These instantaneous inversions of locale allow dramatists to follow Lope de Vega's recommendation, in *Arte nuevo de hacer comedias en este tiempo* (New Rules for Writing Plays at This Time), to avoid stage-clearing scene breaks:

> Quede muy pocas veces el teatro
> sin persona que hable, por que el vulgo
> en aquellas distancias se inquieta
> y gran rato la fábula se alarga;
> que, fuera de ser esto un grande vicio,
> aumenta mayor gracia y artificio.

(The stage should very rarely be left empty,
without a person speaking. If there are
such gaps, you'll find the public will get restless.
Besides, the play will go on much too long,
which is a serious fault, and that apart,
avoiding them displays more skill and art.) (237–42)[9]

Several scholars have noted this midscene inside/outside phenomenon, but none, to my knowledge, have articulated the staging convention that governs it—and the one that governs its inverse: the need to clear the stage to start a new scene to permit a change of location. To put the conundrum in terms of an example: if, in the first scene of Act 2 of Tirso de Molina's *El burlador de Sevilla*, the locale changes from inside the royal palace (the conversation between King Alonso and Don Diego) to a street outside when a woman "*por una reja*" (*through a window grille*) (1291) tosses a letter down to Don Juan, why, in Act 3, must Don Juan and Catalinón leave the stage to go from outside to inside the church: "*Entran por una puerta, y salen por otra*" (*They exit through one door and reenter through another*) (2680)? I have found several dozen cases of the midscene inside/outside switch but will include only a few representative examples here. In each case, the dialogue (often confirmed by the dress) of the characters on stage establishes the platform stage as one locale and the area behind the rear curtains (i.e., "dentro" [offstage]) as the space on the other side of this "wall." At the magic moment, the locales trade places; the stage seemingly revolves 180 degrees to turn inside out.

The most frequent examples of the "reversible" stage feature a shift from outside to inside a woman's house. The first scene of Act 2 of Lope de Vega's *El caballero de Olmedo* starts with Don Alonso and Tello walking toward Inés's house. Alonso then commands his servant to announce their arrival: "Llama, que es hora" (Knock on the door; it's time) (1001). After a brief comic exchange between the maid Ana and Tello, "*Sale Doña Inés*" (*Enter Doña Inés*) (1006). The fact that Inés is not wearing a shawl signals to the audience that the action has suddenly moved into the house. This shift is confirmed later when Alonso and Tello must hide to avoid detection by Inés's father, who has returned home earlier than expected. In the first scene of Act 3 of Lope's *El perro del hortelano*, the servant Tristán leaves the tavern to head home—"A casa voy" (I'm going home) (2506)—and picks up Teodoro en route. After Tristán announces "A casa hemos llegado" (We've arrived home) (2559), Countess Diana enters: "*Sale la condesa*" (2576); the rest of the action takes place in her palace. In each case, instead of the men exiting the stage to enter the house, the women's entrance "brings the house" onto the stage.

The shift can also be from inside to outside, as is the case when Don Sancho Ortiz is released from prison in *La estrella de Sevilla*, attributed to Lope de Vega. Estrella, accompanied by the jailer, enters the cell where Sancho and his servant Clarindo are being held. Estrella's dialogue sets up the expectation that she and Sancho, hand in hand, will exit to leave the prison while the other two men remain behind: "Señor, / venid conmigo … Dadme la mano, y venid … ¡Nadie nos siga!" (Sir, come with me … Give me your hand and come … No one follow us!) (2544–50). Yet Estrella and Sancho remain on stage as the servant and the jailer exit, "taking the prison with them." This "through the looking glass" moment in which dialogue and movement are opposed is also found in the autograph manuscript of Calderón's *El agua mansa*. Juan and Pedro are guests in Félix's house, which is just across the street from the house of Clara and Eugenia. Knowing that the women will have to emerge to attend Mass, Juan leaves the stage to wait "a la puerta de la calle" (outside the front door) (843). Pedro, still in the house with Félix, announces that he will join Juan. However, at this moment the audience sees an entrance instead of the expected exit:

> *Sale Don Juan.*
> Félix: ¿Qué hacéis, don Juan?
> Juan: Esperaros para saber a qué iglesia queréis que vamos a misa.
>
> (*Enter Don Juan.*
> Félix: What are you doing, Don Juan?
> Juan: Waiting for you two to find out to which church you want us to go to hear Mass.) (883–85)

That is, the character in motion claims that he has been waiting—the inverse of the moment in *La dama duende* in which the moving Rodrigo asks the stationary Luis, "¿de dónde vienes?" (Where are you coming from?). These examples confirm Fausta Antonucci's sense that "la acotación 'Sale Rodrigo' (v. 1380) no señala la llegada de Rodrigo al espacio previamente ocupado por don Luis, sino que designa todo lo contrario: la llegada de don Luis al espacio previamente ocupado por Rodrigo" (the stage direction, "Enter Rodrigo," does not signal Rodrigo's arrival to the place where Don Luis is, but just the opposite: Don Luis's arrival to the space already occupied by Rodrigo) ("Sobre" 74n18). The location has surely changed from inside Ángela's quarters to the street.[10]

The opening scene of Juan Pérez de Montalbán's *La centinela del honor* exploits both the unadorned stage's elasticity (the ability to travel distances in excess of the dimensions of the stage) and its inversion capability. With the Marqués delivering letters from the king, the action moves from inside the palace to outside and down the street to inside Leonisa's house to outside and down the street back to the palace (A_1r–B_1r). These multiple changes of location are sequential. I am skeptical about Vitse's contention that the V/Z version of the third act of *La dama duende* contains an example of two locales, one on each side of a door, being staged simultaneously (25). The sequence starts in Ángela's room when Luis hears tinkling glass and grabs a light to follow the noise; he exits the stage. The next scene opens with an entrance through the hidden door: "*Sale por la alacena DON MANUEL y COSME, y ISABEL los mete y se va*" (*Enter through the cupboard DON MANUEL and COSME, and ISABEL leads them in and exits*) (2631). Manuel and Cosme converse in the dark for twenty-six lines. The text continues:

> *Salen DON LUIS y ISABEL con luz.*
>
> DON LUIS   Yo vi un hombre, vive Dios, …
> COSME   (Uno, dijo.)
> ISABEL   ¿Cómo quieresque se haya ido?
> DON LUIS   … y he de hallarle.
> COSME   (Malo es esto.)
> DON LUIS   ¿Cómo tienes desviada esta alacena?
> ISABEL   ¿Yo, señor? No sé quién puede haberla apartado.
> DON LUIS   Quita.
> *Entran por otra puerta y sale DON LUIS por la alacena.*[11]

> (*Enter DON LUIS and ISABEL, with light*
>
> DON LUIS   By God, I saw a man …
> COSME   (Just one, he said.)
> ISABEL   Where do you think he's gone to?
> DON LUIS   … and I will find him.
> COSME   (This is bad.)
> DON LUIS   Why have you left this cupboard ajar?
> ISABEL   Me, sir? I don't know who could have opened it.
> DON LUIS   Get away.
> *They exit through the other door and DON LUIS enters through the cupboard.*) (2658–65)

The logical sequence of events is that Luis, light in hand, intercepts Isabel just after she has left Manuel's room. As Luis and the maid reach the *alacena*, he sees that it is ajar and, through the opening, espies a man. When he advances into the room, Isabel exits again, this time carefully shutting the door. According to the V/Z text, the spectators see Manuel and Cosme *in* the room at the same time that they see Luis and Isabel advance *toward* the room as they cross the stage. I am convinced the last stage direction is a mistake, since it has Luis and Isabel entering from the "bedroom door," crossing the stage and exiting via the "door to the vestibule." If a stage direction is required here at all, it should read something like "*Éntrase Isabel, y llega Don Luis*" (*Isabel exits and Don Luis approaches* [the characters on stage]), a parallel to "*Éntrase Don Juan, y llega Don Luis*" (*Don Juan exits and Don Luis approaches*) (3157) two scenes later. For me, this single stage direction is insufficient evidence that the "escenario múltiple" (simultaneous multiple location) is a standard feature of *Comedia* staging.

Midscene location changes from indoors to outdoors (or vice versa) can occur on the *corral* stage if the following conditions are met:

1. The stage is unadorned (i.e., all the rear curtains are closed and there is no furniture on stage).
2. The characters are wearing the appropriate clothing. In *La estrella de Sevilla*, Estrella's shawl serves both to hide her identity from Sancho and to permit her to move in and out of the prison.
3. The two locales are contiguous spaces, separated only by a door. In any *Comedia* scene, the space traversed is always contiguous, whether it is a few feet or a mile, just as the time is always continuous, even though fictional hours may pass in a few minutes of playing time. Gaps in time and space can occur only between scenes.
4. At the moment of the location inversion, at least one character crosses the threshold between the inside and the outside—that is, enters or exits through a rear curtain—but it is always a case of "reverse movement": the character who should logically be moving to the new location stays in place on stage.

Back to *El burlador*: Don Juan and Catalinón have to exit and immediately reenter because they are they are the only characters available to cross the threshold to make the transition from outside to inside the church; the statue of Don Gonzalo de Ulloa is not yet mobile.

The *Comedia* is, literally, poetry in motion. Because they know the "rules" of Spanish grammar and versification, scholarly editors are able to identify and correct any errors in the dialogue. Once we fully recover Golden Age staging conventions, future editors can be as rigorous in analyzing the stage directions, in identifying staging patterns and predilections of certain dramatists, and in advancing our appreciation of the ingenuity of the playwrights and the professional theater companies in exploiting the possibilities of the "simple" *corral* stage.

Notes

[1] Unless otherwise indicated, all English translations are mine.

[2] I thank Jay Allen for his suggestion (May 18, 1994) that the *bufete* and the *mesa* are the same piece of furniture.

[3] Joan Oleza also locates the *alacena* in the central "cortina de las apariencias" (discovery curtain) (217).

[4] All quotations from *La dama duende* are taken from Antonucci's edition.

[5] The play contains another case of discrepancy between a stage direction and the corresponding dialogue—an inconsistency that no editor has noted. In Act 2, scene 2, when Cosme accidentally leaves behind the important documents that Manuel plans to present to the king, the stage direction places the papers on the chair: "*Pónelos sobre una silla, y Don Manuel escribe*" (*He puts them on a chair and Don Manuel writes*) (1662). But two scenes later, Cosme remembers leaving them on the table—"a la mesa / donde sé que los dejé" (I know I left them on the table) (1972–73)—and in the next scene, Ángela sees them on the table: "Hacia aquí la mesa veo, / y con papeles está" (Over here I see the table with papers on it) (2021–22). Either there really is, as Cosme fears—"no sabré yo adónde / el duende los habrá puesto" (I don't know where the phantom will have put them) (1975–76)—a paper-moving poltergeist, or there is an error in the stage direction. Since Don Manuel likely sits on the chair to write, the logical place for Cosme to leave the documents is atop the table.

[6] Since the brothers have unfettered access to Ángela's apartments in Act 2, they are furious at being locked out in Act 3 during her performance as "Vueseñoría" for Manuel.

[7] Oddly, the 1991 staging by the Compañía Nacional de Teatro Clásico in Madrid put the glass cupboard in the set of Ángela's room and put a bookcase on Manuel's side of the disguised door. Their edition of the play contains still photographs of the performance.

[8] Midscene inside/outside changes are also found in Shakespeare: "[T]he locale could shift without figures even leaving the stage, most notably in *Romeo and Juliet* where Romeo and the masquers '*march about the*

stage' rather than exiting (thereby signaling a change in locale), while *'Serving men come forth with napkins'* (thereby establishing the new locale as the Capulet house); then, after some dialogue among the servants, *'Enter all the Guests and Gentlewomen to the Maskers'* (1.5.15.s.d.). Our expectation of a 'change in scene' or an exeunt-reentry to denote a change in locale is here superseded by another principle, perhaps best described as dramatic economy" (Dessen 93).

[9] The English translation is by Victor Dixon.

[10] Donald Beecher and James Nelson Novoa's English translation adds a stage direction—"In the Street before Don Manuel's Door"—to change the location at this point (96).

[11] The sequence of Luis hearing the noise, grabbing a light, and entering Manuel's suite contains problematic stage directions in both versions of Act 3. In the Madrid version, while still in Ángela's room, the stage direction says that Luis "*Aparta la alacena para entrar con luz*" (*He opens the cupboard in order to exit with a light*) (2702) five lines before he announces: "Luz tomaré" (I'll take a light) (2708). Since the *alacena* is a long way from Ángela's room, it is impossible for him to "open" it at this point. In contrast, the corresponding stage direction in the Valencia/Zaragoza version makes perfect sense: "*Toma una luz de un bufete*" (*He takes a light from a table*) (2608). "*Aparta la alacena*" may be a misprint for "*Aparta la antepuerta*" (*He pulls aside the curtain*) behind which Beatriz had earlier hidden in order to take a light from offstage.

Works Cited

Antonucci, Fausta, ed. *La dama duende*, by Pedro Calderón de la Barca. Barcelona: Crítica, 1999.

———. "Sobre la construcción y sentido de *La dama duende* de Calderón." *Rivista di Filologia e Letterature Ispaniche* 3 (2000): 61–93.

Beecher, Donald, and James Nelson Novoa, trans. *The Phantom Lady*, by Pedro Calderón de la Barca. Ed. Donald Beecher. Ottawa: Dovehouse Editions, 2002.

Calderón de la Barca, Pedro. *El agua mansa; Guárdate del agua mansa*. Ed. Ignacio Arellano and Víctor García Ruiz. Murcia: U de Murcia, 1989.

———. *La dama duende*. Adaptación de Luis Antonio de Villena. Madrid: Compañía Nacional de Teatro Clásico, 1990.

———. *El escondido y la tapada*. Ed. Maravillas Larrañaga Donézar. Barcelona: Promociones y Publicaciones Universitarias, 1989.

———. *Fineza contra fineza: The* Comedias *of Calderón*. Ed. D. W. Cruickshank and J. E. Varey. Vol. 10. London: Gregg, 1973. 518–63.

———. *Love Is No Laughing Matter* (*No hay burlas con el amor*). Ed. Don Cruickshank and Séan Page. Warminster: Aris & Phillips, 1986.

De la Granja, Agustín. "Tras *La dama duende* y sus espacios: a vueltas con la alacena." *Escenografía y escenificación en el teatro del Siglo de Oro*. Ed. Roberto Castilla Pérez and Miguel González Dengra. Granada: U de Granada, 2005. 223–40.

Dessen, Alan C. "Shakespeare and the Theatrical Conventions of His Time." *The Cambridge Companion to Shakespeare Studies*. Ed. Stanley Wells. Cambridge: Cambridge UP, 1986. 85–99.

La estrella de Sevilla. Ed. Raymond Foulché-Delbosc. *Revue Hispanique* 48 (1920): 497–678.

Molina, Tirso de. *El burlador de Sevilla y convidado de piedra*. Ed. James A. Parr. Binghamton, NY: Center for Medieval and Renaissance Texts and Studies, 1994.

Oleza, Joan. "Lugares intangibles: El espacio barroco en la comedia nueva de Lope." *La representación del espacio en la literatura española del Siglo de Oro*. Ed. Eberhard Geisler. Barcelona: Anthropos, 2013. 206–31.

Pérez de Montalbán, Juan. *La centinela de honor: Parte quarenta y tres de comedias de diferentes autores*. Zaragoza: Juan de Ybar-Pedro Ecuer, 1650.

Pérez Magallón, Jesús, ed. *La dama duende*, by Pedro Calderón de la Barca. Madrid: Cátedra, 2011.

Ruano de la Haza, J. M. "The Staging of Calderón's *La vida es sueño* and *La dama duende.*" *Bulletin of Hispanic Studies* 64 (1987): 51–63. http://dx.doi.org/10.1080/1475382872000364051

Ruano de la Haza, J. M., and John J. Allen. *Los teatros comerciales del siglo XVII y la escenificación de la comedia.* Madrid: Castalia, 1994.

Serrano, Antonio, ed. *La dama duende*, by Pedro Calderón de la Barca. Alicante: Aguaclara, 1992.

Stroud, Matthew D., trans. *The Phantom Lady*, by Pedro Calderón de la Barca. At http://www.comedias.org/play_texts/translat/phantom.html.

ter Horst, Robert. "The Ruling Temper of Calderón's *La dama duende.*" *Bulletin of the Comediantes* 27.2 (1975): 68–72. http://dx.doi.org/10.1353/boc.1975.0026

Varey, John E. "*La dama duende*, de Calderón: Símbolos y escenografía." *Calderón: Actas del Congreso Internacional sobre Calderón y el teatro español del Siglo de Oro* (Madrid, 1981). Ed. Luciano García Lorenzo. Madrid: Consejo Superior de Investigaciones Científicas, 1983. 1:165–83.

Vega Carpio, Lope de. *Arte nuevo de hacer comedias en este tiempo.* Ed. Juana de José Prades. Madrid: Consejo Superior de Investigaciones Científicas, 1971.

———. *El caballero de Olmedo.* Ed. Francisco Rico. Madrid: Cátedra, 1981.

———. "New Rules for Writing Plays at This Time." Trans. Victor Dixon. *Arte nuevo de hacer comedias en este tiempo: Edición políglota.* Ed. Felipe B. Pedraza Jiménez. Almagro: Festival de Teatro Clásico de Almagro, 2009. 169–86.

———. *El perro del hortelano.* Ed. Victor Dixon. London: Tamesis, 1981.

Vitse, Marc. "On the Space of *La dama duende*: Don Manuel's Room." *The Calderonian Stage: Body and Soul.* Ed. Manuel Delgado Morales. Lewisburg, PA: Bucknell UP, 1997. 185–207.

———. "Sobre los espacios en *La dama duende*: El cuarto de don Manuel." *Notas y Estudios Filológicos* 2 (1985): 7–32.

5

Antigone on the Border

Kirsten F. Nigro

The University of Texas at El Paso[*]

"We are in the times of Antigone." This statement drew loud applause at the presentation *Cuerpos sin duelo: Iconografías y teatralidades del dolor*[1] by the Cuban Mexican researcher Ileana Diéguez, which deals with the violence unleashed in and on Mexico since the 1990s and its tragic wake of thousands of dead bodies, so many of them unclaimed, unidentified, disappeared, buried in hastily dug mass graves, or simply dumped somewhere to be eaten as carrion or roasted under the scorching desert sun. Diéguez confesses that she was moved to do the difficult research for this book and exhibition by a deep concern with "el *no-lugar* del cuerpo—sin extensión, sin horizontalidad ni verticalidad—que introducen los cuerpos desaparecidos, los amontonamientos de cuerpos desmembrados y acéfalos, las apariciones de fosas comunes, la acumulación creciente de NN [No nominados. No nombre]" (27).

The present essay will look at two Mexican plays concerned with the extreme violence that has wracked the northern border of Mexico since the mid-1990s, starting with the mostly still-unsolved and continuing *femicide*[2] of hundreds of young girls and women, and the narcoterror that is a still a way of life that settled in with former president Felipe Calderón's declaration of war against the cartels soon after taking office in 2006. These plays also have another important commonality: they frame their content by harkening back to the ancient Greek story of the young Antigone that has come down to us from Sophocles's eponymous play text. That the playwrights studied here—Perla de la Rosa and Sara Uribe—should look to Antigone is not surprising, given the long tradition of evoking this heroine in times of violence, state repression, and competing allegiances to family, political ideologies, and ethical beliefs.[3] George Steiner's landmark study *Antigones: How the Antigone Legend Has*

---

[*] Since we were colleagues at the University of Arizona in the 1970s, I have remembered Professor Robert ter Horst fondly as someone who always encouraged me as a young teacher and novice researcher. I cannot fully express how touched I am that he should remember me after all these years and invite me to contribute to this volume in his honor.

Endured in Western Literature, Art, and Thought (1984) is testimony to the long and varied tradition of Antigone rewritings and adaptations during times of political crisis and existential stress; so are the hundreds of Antigones that have been written globally since the publication of Steiner's book. Yet, as was underscored in the call for papers for the March 2014 conference "Occupy Antigone: Tradition, Transition and Transformation in Performance" held at the University of Ghent, "although research on re-stagings of ancient tragedies has continually increased within Theatre Studies, analyses of the performances of Antigone are still significantly underrepresented" ("Occupy Antigone" n.p.).[4]

Within this paucity, there has been an even greater one: the absence of studies of Latin American plays that adapt the Antigone character and seminal themes from Sophocles's play. Recently, however, three studies have helped to fill this gap. The first, Rómulo E. Pianacci's published dissertation, Antígona: *una tragedia latinoamericana* (2008), is a sometimes sketchy review of numerous Antigones in Latin American theater that offers three very important insights: (1) that in the retellings of the Antigone story, it is vital to keep in mind the political and social frames within which they are written; (2) that many Antigone adaptations in Latin America look back in history to the continent's period of independence and subsequent nation building, during which many women played the role of protagonists—this political agency is repeated in plays that recast Antigone to more recent times, in which she becomes emblematic of women in Latin America's current history and culture; and (3) that there is a utopian vision in many of these adaptations and that these Antigones often see beyond the past and the present to what could and should be; in this way, they offer hopeful images of the future. In her dissertation "From Tragedy to Ritual: Latin American Adaptations of Sophocles' 'Antigone'" (2009), Victoria Brunn echoes some of these observations when noting that the plays that she studies "are deeply entrenched in the socio-political context in which they were created, as they encode or decipher contemporary reality, or imagine a different outcome for the social dramas of their times" (n.p). And in her contribution to the excellent collection of twelve essays *Whose Voice Is This? Iberian and Latin American Antigones* (2012), the collection's editor Jennifer Duprey notes that "different accounts of the myth of Antigone represent and embody historical, cultural, and political events in modern and contemporary … Latin America" (2).

The two Latin American Antigones that have received most attention in these studies and elsewhere are *Antígona furiosa* (1986) by the Argentine Griselda Gambaro and the *Antigone* written by the Peruvian poet José

Watanabe, commissioned and performed by Yuyachkani, that country's premier theater group (2000). In both cases, the characteristics noted above are very much in evidence. Gambaro's text very clearly approximates the content of the source text to events in Argentina during the Dirty War of the 1970s and early 1980s, and to the Mothers of the Plaza de Mayo, who organized (and continue to organize) weekly protests against a government that "disappeared" thousands of their husbands, sons, and daughters. The local context is obvious in the very Argentine language the characters speak, in the allusions to horrors and violence visited upon Argentines by Argentines in that period, and in the uniquely Argentine black humor and cruel parody that runs throughout Gambaro's play (the *grotesco criollo* that defines much of Argentina's modern theater). The Watanabe/Yuyachkani *Antigone* is a free version of Sophocles's text that collapses all the major characters into the body and voice of one actress, Yuyachkani's supremely talented Teresa Ralli. The absence of *deictics* pointing to local circumstances does not, however, preclude the theater audience's filling them in, for after years of fratricidal war and homegrown terrorism that "pitted the radical leftist groups Shining Path, in the highlands, and Túpac Amaru, on the coast" (Lambright 8), against an inept and corrupt government, against each other and fellow Peruvians, and, most tragically, against entire indigenous villages, guilty only of being in the way. After this, no one in a Peruvian theater audience could miss the extratheatrical referents.

While the Mexican plays analyzed here have yet to receive such substantial critical attention, they have much in common with the above two adapted texts, for they also indigenize the Antigone story and character. Referring to another famous heroine—Carmen—Linda Hutcheon, in her study *A Theory of Adaptation*, notes that the Carmen story is nomadic, circulating widely and displaying a "decidedly dynamic and fluid rather than static and fixed meaning" (158).[5] Borrowing from the anthropologist Susan Stanford Friedman, Hutcheon uses the term and concept of *indigenization* in relationship to adaptations because they "too constitute transformations of previous works in new contexts. Local particularities become transplanted to new ground, and something new and hybrid results" (150). She adds that this also "implies agency: people pick and choose what they want to transplant to their own soil, adapters of traveling stories exert power over what they adapt" (150). That is to say, they make them their own. Hutcheon notes that there are various ways to indigenize a story, among them historicizing it (158); that is, placing it in a different historical period. So too the Antigone story, which, as Fanny Söderbäck has said, "continues to shed light on the specific problems of every historical generation" ("Why Antigone Today?" 3).

In the case of Latin American versions of *Antigone*, even when the play's dramatic action is located in the past, the time and place are to be read as an analogue for the present; for example, ancient Thebes stands in for Ciudad Juárez today in Perla de la Rosa's *Antígona, las voces que incendian el desierto* (2004), with its wars against women in a country that operates arbitrarily, corruptly, and rarely for the good of the people and victims of violence. The playwright frames the classical *Antigone* within a context that she, as a native of Ciudad Juárez, knows well: the brutal femicides that began to come to light in the early 1990s, despite local, federal, and state agencies' eagerness to cover them up.[6] Or better said, not covering them up; that is, doing their best to *not* find the bodies of disappeared women and thereby not allowing families to give them a proper burial. De la Rosa's play text is among what Michael Alexander has called "palimpsestuous works, haunted at all times by their adapted texts (qtd. in Hutcheon 6). The story line and its tone follow closely those of Sophocles's text; and a goodly part of the dialogue is also taken from the latter, although there are speeches cited from real newspapers and television interviews with local and state officials, as well as with relatives (especially mothers) of missing girls. In addition, there are two other outside quotations, one from Jean Anouilh's *Antigone*, first performed in 1944 during the Nazi occupation of France, and the second from Bertolt Brecht's *Antigone* (1947–1948), with its direct references to fascist Germany. As another *juarense* playwright, Guadalupe de la Mora, explains in her prologue to de la Rosa's text: "Más allá de la cita directa o indirecta, la alusión o la reelaboración, lo que en definitivo vincula el texto de Perla de la Rosa con las versiones de Brecht y Anouilh, es que la autora se plantea el teatro a partir de su función social, a través de un discurso dirigido a condenar la tiranía y defender la libertad y la justicia, pero a partir de sucesos concretos, de personajes de carne y hueso y de frente a un público que comparte este momento histórico y político" (182).[7]

While critical and theoretical terminology can vary, in her study *Adaptation and Appropriation*, Julie Sanders opts for those that Gérard Genette proposes in *Palimpsests: Literature in the Second Degree* (1982; English translation 1997): *hypotext* for the source text of any appropriation or rewriting; *hypertext* for the appropriative or adaptive text; and *proximation* for an updating or the cultural relocation of a text to bring it into greater proximity to the cultural and temporal context of readers or audiences (qtd. in Sanders 6, 19, 162–63). According to these terms, then, de la Rosa's hypertext has a double frame: within Sophocles's hypotext, but also within the proximate frame of the Mexican border today (and a quadruple frame, if we count the citations from Anouilh and Brecht). There is here, therefore, repetition without replication, repetition with change, which Hutcheon argues is the essence of adaption as *adaptation* (xviii): "We retell—and show again and interact anew with—stories over and over; in the process, they change with each repetition, and yet they are recognizably the same" (177).

The major change in Perla de la Rosa's *Antígona* is that the body to be buried is not of a brother but instead of a sister, one who dares to venture forth from the underground caves where women have taken refuge from the war being waged against them by Creón, in the dry desert city of Thebes:

> MUJER 1: Soy una mujer en esta ciudad, donde todo es de arena. Desde hace años enfrentamos la Guerra. Ser mujer aquí es estar en peligro. Por ello decidimos construir refugios bajo la arena. Ampararnos bajo la arena para continuar viviendo. Se trata de ocultarnos, de desaparecer de la vista del enemigo. No todas han tomado la decisión, algunas piensan que están a salvo ... hacer como que pasa nada ... o como Clara, se arman de valor y salen a las fábricas. ... Alguien tiene que trabajar. (187–88)

Clara is Isabel's sister, and, like so many of the women killed in Ciudad Juárez, she is employed by one of the border maquiladoras. She is murdered just outside the front door of the house where she lives with Isabel and her other sister, Elena; neither sister comes to her aid, despite her screams for help.[8] When they see Clara's dead body, tied up in the same fashion of many of the victims of femicide, Elena runs out of the house after the soldiers who are taking the corpse; Isabel, on the other hand, denies knowing her dead sister, slams the door shut, and asks herself if it is worth risking her own life to go after Elena, who by leaving their house and breaking curfew is most probably facing a fate similar to Clara's.

This first scene, or prologue, segues into scene 2, "El regreso de Antigona," and from then on the play's dramatic action follows, but not always faithfully, its hypotext. According to de la Mora's analysis of the play, the titles of the eighteen brief scenes follow the hypotext's plot line, with three scenes that do so quite closely: the dialogues between Antigone and Ismene, Antigone and Creón, and Creón and Hemón (179). Still, the proximations to the hypotext of femicide in Ciudad Juárez are notable throughout the play: for example, Creón's refusal (like those of local and national Mexican government officials) to acknowledge the murder of the women, which is tantamount to erasing their existence, to making them invisible (the denying of the reality of unburied bodies to which Diéguez refers); or scene 18, "El engaño y el rencor," which echoes the words of plaintive mothers in Ciudad Juárez whose dead daughters are treated like so much trash:

> Generosamente pagan los gastos del funeral y aun así exhiben su mezquindad. En realidad lo que hace Creón es deshacerse de los cuerpos, que ya no puede negar. Los saca de la ciudad, les otorga un espacio entre los muertos de pobreza. Hasta al infierno mismo nos persiguen para dejar claro que no somos iguales. En esta maldita ciudad de siete puertas, hay muertos de primera ydequinta clase. Confinan a nuestras hijas al olvido. (208–9)

Like so many other speeches in the play, this one has clear extratheatrical references to the way in which, for years, the murdered women in and around Ciudad Juárez were dismissed as part of an underclass of prostitutes and similarly loose women who left their homes to work in maquiladoras, who went to bars dressed provocatively, and who basically got what they asked for—their mutilated corpses registered as mere statistics, as just a few more among hundreds and hundreds of "NN."

While in de la Rosa's *Antigone* women are most certainly brutalized victims, they are, however, also positive agents of the future. As Pianacci underscores in his study, "Si la interpretación mítica constituye un pensar en imágenes como realidades, las Antígonas latinoamericanas construyen sus imágenes como futuro" (178). This is where *Antígona, las voces que incendian el desierto* makes its most radical salvaging or re-creation (Hutcheon 8) of its hypotext; for in this play not only does Antigone fail to find her sister's body and give it a proper burial, she does not die. This Antigone survives; she chooses life in order to continue her quest for justice and the creation of a new reality (the utopia to which Pianacci refers). As testimony to her agency, de la Rosa's Antigone delivers the closing words of the play, in which she speaks directly to the audience and to all of us, in an exhortation that we join together in demanding the restitution of justice and the restoration of order and balance to a world spinning out of control into chaos: "Estás de luto ciudad mía. Debes estar de luto. Han asesinado toda esperanza. Te ha abandonado la ley. ... Te abandonó la justicia. ¿Te das cuenta? No hay justicia. Y no lo habrá hasta que todos ciudadanos, todos, ¿lo oyes? laven las culpas de estos crímenes. Hasta que todos tus hijos lloren las amargas lágrimas de las muertas del desierto" (227–28).

This new reality is still to be, as women in Ciudad Juárez and elsewhere in Mexico continue to be brutalized and murdered with impunity. [9] Mexican Antigones have a daunting challenge and mission, to be sure; and while de la Rosa's adaptation is open to positive outcomes, these outcomes are still to be realized.[10] Sadly, however, news of the femicides has taken second place to another kind of violence on Mexico's northern border: the narco wars, which for years just simmered and were mostly self-contained among cartels, with the tacit approval and complicity of the Mexican government, even though the butchery had begun to spill over into the civilian populations of border cities and states, which slowly but surely had been taken over by the cartels. When newly elected president Felipe Calderón declared open warfare on the drug lords in 2006, they responded in kind, understanding the declaration of war as carte blanche to fight back in the most barbaric manner with beheadings, bodies hanging from bridge posts, innumerable mutilated cadavers tossed out like garbage in black plastic bags, collateral damage among the civilian population, mass graves, and many, many disappeared. One particularly monstrous episode was the murder of a busload of migrants who were massacred by Los Zetas, deserters of the federal army who have brought their crack military expertise to drug trafficking; they are considered among the most extreme of the cartels. The massacre took place the small town of San Fernando in the northern state of Tamaulipas, which has experienced some of the worst drug-related violence of recent years.[11] Tricked into thinking that they were headed for an illegal border crossing into the United States, these mostly Central American migrants were, it is believed, to be used as potential mules or assassins by Los Zetas. Things apparently did not work out as planned, and the men on the bus were slaughtered and hastily buried in mass graves in the desert.[12] This incident is the basis for Sara Uribe's *Antígona González* (2012), and the playwright makes known up front her intention for the text to be a "deliberate, announced re-visitation" (Hutcheon 170) of Sophocles's *Antigone* as well as an indigenization into a Spanish-speaking world. Like the last name "Smith," González stands for a kind of everyman, but as the title makes clear, this González is marked by gender. As the text goes on to show, this Antigone is a Mexican everywoman who despairs of receiving news about her brother Tadeo, who was on the bus heading north. Once she hears of the bus's fate, she seeks to sort out her brother's remains from among the pile of disinterred corpses, to then bury him again.

Uribe's adaptation is quite different from Perla de la Rosa's in that the Antigone story here is more like a framework that is filled in with a mosaic of secondary quotations from a wide variety of sources. It most resembles what Sanders has identified as *collage*, an "assembling of found items to create a new aesthetic object" (4). Sanders proposes that for such a hypertext to constitute an adaptation, it must be in an extended, continuous dialogue with its hypotext (4), which indeed is the case with *Antígona González*, where the propelling dramatic force is the search for a brother felled in a war zone and the burying of his body; in so doing, Antígona must confront the ways of a corrupt official state apparatus as well as that of a new state-within-a-state, the vicious drug cartels: "¿Justicia? ¿Qué si espero que se haga justicia? ¿En este país? (40).

The text of *Antígona González* is written in a series of brief, and sometimes longer, almost poetic enunciations, which start with three instructions for finding and counting the dead:

> *Uno, las fechas, como los nombres, son lo más importante. El nombre por encima del calibre de las balas.* / Dos, sentarse frente a un monitor. Buscar la nota roja de todos los periódicos en línea. *Mantener la memoria de quienes han muerto.* / *Tres, contar inocentes y culpables, sicarios, niños, militares, civiles, presidentes municipales, migrantes, vendedores, secuestradores, policías.* / Contarlos a todos. / Nombrarlos a todos para decir: este cuerpo podría ser el mío. / El cuerpo de uno de los míos. / Para no olvidar que todos los cuerpos sin nombre son cuerpos de nuestros perdidos. (3; italics in original)

While many of the enunciations are free floating, their source is never clearly identified.[13] However, this opening sequence is clearly voiced by the eponymous character: "Me llamo Antígona González y busco entre los muertos el cadáver de mi hermano" (3). In the process of this search, this Antígona is identified with Sophocles's character but also with many of the other Antigones in Latin American drama; for example, there are citations from Pianacci's study: "La interpretación de Antígone sufre una radical alteración en Latinoamérica—endonde Políníces es identificado con los marginados y despararecidos" (10) and other academic studies. During her journey, Antígona González reconstructs the story of her brother through her own memories, and that of the ill-fated migrants through citations from newspapers in Tamaulipas, among other sources; other newspaper citations refer to the disappeared in different areas of Mexico. Most interesting in this string of quotations is how Sophocles's hypotext is mediated through yet another hypotext (which is also a hypertext): Griselda Gambaro's *Antígona furiosa*, especially through the reiteration of two citations: "*Siempre querré enterrar* a Tadeo. Aunque nazca mil veces y muera mil veces" (56) and "No, Tadeo, yo no he nacido para compartir el odio" (40). By quoting directly from Gambaro's *Antígona furiosa*, Uribe indigenizes Sophocles's text not just into a Mexican context but also into a wider Latin American one; in so doing, she proximates Mexico's dirty drugs wars to Argentina's fratricidal Dirty War of the 1970s and early 1980s.

Antígona González's structure of texts within texts, of quotations within quotations enunciated by seemingly disembodied, free-floating voices is very powerful in the way that it reiterates themes that run throughout the text, including those of the disappeared, of bodies in suspension, waiting to be found, buried and finally put to rest: "Rezo para que tu cuerpo ausente no quede impune. Para que no quede anónimo. Rezo para tener un sitio a dónde ir a llorar" (17); "eso es lo único que espero ya, un cuerpo, una tumba. Ese remanso" (37); "¿Qué cosa es el cuerpo cuando alguien lo desprovee de nombre, de historia, de apellido? ... Cuando no hay faz, ni rastro, ni huellas, ni señales. ... ¿Qué cosa es el cuerpo cuando está perdido?" (45). Even in its written form, the text captures this sense of absence, with the "parts" for voice placed on the page with often extensive blank spaces between them and occasionally with only one or two lines on a single page. The visual effect is that of concrete poetry, and the poetic nature of the written play script is also accentuated by the use of various techniques associated with poetic rhythm, for example the stichomythia of Greek tragedy: "Llenos de muertos. / Los caminos. / Por aquí también a usted. / Si entierra a sus muertos. / Dan más miedo ¿no?" (33); and the reiterated use of *estribillos* or refrains: "¿No hay un sol de los muertos? / Este sol ya no es el mío," which is repeated by various voices four times on pages 47 and 48.

The motif of voices is key in the plays studied here. It appears in the title of Perla de la Rosa's *Antígona, las voces que incendian el desierto*, and it functions as a thematic and structuring element in Uribe's *Antígona González*. These are the voices of strong women, descendants of Sophocles's Antigone, who struggle with the laws of tyrants (Creón in de la Rosa's adaptation, and the sinister capos of the drug trade and Mexico's corrupt politicians in Uribe's text). Antígona González also voices the utopian dream of a place where one can live a dignified and compassionate life, an ethical life in the face of almost inconceivable violence. While de la Rosa lets her Antigone have the last word and exhort all of us to take action, Uribe has her Antigone close the play by asking us to lend a helping hand: "¿Me ayudarás a levantar el cadáver?"(57). Both plays end by going beyond the "I" of the individual heroine to the collective "we": "Todos aquí iremos despareciendo si nos quedamos inermes sólo viéndonos entre nosotros, viendo cómo desaparecemos unoa a uno" (Uribe 54). Sanders notes that "[a]daptation is frequently involved in offering commentary on a source text; this is achieved most often by offering a revised point of view from the 'original,' adding hypothetical motivation, or voicing the silenced and marginalized" (18–19). Clearly this is often the case with adaptations of classical drama as practiced by Latin American playwrights, whose works have tended heavily toward the social and the political. It is understandable, then, that adaptations of Antigone undergo a radical alteration in the hands of these playwrights, who transform her into a champion of the marginalized and the disappeared. The "searcher" and the "searched" become everyday people caught up in circumstances not of their making and most certainly not of the gods' making, either. At this moment in Mexican history, these two Antigone adaptations are effective, necessary ways of confronting corrupt powers, gross and flagrant impunities, and a landscape littered with unburied bodies, or those quickly interred only to be dug up again and reinterred; of protesting violence against the powerless and the voiceless, be they women and young girls or those who perish in the cross fire of drug wars in which they are not major players, if players at all. Hutcheon poses the question, Why another adaptation? (95); and, in her introduction to *Feminist Readings of Antigone*, Fanny Söderbäck asks: "Why Antigone Today?" (1). Present realities of Mexico offer one very compelling answer to both these questions.

Notes

[1] The presentation, also published as a book, was at the Muestra Nacional de Teatro, in the city of Durango, Mexico, in November 2013. Diéguez's study is not concerned only with Mexico's disappeared but also those of Argentina, Colombia, Peru, and other Latin American countries that have endured extreme political and drug-related violence. She concentrates mostly on performance and installation art, as well as various forms of images, including photography. Her references are to a wide body of theoretical sources regarding violence, the body, and the arts (Walter Benjamin, Jean-Luc Nancy, Jacques Rancière, Slavoj Žižek, Beatriz Sarlo, Nelly Richard, Susan Sontag, and Judith Butler, among many, many others). Diéguez's is the most comprehensive study of its kind addressing this subject matter in Mexico and Latin America.

[2] *Femicide* (as opposed to *feminicide*) is the term often used among researchers of the murder of women of Juárez. The term was popularized by the Australian sociologist Diana E. H. Russell as a way to politicize the murder of women qua women, because they are women (thereby defining the act as a hate crime); see Russell's book, coedited with Jill Radford, *Femicide: The Politics of Woman Killing* (1992). See also her "The Origin and Importance of the Term *Femicide*," in which she talks about her unhappiness about how the term has sometimes been used in Latin America.

[3] In her review of Uribe's *Antígona González* (one of the plays studied here), Sylvia Aguilar Zéleny says: "En un país donde la violencia se vuelve el sistema operativo, en un país donde amanecen cadáveres de civiles en las primeras planas de los periódicos, en un país que es más un estado de sitio que otra cosa, no es de asombrarse que los autores vuelvan los ojos a la tragedia griega. ... Este es el caso de Sara Uribe quien toma en sus manos a la figura de Antígona y la coloca en un tablero actual para hablar de una *tragedia* real" (n.p.; italics in original).

[4] In fact, the Antigone figure has experienced something of a revival in critical studies in recent years, although not always as she reappears in contemporary theater; for example, Judith Butler's *Antigone's Claim: Kinship between Life and Death*, and her essay "Promiscuous Obedience" in the collection *Feminist Readings of Antigone*, edited by Fanny Söderbäck. ("Promiscuous Obedience" is also the final chapter of *Antigone's Claim*.)

[5] In her prologue to *Feminist Readings of Antigone*, Moira Fradinger also uses the image of a traveling Antigone, as she traces the character's journey throughout world literature; see "Nomadic Antigone."

[6] The bibliography concerning the femicides in Ciudad Juárez is very extensive. The following three studies are recommended: Sergio González Rodríguez, *The Femicide Machine* (2012); Teresa Rodríguez (with Diana Montané and Lisa Pulitzer), *The Daughters of Juárez: A True Story of Serial Murder South of the Border* (2007); and Diana Washington Valdez, *The Killing Fields: Harvest of Women; The Truth about Mexico's Bloody Border Legacy* (2006).

[7] Guadalupe de la Mora's prologue to the published text of *Antígona, las voces que incendian el desierto* remains one of the most thorough and insightful commentaries about de la Rosa's play. The analysis done by the classical scholar Jesse Weiner is also very valuable: "*Antigone* in Juárez: Tragedy, Politics, and Public Women on Mexico's Northern Border."

[8] This opening scene, entitled "Prólogo," is a clear citation from Brecht's *Antigone*, which also starts with a prologue, which takes place during World War II. Two sisters open their door to their brother, who has returned from the front. They take him in (unlike the scene in de la Rosa's text), but he has deserted the German front and, after being found at his siblings' house, is hung from a lamppost. Brecht's purpose, like de la Rosa's, is to proximate his text to contemporary events and to make of Antigone and Polyneices political heroes who fight against the tyranny represented by Creon. It should be stressed, however, that few scholars believe that this was Sophocles's purpose. Rather, his Creon is described as a ruler who champions the laws of the polis, and it is against these

laws that his Antigone rebels; both are presented as blinded by hubris, and this leads to their tragic downfalls. However, as both Hutcheon and Sanders argue, adaptations and appropriations are not bound to their original hypotext.

[9] In August 2015, in what was billed as "el juicio del siglo" in Ciudad Juárez, five men were found guilty of kidnapping, prostituting, and then killing eleven women between the ages of eighteen and twenty-five; they were sentenced to a total of three hundred years behind bars. This has been a landmark case that breaks with the impunity that those involved in femicide (killers, law enforcement, and politicians) have enjoyed.

[10] According to recent statistics, femicide in Mexico continues at an alarming rate. As reported by Judith Matloff, in 2012 and 2013 only 24 percent of 3,892 femicides were investigated by authorities, and of these, only 1.6 percent led to sentencing. On average, six women are murdered in Mexico every day.

[11] There were two massacres: the first in 2010, with 47 known dead, and the second in 2011, with 193 bodies found in clandestine graves. It has been proven that Los Zetas were behind both massacres, with little doubt that local police were also complicit. Alma Guillermoprieto, in "The Murderers of Mexico," talks about four important books dealing with the drug cartels, and she gives a good sense of how Los Zetas operate. Coverage of the 2011 massacre, especially, has been worldwide, with stories appearing in just about every major newspaper.

[12] On September 26, 2014, another flagrant and shocking violation of human rights took place in the town of Iguala in the state of Guerrero, where forty-three students from a rural teachers college were disappeared; as of summer 2015, their fate is still not known for sure. At one point, it was believed that they had been kidnapped by a local drug gang (at the behest of the mayor) and that their bodies were incinerated at a local dump; despite the federal government's initial acceptance of this story, forensics have been able to identify the incinerated remains of only one student. Federal officials point fingers at local authorities and vice versa. In the meantime, the case has brought international investigative teams to the area, and parents of the disappeared keep pushing for the truth about happened to their children. The Iguala disappearances continue to receive wide coverage internationally.

[13] While Uribe does not identify the sources of her citations within the text of her play, she often uses normal script for her original text and italics for what she is citing. However, the last page of Uribe's text includes a long list of sources, although they do not seem to be listed in the order in which they appear in the play text.

Works Cited

Aguilar Zéleny, Sylvia. "*Antígona González* de Sara Uribe." *Borderzine*, August 8, 2013. At http://borderzine.com/2013/08/12-antigona-gonzalez-de-sara-uribe/.

Brunn, Victoria. "From Tragedy to Ritual: Latin American Adaptations of Sophocles' 'Antigone.'" Diss. Columbia U, 2009.

Butler, Judith. *Antigone's Claim: Kinship between Life and Death*. New York: Columbia UP, 2002.

———. "Promiscuous Obedience." *Feminist Readings of Antigone*. Ed. Fanny Söderbäck. Albany: State U of New York P, 2010. 133–53.

De la Mora, Guadalupe. "Las voces de Antígona en Ciudad Juárez." *Cinco dramaturgos chihuahuenses*. Ed. Víctor Hugo Rascón Banda et al. Ciudad Juárez: Fondo Municipal Editorial Revolvente, 2005. 169–83.

De la Rosa, Perla. *Antígona, las voces que incendian el desierto. Cinco dramaturgos chihuahuenses*. Ed. Víctor Hugo Rascón Banda et al. Ciudad Juárez: Fondo Municipal Editorial Revolvente, 2005. 187–228.

Diéguez, Ileana. *Cuerpos sin duelo: Iconografías y teatralidades del dolor*. Córdoba: Ediciones DocumentA/Escénicos, 2013.

Duprey, Jennifer. "Antigone and the Poliethical Life." *Whose Voice Is This? Iberian and Latin American* Antigones. Ed. Jennifer Duprey. *Hispanic Issues On Line* (Fall 2013). 1–23. At https://cla.umn.edu/sites/cla.umn.edu/files/hiol_13_00_duprey_antigone_and_the_poliethical_life.pdf.

Fradinger, Moira. "Nomadic Antigone." *Feminist Readings of Antigone*. Ed. Fanny Söderbäck. Albany: State U of New York P, 2010. 15–23.

Gambaro, Griselda. *Antígona furiosa. Teatro 3*. Buenos Aires: Ediciones de la Flor, 2011.

Genette, Gérard. *Palimpsests: Literature in the Second Degree*. Trans. Channa Newman and Claude Dubinsky. Lincoln: U of Nebraska P, 1997.

González Rodríguez, Sergio. *The Femicide Machine*. Trans. Michael Parker-Stainback. Cambridge: MIT P, 2012.

Guillermoprieto, Alma. "The Murderers of Mexico." *New York Review of Books*, October 28, 2010. At http://www.nybooks.com/articles/2010/10/28/murderers-mexico/.

Hutcheon, Linda, with Siobhan O'Flynn. *A Theory of Adaptation*. 2nd ed. London: Routledge, 2013.

Lambright, Anne. "Woman, Body and Memory: Yuyachkani's Peruvian *Antigone*." *Women in Theater and Film*. Spec. issue of *Feminist Scholarship Review* 11.1 (Fall 2001): 7–11.

Matloff, Judith. "Six Women Murdered Each Day as Femicide in Mexico Nears a Pandemic." Al Jazeera, January 4, 2015. At http://america.aljazeera.com/multimedia/2015/1/mexico-s-pandemicfemicides.html.

"Occupy Antigone: Tradition, Transition and Transformation in Performance." At http://www.theaterwetenschappen.ugent.be/occupyantigone.

Pianacci, Rómulo E. *Antígona: una tragedia latinoamericana*. Irvine, CA: Ediciones de GESTOS, 2008.

Rodríguez, Teresa, with Diana Montané and Lisa Pulitzer. *The Daughters of Juárez: A True Story of Serial Murder South of the Border*. New York: Simon & Shuster, 2007.

Russell, Diana E. H. "The Origin and Importance of the Term *Femicide*." December 2011. At www.dianarussell.com/origin_of_femicide.html.

Russell, Diana E. H., and Jill Radford, eds. *Femicide: The Politics of Woman Killing*. New York: Twayne Publishers; Milton Keynes, Buckinghamshire, England: Open University P, 1992.

Sanders, Julie. *Adaptation and Appropriation*. London: Routledge, 2006.

Söderbäck, Fanny, ed. *Feminist Readings of Antigone*. Albany: State U of New York P, 2010.

———. "Why Antigone Today?" *Feminist Readings of Antigone*. Ed. Fanny Söderbäck. Albany: State U of New York P, 2010. 1–13.

Steiner, George. *Antigones: How the Antigone Legend Has Survived in Western Literature, Art, and Thought*. Oxford: Oxford UP, 1984.

Uribe, Sara. *Antígona González*. Mexico City: Surplus Ediciones, 2012.

Washington Valdez, Diana. *The Killing Fields: Harvest of Women; The Truth about Mexico's Bloody Border Legacy*. Burbank: Peace at the Border, 2006.

Watanabe, José. *Antígona: Versión libre de la tragedia de Sófocles*. Lima: Yuyachkani/Comisión de Derechos Humanos, 2000.

Weiner, Jesse. "*Antigone* in Juárez: Tragedy, Politics, and Public Women on Mexico's Northern Border." *Classical Receptions Journal* (December 2014): 1–34. At http://crj.oxfordjournals.org/content/early/2014/12/04/crj.clu021.

6

Toward an Epistemology of Enchantment:
Don Quixote and the Limits of Cinema

Adrián Pérez Melgosa

Stony Brook University

Cervantes's *Don Quixote* has established a prolonged and revealing relationship with cinema. First of all, it has become the literary work most frequently adapted to film throughout the history of cinema (Mancing 176).[1] Since 1898, when French producer Léon Gaumont filmed a few fragments of Don Quixote's story in a silent short, and until 2016, when Terry Gilliam has new hopes of finishing his long-promised *The Man Who Killed Don Quixote*, more than 350 films have attempted to render the novel visually for the big screen and for a variety of smaller ones.[2] If we widen our conceptual sieve to include those movies that without properly adapting the novel still convey what Pedro Javier Pardo García calls Cervantine, Quixotic, and Quixotizing artistic visions, the influence of this novel reveals itself as a preeminent force throughout world cinema.[3] There is also a substantial critical bibliography devoted to analyzing these adaptations and the novel's connection to film from multiple perspectives that have now developed into recognizable strands in both Cervantine and film studies.[4] Most importantly for our purposes are two other points of contact between *Don Quixote* and cinema. One concerns the theoretical discussion, disseminated throughout the novel itself, about the distinct virtues that image and letter hold as tools to represent, understand, and interpret the world. The second stems from a retroactive reading of these reflections within a novel that becomes possible when considered from the point of view of the many failures and limited successes that characterize the corpus of films that have attempted to render into images and sounds *Don Quixote*'s words. Looking at these two points of contact—a reading of cinema that springs from *Don Quixote*'s attention to the description and theorization of sight and sound, and a retroactive reading of the novel departing from the films it has inspired—this paper traces the existence within Cervantes's text of a theory of visuality that we may term an epistemology of enchantment.

The novel describes a way of understanding the act of looking that transcends the hierarchies of the traditional gaze to show the interdependence of the looking subject and the looked-at object as they engage in a sustained struggle between what the subject desires to see and how the object desires to be seen. As we will see below, this theory of audiovisual images and their reception becomes particularly evident when the novel is read in light of the many failed attempts at adapting the book to the film media. Professor Robert ter Horst used to open his classes on *Don Quixote* describing it as the inauguration, culmination, and exhaustion of the narrative possibilities of the novel. He frequently went on to explore the visuality of this work by calling our attention to the recurrent efforts of the characters to see in situations where darkness was frequently the norm. In many ways, this essay finds its origin in the transposition of ter Horst's insightful assessment of Cervantes's work to its interaction with film.

I will pay special attention to four films from different periods, by directors of different nationalities. Two are completed adaptations of the novel: Georg Willem Pabst's *The Adventures of Don Quixote* (1933) and Manuel Gutiérrez Aragón's Spanish television series *El Quijote de Miguel de Cervantes* (1992). The other two remain uncompleted to this date: Orson Welles's *Don Quixote* (USA/Spain) and Terry Gilliam's *The Man Who Killed Don Quixote* (USA/UK). Film adaptations of *Don Quixote* such as these make visible the traces of a map charting the visual and auditory realms embedded in Cervantes's novel. As this map registers the contours, accidents, and edges of the audio-visual, it also signals the location of the representational limits of cinema. In turn, these film adaptations of *Don Quixote* become material manifestations of a theory of looking based on enchantment. As they do so, the film adaptations as a whole provide the necessary symbolic environment to engage in a double rereading of Cervantes's novel: first, as what Darío Villanueva has identified as "pre-cinema," namely employing narrative techniques that would become central to cinema; and second, as post-cinema, marking the contours of cinema and signaling that which exceeds its representational possibilities.

Haunted Cinema: When *Don Quixote* Becomes Film

The history of *Don Quixote*'s film adaptations is plagued with a variety of paradoxical failures. Among the successfully completed films (produced, finished, and released) based on the novel, we find a profusion of disappointing selective reductions, elisions, and elaborations of arbitrarily chosen passages. These are simplifications that strive to be faithful to the narrative surface of the original text but frequently resulting in unremarkable films. The great number of these disappointing adaptations implicitly conveys the sense of an impossibility, of a limit to what it is possible to represent from this novel by merely relying on visual and auditory impressions captured by a camera. As a group, these films contain the implicit message that if an adaptation of *Don Quixote* is to reach completion, the directors must trivialize the novel aesthetically, thematically, or both. Thus, the great majority of films successfully completed have met with varying degrees of aesthetic, critical, and commercial failure.

A second group of films comprising uncompleted and fragmentary attempts at adaptations have become famous failures. Halted at the preproduction or production stages, these films appear haunted by a curse that prevents their production teams, for whatever reason, from finishing their work. These films' backstage stories, frequently drawn out over several decades, are plagued with financial hurdles, production missteps, and a variety of calamitous accidents. The best examples of the extreme effects of *Don Quixote*'s combination of inspiration and curse are Orson Welles's *Don Quixote* and Terry Gilliam's *The Man Who Killed Don Quixote*, two never-completed films that, as we will analyze below in more detail, could be characterized as successful failures.

Even more lineal films like Georg Willem Pabst's *Don Quixote* and Manuel Gutiérrez Aragón's several attempts to adapt the book, first into the television series *El Quijote de Miguel de Cervantes* (1992) and second in his feature film *El Caballero Don Quijote* (2002), are good examples of works that, the more they tried to become adequate representations of Cervantes's novel, the further they became mired in a labyrinth of technical impossibilities and material obstacles. Paradoxically, the films that failed to reach completion both contain and have become through their intimate acquaintance with protracted failure worthy representations and continuations of the dilemmas, complexities, and artistic vision conveyed in Cervantes's novel. Arthur Penn summarizes this double irony (failed successes versus successful failures) when he states, referring to his reluctance to make a film inspired by *Don Quixote*, that "with this work failure is a must" (*El Universal*).[5]

Penn here makes two statements that capture the doubly haunting hold that Cervantes's text casts on film. First, he says that anyone attempting to adapt *Don Quixote* to film "must fail"; that is, they will necessarily produce an inadequate rendition of the novel. Second, he conveys the idea that "failure" itself is a central concept in *Don Quixote*'s narrative. In other words, to produce an adequate rendition of the novel, the director "must fail" to complete the film. In spite of this, the film adaptations of *Don Quixote* keep appearing with astounding regularity. The desire to adapt

Don Quixote into a movie is already encoded and set in motion by the novel itself. Early in the second chapter of the first volume, as Don Quixote leaves his unnamed village for the very first time, his thoughts reach forward:

> Dichosa edad, y siglo dichoso aquel adonde saldrán a luz las famosas hazañas mías, dignas de entallarse en bronces, esculpirse en mármoles y pintarse en tablas para memoria en lo futuro. ¡Oh tú sabio encantador, quienquiera que seas, a quien ha de tocar el ser cronista desta peregrina historia! (71)
>
> (Fortunate the time and blessed the age when my famous deeds will come to light, worthy of being carved in bronze, sculpted in marble, and painted on tablets as a remembrance in the future. O thou, wise enchanter, whoever thou mayest be, whose task it will be to chronicle this wondrous history!) (25)[6]

Through this exhortation, Don Quixote enters the realm of performative aesthetics. Reversing the traditional hierarchy between creator and creation, these words set in motion a powerful rhetoric designed by the character to take control over his future life in a variety of artistic reproductions. As he invokes the figure of the "sabio encantador," Don Quixote reaches forward in time to interpellate future writers, painters, and film directors. Filmmakers and their films thus become projections of Don Quixote's desires, already anticipated by the novel's protagonist.

Perhaps the abundance of film adaptations of the novel does obey the will of Don Quixote, or perhaps each new adaptation is spurred by the ambition to succeed where others have failed. From a purely formal point of view, however, the widespread desire to embark on a *Don Quixote* film project stems from the overt visual and auditory character of the novel's language, an aspect well commented upon among Cervantes scholars. For example, in his study of the transition of Don Quixote from character to icon, E. C. Riley describes the book as "a novel conceived in strongly visual terms" (111). Darío Villanueva studies the novel's reliance on the ear and the eye as proof of its status as "toda una enciclopedia narrativa genuinamente precinematográfica" (a whole narrative encyclopedia genuinely pre-cinematographic) (88).[7] In this regard, he specifically identifies *Don Quixote*'s attention to dialogue, its reliance on comic situations that parallel the structure of cinematic gags, and the novel's montage-like narrative structure (76, 89). Paradoxically, many of the critics who highlight the work's visual deftness also mention the failure of most film adaptations to capture the richness and complexity that breathes through the novel. Howard Mancing, for example, concludes his evaluation of the filmic adaptations of the novel by stating: "Cervantes wrote for the imaginative and creative reader and can only truly be understood by reading his novel" (179). Thus with the same poignant ease with which both promise and failure coexist within the adventures of Don Quixote itself, these two opposites also blend with each other in the book's exegesis and in its corpus of film adaptations. Yet the significance of this apparent performative contagion, in which critics and film adaptations end up mimicking in their commentary and their production histories the paradoxical nature of Don Quixote's quest to become a knight errant, remains to be interpreted.

Enchanted Images: Looking Beyond Plato and Narcissus

I would like to suggest a third way to read this contrast between the cinematic promise of the novel and the paradoxical failures of its film adaptations. More than examples of the inadequacies of the film medium to capture the novel, as a whole the film adaptations of *Don Quixote* are material evidence of a theory of perception set in motion by the novel itself. This theory emerges from the novel's sustained questioning, destabilization, and eventual reversal of a variety of hierarchical relations, especially those between image and letter, eye and vision, ear and sound, subject and object, past and future, author and character. The concept of enchantment stands at the center of this theorization. In the novel, the abstract referent of this concept is a mysterious force that manipulates, corrupts, meddles with, and alters both images and sounds. Don Quixote frequently uses this concept to explain the gap existing between what he sees and what others see. Within the novel, enchantment renders visual and auditory images as unstable, pleasurable, yet deceptive sources of information about the world. They are both a source of wonder and the origin of tragedy. Enchantment allows for glimpses of the grandeur hidden beneath decrepit appearances, and also places Don Quixote in continuous physical danger.

Through this concept, *Don Quixote* intervenes in a classical discussion about visuality began by two other pre-cinematic texts: the Greek myth of Narcissus and Plato's parable of the cave. As many critics have suggested, these texts are not only central to the development of Western thought, they also contain the conceptual seeds for the development of film. Plato's myth suggests that in our perceptions of the world we are all prisoners of a carefully crafted deception. Like slaves in a cave who are only allowed to see the shadows of the real world outside, our senses only allow us to experience imperfect copies of the flawless elements from the ideal world, a world more real than the one in which we live.[8] Beautiful Narcissus fell in love with his own image reflected on the surface of clear water and with the sounds of his voice's echo. The water in this story, a natural screen, not only foreshadows the invention of cinema but forces the question "is the cinema screen a window into the world or a mirror inviting us to step through it?" (Gardies 111). These two stories anticipate the powerful spell that reproduced images and sounds have upon us. They also have been deployed to theorize the role of the spectator, the powerful process of identification that takes place in a film, and the ability of reflected images and sounds to masquerade as reality.

Looking at the long history of influence that these parables have had on Western thinking, some critics defend that cinema had to be invented in order to provide legitimacy to the centrality of the eye within Western epistemology. Others, most prominently Kaja Silverman, see in film, especially in experimental cinema, a performative critique of these two foundational theories of the visual. Silverman coins the expression "world spectatorship" to represent a new conceptualization of seeing and being seen. "The world," concludes Silverman, "'intends' toward being seen; it aspires or moves toward appearance. When we look at other creatures and things [as world spectators] it is also in response to their very precise solicitation to us to do so" (129). By pointing at the inherent desire of the world "to be seen," Silverman is endowing the object with a particular kind of agency, and both seer and seen as co-collaborators in the negotiation of meaning and identity.

Silverman's critique of traditional Western notions of visuality provides a conceptual background to discuss the specificity of the epistemology of enchantment embedded in *Don Quixote*. The novel takes up on the ideas of Plato and the myth of Narcissus and constructs yet another level of thinking upon them. It is in the use of the word "encantamiento," a dynamic concept whose meaning evolves and becomes more complex as the book advances, where Don Quixote's cinematographic promise lies. It also contains the seeds that have yielded so many of its production difficulties.

One of the early episodes of the novel, the manufacturing of a visor made out of pasteboard to complete the defenses of the main character's dilapidated armored helmet, contains an insight about the initial relation of *Don Quixote* to vision and enchantment. This episode has been commented upon by both John Barth and his teacher Pedro Salinas as the very first quixotic adventure in the novel (Barth 23): quixotic because, after the visor breaks in an initial test of its strength, our protagonist "la tornó a hacer de nuevo, poniéndole unas barras de hierro por de dentro, de tal manera que él quedó satisfecho de su fortaleza; y, sin querer hacer nueva experiencia della, la diputó y tuvo por celada finísima de encaje" (67–68) ("made another one, placing strips of iron on the inside so that he was satisfied with its strength; and not wanting to put it to the test again, he designated and accepted it as an extremely fine sallet") (22). For Barth, this episode is a demonstration that true quixotism is not the "misperception of things, a way of acting on those misperceptions" (23). There is, however, not only a reflection on action here but on the very action of seeing. This episode reveals the starting point of a complex relationship with visuality and an intimate relation with failure. It is not inconsequential that the piece of armor he is repairing will perform the function of a visor, as the screen through which our protagonist will see the world.

Few film adaptations have captured this apparently straightforward and easy-to-visualize scene. Perhaps the reason is that it captures Don Quixote alone, without contrasting witnesses, deploying simultaneously two ways of looking. After finishing the first pasteboard visor, he trusts in the correspondence between image, function, and identity. If it looks like a good piece of armor, it will certainly act as a strong protection against the strike of a sword. But the test itself also signals the existence of a doubt, that the pasteboard defense may not be as strong as it looks. Here, Don Quixote simultaneously looks with a narcissistic gaze (things reflect my desires) and a platonic one (things are always imperfect reflections of the ideal they emulate). These two ways of looking are also present in the second attempt to manufacture a visor: in the platonic resignation to "reinforce" the inadequate copy of a visor, and in the narcissistic "satisfaction" that his reinforcement will be sufficient. As he accepts the makeshift visor as a fine one and moves on with other preparations, Don Quixote is also tacitly announcing that neither of these two codes of interpretation of the visual world provides the kind of understanding of visuality that he needs to proceed with his plans.

One of the few film renditions of this visor episode appears in Manuel Gutiérrez Aragón's *El Quijote de Miguel de Cervantes*. On the screen, the scene presents Don Quixote (played by Fernando Rey) as a decrepit, possibly mad, old man who still holds onto some figments of a former dignified bearing. He sits in his library dressed in his white linen nightgown and surrounded by large books. In Gutiérrez Aragón's images, the manufacturing of the visor (fashioning, testing, remaking, being satisfied) becomes a process of identity transformation. It is Alonso Quixano whom the scene shows alone repairing the visor first and then witnessing its failure. By the end, while talking to his maid (played by Terele Pávez), the protagonist reveals to her, and to the audience, his newly minted identity as Don Quixote of La Mancha. Through the eyes of this witness, Alonso's transformation becomes the delusion of a mad old man, even if the camera's heroic depiction of Don Quixote's silhouette backlit by the glowing rays of the summer sun lend him for a brief moment the semblance of possessing the appearance of a strong hero.

In the novel, by contrast, the whole scene is one of solitude, trial, failure, and moving onto the next task. While it represents a turning point in the process of transformation of Alonso Quixano into Don Quixote, the novel does not show its completion. The very scene that announces the beginning of Don Quixote's search for adventures also chronicles his search for a third understanding of the relationship between vision and the world, one that transcends the narcissistic and the platonic gazes. Implicit in this pairing of the chivalric quest and the search for an adequate theory of perception is the epistemological character of Don Quixote's adventures. What he finds immediately after his first sally is a world full of deceptions that force things to appear as less than what they really are. In this world, princesses acquire the appearance of common peasants, castles look like country inns, and he himself seems an old, weak, and delusional man. This awareness explains why, during his first night out, when a group of country women he addresses as noble ladies help him off his armor, he refuses to take off his helmet. He says he does not deserve to be seen until he has performed enough feats such that he will not need an introduction. In light of the visor event, it is possible to see that Don Quixote knows that these young women will (imbued of a platonic gaze) see the old decrepit man he is as a degraded version of the ideal knight they might have in their imaginations. He predicts that once he becomes famous, people will look at him with different eyes and look beyond his decrepit appearance to see him as a strong, heroic figure.

Beyond World Spectatorship: Enchantment and the Limits of Film

Film directors must certainly have felt, and will probably continue to feel, seduced by the misalignment between Don Quixote's vision and what Sancho, the rest of the characters, and the narrator, see. Once they attempt to film those same events, they must confront a "dreadful" dilemma: the camera must either portray the reality as described by the narrator by showing the scene through the eyes of some witnessing characters like the maid, Sancho, or others, while allowing Don Quixote's words to describe his vision; or it must portray his words in images, endowing them with the "effect of the real" that characterizes cinema as a medium. In this second alternative, the "real" point of view of the narration must appear portrayed in the voice of Sancho, the narrator, or the other characters. Directors therefore must either align themselves with the spectacle of seeing an aging man fighting windmills, or find the ways to render in film the magical enchantment of finding an army of giants in the deserted plains of La Mancha. A third path that would intertwine the two visions seems also possible, but once cast in images the result puts the movie straight in the very fantastic world that Cervantes is leaving behind. This approach has been frequently used in adaptations of the novel rendered in animated cartoons.

Let's analyze how this has worked in a few versions by looking at their rendering of the famous adventure of the windmills. In the novel, the episode starts when Don Quixote and Sancho run into some thirty windmills on a deserted plain. Alone with Sancho, Don Quixote announces that these are giants and that he intends to fight them. Sancho conveys that all he sees are windmills. Eventually, Don Quixote attacks a sail, which hits him back, sending him to the ground. Humiliated both physically and in his pride, Don Quixote now sees the windmills but declares the transformation to be part of a trick played on him by his enemy enchanter, Festón.

In 1933, Pabst's film *Adventures of Don Quixote* took the route of emphasizing Sancho's and the narrator's perspectives, banning from the images Don Quixote's vision of the giants. The scene is beautifully filmed, including a technically unusual and highly dramatic shot of Don Quixote (played by Feodor Chaliapin Sr.) shown from the point of view of the turning sails, as he turns a full circle while being stuck in one of them. Pabst has populated the scene with lines of laborers loading sacks of flour away from the mills, the priest, the barber, and Sansón Carrasco. Their presence reinforces Sancho's ways of seeing. Furthermore, Pabst's scene suppresses any possible metaphoric value of the mills by showing the peasants controlling the sails with a large piece of wood. Thus, Pabst stresses the impossible existence of Don Quixote's vision of the giants. In doing so, he dismisses the enchanted gaze as an error. Peculiar to this adaptation is the placement of this scene at the end of the movie. This defeat of Don Quixote marks the end of his adventures and his repentant return to his village. Thus Pabst's adaptation, rather than showing the adventure of the windmills as a first attempt by Don Quixote to impose his vision of the world, presents it as the challenge that completely unravels Don Quixote's mode of perception.

In 1992, Gutiérrez Aragón's television series *El Quijote de Miguel de Cervantes* emphasized the dangerous appearance of the mills through camerawork and the mise-en-scène. Low-angle shots show the mills towering over the frail figure of Don Quixote. Close-ups of the moving sails highlight the danger of their relentless motion. By grouping more than twenty windmills on the frame and coordinating the movement of their sails, the director uses the images to convey a sense of orderly formation that resembles that of an army. Rather than portraying the windmills as the famous whitewashed, quaint cylindrical buildings commonly associated with La Mancha, the walls of Gutiérrez Aragón's windmills are covered in brown dust, and their stucco is cracked, showing many of the stones underneath. The windmills look both like well-worn constructions and like a camouflaged contraption from a fantasy army. The duality of the vision of Don Quixote is further emphasized by his walking sword in hand among the threatening windmills, identifying each with the name of a giant. Somehow, he knows that these "giants" are stuck to the ground and will not advance to meet him. When Sancho warns Don Quixote that they are indeed windmills, his response, "they are giants," indicates more a will to see what is not visible than a statement of misrecognition. In this way, this adaptation manages to keep some of the tension between the enchanted vision of the knight and the one of his esquire. By contrast with Pabst's film, there are no outside witnesses here. Eventually the camera chooses Sancho's point of view as the one that portrays reality, but in the dialogue Don Quixote introduces the figure of the "encantador," signaling his first attempt to bridge the gap between his vision and that of Sancho. The images still anchor our perception on what Sancho sees.

Moving onto the "unfinished" adaptations, Orson Welles's version, as seen in the compilation made by Jesús Franco in 1992, is the only one that chooses to deviate from the conventions of cinematic realism. As in Gutiérrez Aragón's adaptation for television, Welles shows Don Quixote (played by Francisco Reiguera) and Sancho (Akim Tamiroff) facing the windmills in a deserted plain, but Welles attempts to show Don Quixote's vision by animating the sails: first through mechanical props that bend them forward and backward as if the sails were arms trying to reach an opponent, then by editing multiple images of the moving sails superimposed together. Both techniques convey the unpredictability and danger of something alive. Welles also places special emphasis on Don Quixote's processing of his defeat, showing him contemplating with indignation the giants-turned-mills and condemning the "enchanter" who conceived this affront to his courage.

Lost in La Mancha (Keith Fulton and Louis Pepe, 2002) is a documentary that chronicles Terry Gilliam's repeated attempts and failures to film his version of *Don Quixote*. His adaptation presents the most accurate depiction of the different points of view concurring in the adventure of the windmills and, therefore, preserves some of the tension between reality and imagination that Cervantes portrays, but it does so at the price of rendering the whole scene in animated cartoons, opting for highlighting the allegorical dimension of the fight with the mills while downplaying the realism that Cervantes cultivated. The written text simultaneously embraces and praises both spectacle and enchantment while taking any chance to critique their contributions to the misrepresentation of the world. The film versions, so far, have either aligned themselves with the portrayal of the fight against the mills as a spectacle as in Pabst and Gutiérrez Aragón, or as a reflection on the power of allegory as in Gilliam's and Welles's versions. As films, each of these four adaptations is a skillful and engaging work. As renditions of the novel, however, they fail to fully engage with the book's complex notion of "encantamiento." After the manufacturing of the visor, the windmills episode represents the second stage of the development of this notion. Here, enchantment points to the ability of magical powers to change the appearance of things. Either as windmills or as giants, these are not degraded versions of a platonic ideal, nor do they represent a narcissistic projection either of Sancho or Don Quixote.

As the first part advances, enchantment gradually becomes a signifier that reveals the subtle way in which things are not what they appear: pasteboard that becomes a visor in a suit of armor, characters acting as authors, giants disguised as windmills, armies as herds of sheep, prostitutes who become princesses, a helmet that appears a barber's basin. The connection between what Sancho and the narrator see, and what Don Quixote perceives, is a rhetorical one based on analogy. It follows the lines of Silverman's notion of "world spectatorship" in that "visual perception is not located 'in' us. It is situated rather at the point at which memory meets external stimulus" (128). The world of which Don Quixote becomes a spectator is connected through his memory and analogy to the world he has read in his favorite books.

Throughout the second part of *Don Quixote*, and following the path outlined in his refusal to test the strength of his helmet piece for a second time, Don Quixote gradually refrains from assessing his visions experientially. Also throughout this second part, Sancho learns the strategic use of the concept of "enchantment" in order to negotiate the difficult task of finding Dulcinea. In his most extreme rejection of the stubborn "real," Don Quixote willingly returns to a simulacrum of Plato's scenario, here known as Montesinos's cave, where he is to find the most "real" and therefore "ideal" of his adventures. There, he avoids the interference of other witnesses by descending by himself into the darkness of the cave. No one, not even the narrator, can pass judgment on the truth of what Don Quixote has seen there. It is in the darkness of this cave that spectacle will stop coming from the confrontation between Don Quixote's vision and reality and begin to spring only exclusively from "encantamiento." In Montesinos's cave, Don Quixote's senses stop receiving information from the outside world, and reality springs completely from the mind. Under these conditions, spectacle and enchantment become the tools for a critique of both the real and the platonic ideal. The visions that Don Quixote relishes in the cave do not come from shadows but exclusively from dreams and memory.

From 1955 until his death in 1985, Orson Welles searched for a suitable way to render these three elements in film: reality, spectacle, and enchantment. In the remaining footage of his uncompleted project, we find scenes in which the path of the characters meets with that of the author (Welles) as Sancho, who has managed to survive until the twentieth century. In one of these anachronistic scenes, Sancho watches a real Noticiarios y Documentales, or "No-Do," the weekly newsreel that, under Franco, was shown in every cinema before the main feature was projected. On screen, we see the announcement of a new "infallible" air missile and images of Orson Welles as he receives a prize in Jerez. Here, the film is actualizing a motive already present in the novel. Welles maintains that balance between creation and creator, between the visual and the material, and becomes a "dichoso cronista y encantador." Welles could not fully escape *Don Quixote*'s curse. By focusing on transferring Cervantes's loving critique of Western culture's infatuation with Platonism and narcissism, Welles went so far astray from the story of the novel that he could never find an understanding producer who would provide financial backing for his project.

In his early prophetic words, Don Quixote referred to future artists using the terms "cronistas" and "encantadores" as synonyms. But the narrator of the book constantly works to separate them into two different personas: Cide Hamete Benengeli and a narrator homonymous with Cervantes. This allows Cervantes, the author, to both praise and critique the labor of each writer as well as their purely materialistic or magical views of the world. Unlike Cervantes, directors have only rarely been willing to inhabit that double space, and when they do, they end up feeling so close to the text that no actual image contains enough of *Don Quixote* to satisfy them.

Miguel de Unamuno, in his *Vida de Don Quijote y Sancho*, observed how many of the adventures related in the novel contain stern warnings about the dangers that would issue from the technification of society. For Unamuno, the windmills Don Quixote fights as giants are the forebears of steam, electric, and combustion engines, all of which "siembran mal por la tierra" (seed evil throughout the earth) (78). As a prominent link in this lineage of technical inventions, cinema would certainly not escape the denunciation of the pitfalls of modernity that Unamuno perceives in the novel. Yet film is also a plastic media of expression, and, as such, its relationship with the original book not only is one of "quarrelsome giant" but also encodes information about the original work and transforms it. It is through cinema that we are able to access Don Quixote's struggles to transcend Plato's and Narcissus's ways of seeing by becoming a "world spectator." Through this concept, Silverman attempts to debunk "the fiction that the look always effects an unpleasurable subordination of what it sees" (Pachmanová 38). Reciprocally, it shows that when the look abandons commonsensical ways of seeing, what is seen effects an unpleasurable subordination upon the look. This is where *Don Quixote*'s epistemology of enchantment departs from Silverman's concept of world spectatorship. Silverman locates in the visual realm the possibility to undo the chain of social hierarchies that derive from the platonic split between an object and its shadow, between the idea and the real. Silverman concludes:

> If words represented our only form of symbolization, we would indeed be hopelessly estranged from the world. Not only would we be unable to determine with any assurance whether anything else existed, we would also remain forever in irresolute doubt as to whether we ourselves did. Like Descartes, we would be obliged to verify our reality exclusively by our capacity to think. However, words do not constitute our only or even our primary means of symbolization. Visual perception comes first, and visual perception is not located "in" us. It is situated rather at the point at which memory meets external stimulus. (128)

In *Don Quixote*'s epistemology of enchantment, visual perception remains a raw material in need of a code that may allow it to become significant. As the knight employs memories of his chivalric books to render visible the giants where others see windmills, he is also making visible the invisible conventions that haunt the looks of the other characters. The visual meets its limits in the letter of the ideology each character has internalized. The letter remains the key to the visual in Don Quixote, and the extent of its power is what the film adaptations allow us to see.

At the closing of the documentary *Lost in La Mancha*, Terry Gilliam reflects about the process of adapting *Don Quixote* to film. He is speaking right after realizing that production for his *Don Quixote* project has been canceled by the consortium of European companies and institutions that had been financing it. The insurance company has taken Gilliam's script for the film as collateral, and, somewhere in the historic center of Madrid, the director reflects: "I have done the film too often in my head, too many times I've seen it. I've been through it. I know how it goes. Is it better just to leave it there? I really don't know." Gilliam's question remains: Is it better just to leave it there in the images conjured by Cervantes's words on the imagination of the reader? Perhaps, but it is also too much of a temptation to stop trying to render visually, in film or video, the world that, according to Cervantes (and Cide Hamete Benengeli), Don Quixote believed that he saw.

Notes

[1] For a comprehensive list of films made as adaptations of the original novel, see José María Bravo's "Los viajes mágicos de Don Quijote de la literatura al cine."

[2] According to Matt Kamen, Gilliam is scheduled to finish shooting *The Man Who Killed Don Quixote* early in 2016. Jack O'Connell and John Hurt are confirmed as the lead actors. Gilliam has attempted to complete the film on several occasions since first starting production in the early 1990s. Amazon.com has provided financial backing for the project (Kamen).

[3] Pedro Javier Pardo García reflects on the nature of the many relationships existing between films that are not direct adaptations of *Don Quixote* and the narrative universe created by Cervantes in his novel. Thus, "Cervantine" films would share with the novel its metafictional, self-conscious, and reflexive dimensions. A "Quixotesque" film, by contrast, contains heroic characters who are at odds with the value system of the society that surrounds them and who set out to make things right against impossible odds (Pardo 237–46).

[4] For a selected collection of recent academic studies on the interaction between *Don Quixote* and cinema, see Albrecht, Pardo García, Utrera Macías, and Bravo.

[5] Arthur Penn made this declaration during a roundtable discussion of film versions of *Don Quixote* in Mexico City in 2005. I am quoting from the newspaper article in Spanish in which his comment appears, within a longer reflection about the role of words and images in the novel. Here is the full text as it appeared in the newspaper *El Universal*:

"Yo no me atrevería a llevar *El Quijote* al cine porque con esta obra es obligado el fracaso," señaló en esta ciudad Arthur Penn en una mesa redonda sobre la obra de Cervantes y su relación con el cine. "El lenguaje hablado es esencial en *El Quijote* y en cine éste tiene que ser secundario ante lo visual, por eso fracasaríamos. La falta de esa arma tan eficaz como es la palabra en la obra sería tan patente que me desmayaría." (*El Universal*)

As we will see below, this pre-cinematic nature of *Don Quixote* is more complex than a mere precursor, or even announcer of future media. It also contains prophetic attempts at controlling that future even when it remained uncharted and mostly unimagined.

[6] All quotations in English from the novel are from Edith Grossman's translation.

[7] Darío Villanueva calls attention to the frequency in the text of words related to the senses. Using the database compiled by Juan Torruella for Francisco Rico's edition of *Don Quijote*, Villanueva finds that the word *ver* (to see) appears 410 times in the text, *vio* (he or she saw) 250 times, *visto* (seen) 288 times, *vea* (look) 61 times, and *ojos* (eyes) 287 times (Villanueva 86–87).

[8] For a critical elaboration of the centrality of Plato's parable of the cave to Western visual practices, see Susan Sontag's essay "In Plato's Cave." For a discussion of its impact on cinema, see the excellent monograph on this topic by Nathan Andersen, *Shadow Philosophy: Plato's Cave and Cinema*.

Works Cited

Albrecht, Jane W. "Theater and Politics in Four Film Versions of the 'Quijote.'" *Hispania* 88.1 (March 2005): 4–10. http://dx.doi.org/10.2307/20063070

Andersen, Nathan. *Shadow Philosophy: Plato's Cave and Cinema.* London: Routledge, 2014.

Barth, John. "The Spanish Connection." *Studies in American Literature.* Ed. Antonia Sánchez Macarro. Valencia: Universitat de València, 1991. 17–26.

Bravo, José María. "Los viajes mágicos de Don Quijote de la literatura al cine, 1898–2005." *La huella de Cervantes y del Quijote en la cultura anglosajona.* Ed. José Manuel Barrio and María José Crespo Allué. Valladolid: Universidad de Valladolid, 2007. 517–46.

Cervantes Saavedra, Miguel de. *Don Quijote de la Mancha.* Intro. Felipe B. Pedraza Jiménez. Madrid: Algaba Ediciones, 2004.

———. *Don Quixote.* Trans. Edith Grossman. New York: HarperCollins, 2003.

El Universal. "*El Quijote* en el cine, batalla perdida." August 7, 2005. At http://archivo.eluniversal.com.mx/cultura/43905.html.

Gardies, André. "Cinema on Show in the Work of the Lumière Brothers." *Echoes of Narcissus.* Ed. Lieve Spaas and Trista Selous. New York: Berghahn, 2001. 111–20.

Kamen, Matt. "Amazon Commits to Terry Gilliam's 'Lost' *Don Quixote* Movie." *Wired*, June 11, 2015. At http://arstechnica.com/the-multiverse/2015/06/amazon-commits-to-terry-gilliams-lost-don-quixote-film/.

Mancing, Howard. *Cervantes'* Don Quixote*: A Reference Guide.* Westport, CT: Greenwood Press, 2006.

Pachmanová, Martina. "The World Wants Your Desire: Interview with Kaja Silverman." *N-Paradoxa Online* 19 (2006): 31–41.

Pardo García, Pedro Javier. "Cine, literatura y mito: Don Quijote en el cine, más allá de la adaptación." *Arbor: Ciencia, Pensamiento, Cultura* 187.748 (2011): 237–46.

Riley, E. C. "*Don Quixote*: From Text to Icon." *Cervantes* 8 (1988): 103–15.

Silverman, Kaja. *World Spectators.* Stanford: Stanford UP, 2000.

Simson, Ingrid. "Don Quijote y el cine de América: Sancho, el humor y proyectos fracasados." *Foro Hispánico* 40 (2010): 281–312.

Sontag, Susan. "In Plato's Cave." *On Photography.* New York: Picador, 1990. 3–26.

Unamuno, Miguel de. *Vida de Don Quijote y Sancho.* Madrid: Renacimiento, 1914.

Utrera Macías, Rafael. "*El Quijote* en cine y televisión." *Ínsula: Revista de Letras y Ciencias humanas* 48.558 (1993): 25.

Villanueva, Darío. *El "Quijote" antes del cinema.* Madrid: Real Academia de la Lengua, 2008.

7

The Mute Testimony of Portraits in Calderón's and Unamuno's Work

Randolph D. Pope

University of Virginia

A remarkable article by Robert ter Horst, "The Second Self: Painting and Sculpture in the Plays of Calderón," is notable not just for its erudition and elegance of expression, customary in all his work, but for a profoundly insightful consideration of one aspect of Calderón's life: the pleasure the playwright derived from aesthetic contemplation, reflected in his art collection and in the frequent protagonism of portraits in his plays. It would appear against the grain to highlight the personality of an author at a time when, for a variety of reasons, some commendable, most of us have turned away from the life and work schema so prevalent in the past.[1] From the appraisal of Calderón's estate, made nonetheless by the painter Claudio Coello, ter Horst convincingly proves that the dramatist highly valued painting and sculpture, so their presence in his plays can be seen not only in the service of a dramatic ploy but also as a manifestation of his aesthetic appreciation of art. Ter Horst concludes that Calderón "was not merely 'interested' in art. Rather, beauty in all its forms was with him a passion" (176). What I wish to highlight in ter Horst's lucid observations is the distinction he makes in his argument between language and an irreducibly different presence of the world. Thus, Calderón's estate is not just a passive object of contemplation made of strewn objects left behind for enumeration and cataloguing, but an active intervention that should make us consider the writer in a different light—not as a cold intellectual proudly deploying the complexity of language and concepts but, maybe especially, as "the great depicter of the cognate passions of body and mind" (177).

It could appear obvious that, in a play, the bodies of actors or characters speak their mind, but the point here is more complex, and mostly not about words. This disjunction between "the cognate passions of body and mind" points to a sort of communication that needs no translation and could be betrayed and diminished in the attempt to flatten it to regular spoken vocabulary. The full import of ter Horst's evaluation of Calderón's estate and the presence of portraits in his plays can only be understood when one considers the implications of his observation that "their mute testimony is compelling" (176), plus his quotation from Calderón's *Fuego de Dios en el querer bien* in which a character, Don Álvaro, frustrated by trying to reduce his painful experiences to discourse, gestures toward a different way of relating to others and the world: "Entiéndame quien entiende / los idiomas del silencio" (178).

As literary critics, most of us probably are less versed in the language of silence than in the flourishes allowed by the many possible combinations of known and shared words, even if recent generations of students have confirmed, stressed, and even demanded the need for greater attention to the visual. But Calderón properly did not say "el idioma del silencio," but instead "los idiomas del silencio," which perhaps Simon and Garfunkel's 1964 hit song "The Sounds of Silence" unwittingly echoed (even if the plural is in the title, but not in the lyrics, where we find only "the sound of silence"). [2] Recent advances in cognitive science have established the importance of perceptions and of decisions that are made much earlier than information is processed by the conscious mind, at times beyond the realm of conscious retrieval and understanding. In George Lakoff and Mark Johnson's readable and informative *Philosophy in the Flesh: The Embodied Mind and Its Challenge to Western Thought*, we find the following recommendations that can with some modification apply to literary criticism:

> The very existence of the cognitive unconscious, a fact fundamental to all conceptions of cognitive science, has important implications for the practice of philosophy. It means that we can have no direct conscious awareness of most of what goes on in our minds. The idea that pure philosophical reflection can plumb the depths of human understanding is an illusion. Traditional methods of philosophical analysis alone, even phenomenological introspection, cannot come close to allowing us to know our own minds. (12)

Phenomenology, especially as developed by Maurice Merleau-Ponty, alerts us to the fact that our experience of the world is embodied. Merleau-Ponty wishes to "restore the world of perception" (*The Primacy of Perception* 3) when he observes that there has been a forgetting of how "the perceiving mind is an incarnated mind" (3). His concern is that most people slide too easily into abstract ideas, leaving behind the uniqueness and complexity of lived experience. As he puts it, the self becomes blended into the general, and its specificity is washed away:

I take flight from my experience and I pass over to the *idea*. Like the object, the idea claims to be the same for everyone, valid for all times and for all places, and the individuation of the object as an objective point of time and space appears, in the end, as the expression of a universal positing power. I no longer pay attention to my body, to time, or to the world such as I live them in pre-predicative knowledge, that is, in the inner communication that I have with them. I only speak of my body as an idea, of the universe as an idea, and of the idea of space and of time. (*Phenomenology of Perception* 73–74)

This tension between the useful abstractness of ideas and the immediacy of our experience is one of the reasons why some philosophers—for example Kierkegaard, Nietzsche, Unamuno, and Sartre, concerned about understanding the living individual self—have often resorted to the novel or the theater. More radically and very recently, Hubert Dreyfus and Charles Taylor, in their *Retrieving Realism*, have developed a strong case for the importance of "re-embedding thought and knowledge in the bodily and social cultural contexts in which it takes place" (18), not so that it can be immediately displaced into a traditional sociological or cultural studies approach but so that observing and understanding the self can take into account the non-thought and pre-predicative aspect of our experience (where much of the aesthetic experience takes place): "The contact here [with the world] is not achieved on the level of Ideas, but is rather something primordial, something we never escape. It is the contact of living, active beings, whose life form involves acting in and on the world which also acts on them" (18). Dreyfus and Taylor are not aiming to a form of primitivism but toward a more integrated and dynamic account of experience.[3]

On a different front, yet clearly related, several feminist thinkers have stressed the importance of taking into account the embodied self. For example, Elizabeth Grosz writes in *Volatile Bodies: Toward a Corporeal Feminism*: "This book is a refiguring of the body so that it moves from the periphery to the center of analysis, so that it can now be understood as the very 'stuff' of subjectivity" (ix). Moira Gatens in *Imaginary Bodies* makes very clear the importance of the changing philosophical understanding of the body for feminist thought, especially in the chapter "Towards a Feminist Philosophy of the Body," in which she argues that "the traditional philosophical conceptions of corporeality are counterproductive to the aim of constructing an autonomous conception of women's bodies along with the possibility of women's active participation in the politico-ethical realm" (49). Prudently, Gatens realizes that the conception of women's bodies, as newly constructed as it may be, needs to be constantly counterbalanced and corrected by active participation in life so that it does not become a frozen universal notion.[4]

Portraits and sculptures in the plays that ter Horst analyzes mark this importance of the body; they serve a moral function and inspire characters to attain a better self. Yet the very gesture of generating a second self, or at least a second image of the body, can be disquieting, producing some confusion, as Rosaura's portrait that Astolfo carries in *La vida es sueño* does, and ultimately the two characters are toying with the impossible desire of becoming free from time.

There can be no better formulation of the threat represented by the comparison between the model and the portrait, the original and the copy, than Oscar Wilde's *The Picture of Dorian Gray*. The young and very beautiful Dorian Gray hears an impassioned admonition from the worldly Lord Henry about how beauty is a form of genius that will allow Dorian many a triumph but eventually will fade away: "You have only a few years in which to live really, perfectly, and fully. When your youth goes, your beauty will go with it, and then you will suddenly discover that there are no triumphs left for you, or have to content yourself with those mean triumphs that the memory of your past will make more bitter than defeats" (22). This is a recycled carpe diem, but set up here in a contest of the living body with the painting for which Dorian is sitting when he hears these meditations from Lord Henry. The confrontation of his unavoidably aging body and the painting leads him to a bitter realization and an expression of hope that will eventually prove disastrous:

> "How sad it is!" murmured Dorian Gray, with his eyes still fixed upon his own portrait. "How sad it is! I shall grow old, and horrible, and dreadful. But this picture will remain always young. It will never be older than this particular day of June. ... If it were only the other way! If it were I who was to be always young, and the picture that was to grow old! For that—for that—I would give everything!" (25)

This ardent expression of desire contains a double echo—"How sad it is!" and "For that" are each found twice—which is in turn an echo of the duplicitous painted and real bodies that are about to start a struggle for possessing the privilege of being immune to the ravages of time. The decades-long but nevertheless temporary fulfillment of Dorian's wish does not prove satisfactory. His conclusion is that "[l]ife is a great disappointment" (179). Being embodied is to be mortal, transient, evanescent.

Speaking about the phenomenon of the phantom limb, Merleau-Ponty notes that for people who still believe they have something they have actually lost, "impersonal time continues to flow, but personal time is arrested" (*Phenomenology of Perception* 85). Belief cannot truly restore the gone beauty or the lost limb. Therefore, one can see in the mute testimony of all these portraits circulating within plays the seriousness of a sublime battle destined to be lost when the bodies are gone, only memorialized by the text.

Miguel de Unamuno, who was well aware of Calderón and the concept of our flimsy hold on and understanding of being, made of a portrait also a mute testimony of indubitable power. [5] Augusto Pérez, the main character of *Niebla*, does not feel quite in control of his life, and since he is considering the idea of suicide he decides to travel to Salamanca and visit Don Miguel de Unamuno, who figuratively steps into the novel. There is much that can be said about the different ways in which a bond of frail identity is forged between the historical author of a book or the director of a movie and a character in his or her work, from the full-blown autobiographical approach to walk-on cameos such as those favored by Alfred Hitchcock, but for our purposes here it will suffice to say that they are the equivalent of leaving one's own portrait within one's work. Unamuno, well known for his deep and abiding concern with his own self—not fairly simplified as egocentrism or narcissism—represents himself in *Niebla* twice, once as a character and once as an oil portrait that has gone largely unnoticed in spite of the importance I believe it has in the famous concluding scene between Augusto, the main character in the novel, and his fictional creator.

After Augusto is deceived and ditched by his bride-to-be, Eugenia, he is surprised not to feel the event more deeply, starting to doubt his existence, "aquella calma le hacía que hasta dudase de su propia existencia" (*Niebla* 269). Were he a full human being, wouldn't he be devastated by Eugenia's rebuff? As with the character in Borges's "Las ruinas circulares," who realizes that he is just the creation of a dreamer when he is able to walk through a ring of fire without getting burned, the message of nonexistence comes from the perception of his body, from a missing reaction. As in many of Oliver Sacks's case studies, a nonfunctioning ability of the body reveals the usual conditions of existence: feeling pain indicates that the living body is alert and the *propia existencia* confirmed. Having decided that he will commit suicide, Augusto takes a train to Salamanca, where the author of an essay about suicide, a Mr. Unamuno, has lived for over twenty years. At this point, the narrator announces that he is that renowned Unamuno, the author of the text we are reading, and settles confidently into a first-person narration. When Augusto arrives to Unamuno's house and is announced, two mentioned actions are worthwhile commenting on: "Cuando me anunciaron su visita sonreí enigmáticamente y le mandé pasar a mi despacho-librería" (277). Why is he smiling enigmatically? It is not the first time we find this expression in the novel. Chapter 25 is given over to a conversation between Augusto and his friend Victor, who is writing a novel over whose characters he believes he has full control, even if he is not sure he makes them say or do what corresponds to their nature. At this point, abruptly, the reader is confronted with a few blank lines, followed by a paragraph in italics:

> *Mientras Augusto y Victor sostenían esta conversación nivolesca, yo, el autor de esta nivola, que tienes, lector, en la mano y estás leyendo, me sonreía enigmáticamente al ver que mis nivolescos personajes estaban abogando por mí y justificando mis procedimientos, y me decía a mí mismo: "¡Cuán lejos estarán estos infelices de pensar que no están haciendo otra cosa que tratar de justificar lo que yo estoy haciendo con ellos! Así cuando uno busca razones para justificarse no hace en rigor otra cosa que justificar a Dios. Y yo soy el Dios de estos dos pobres diablos nivolescos."* (252)

This God, though, eventually will be dragged down to the same level as the other characters with Augusto's visit, but at first the character Unamuno is still confident of his superiority and control over his creation, Augusto. It is curious, and not insignificant, that the word "enigma" appears, secondhand, when Unamuno discusses Calderón—and rebukes most of Marcelino Menéndez y Pelayo's opinions about Calderón—in his 1895 "En torno al casticismo." For Unamuno, Calderón's theater lacks life, the action becomes frozen, leading us not, as with Shakespeare, to "al fondo del mar lleno de vida, sino a un cielo frío y pétreo" (29). In the distinction he stresses between Calderón and Shakespeare, we may find the triggering cause for the eventual melting away of his *enigmática sonrisa*:

> La mera ocurrencia de sacar a tablas conceptos abstractos delata toda la flaqueza de este ingenio, como lo empedernido de su idealismo el encontrarse resuelto (¡!!) en sus obras "el enigma de la vida humana … sin luchas, sin vacilaciones, sin antinomias, sin dudas siquiera."
> No es de extrañar que se sobreponga el idealismo de Calderón al de Shakespeare, y aun que no se le vea bien en éste. El inglés pone en escena a que desarrollen su alma hombres, hombres, *ideas* vivas, tan *profundas* cuanto *altas* las más elevadas del castellano. (31; emphasis in original)

Life, then, for Unamuno is unpredictable and an unresolvable problem, with hesitations and antinomies. Characters must come to life and become hombres, real human beings, a word he repeats as though one mention were not enough: "que desarrollen su alma hombres, hombres." The supercilious attitude of Unamuno as he receives Augusto, still for him a puppet-like character and not an hombre, is accompanied by another arrogant gesture, receiving him in his study, which doubles as his library. (There is in fact a similar room in the real Unamuno's Salamanca house, and in one of my visits there the person showing me around confided in me with a hushed voice that "this is the very room in which Unamuno received Augusto Pérez.") It all starts as ostentation of the author's power over his character:

> Cuando me anunciaron su visita sonreí enigmáticamente y le mandé pasar a mi despacho-librería. Entró en él como un fantasma, miró a un retrato mío al óleo que allí preside a los libros de mi librería, y a una seña mía se sentó, frente a mí. (277)

Augusto is following all of Unamuno's instructions, and his perception of the oil portrait is just a glance that does not seem to have any special meaning attached to it. He is devastated when informed that he does not exist except as fictional character, and therefore has no capacity for independent decisions and actions. But now a drastic change will occur, and the author's *enigmática sonrisa* will find a pointed reply:

> Al oír esto quedóse el pobre hombre mirándome un rato con una de esas miradas perforadoras que parecen atravesar la mira a ir más allá, miró luego un momento a mi retrato al óleo que preside a mis libros, le volvió el color y el aliento, fue recobrándose, se hizo dueño de sí, apoyó los codos en mi camilla, a que estaba arrimado frente a mí y, la cara en las palmas de las manos y mirándome con una sonrisa en los ojos, me dijo lentamente:
> —Mire usted bien, don Miguel, ... no sea que esté usted equivocado y que ocurra precisamente todo lo contrario de lo que usted se cree y me dice. (279)

To fully understand why this second glance at the oil painting, this revision, allows Augusto to recover and become his own master, *dueño de sí*, with smiling eyes, it helps to remember that, three years after *Niebla*, several portraits will play an important role in *Abel Sánchez: Una historia de pasión*. The novel is about the conflict between the doctor Joaquín and the painter Abel, both talented in their different fields but with Abel having the advantage, bitterly resented by Joaquín, of a graceful and engaging personality. When a woman whom Joaquín fancies, Helena, models for a portrait by Abel, he captures not only her body's image but also her affection, marrying her. The success of the portrait, as described by the narrator, opens to Helena a redefined life, twinned, as Dorian Gray, in an existence within and without time:

> El éxito del retrato de Helena por Abel fue clamoroso. Siempre había alguien contemplándolo frente al escaparate en que fue expuesto. "Ya tenemos un gran pintor más," decían. Y ella, Helena, procuraba pasar junto al lugar en que su retrato se exponía para oír los comentarios y paseábase por las calles de la ciudad como un inmortal retrato viviente, como una obra de arte haciendo la rueda. ¿No había acaso nacido para eso? (66)

Her confusion, indicated by the "como" implying similarity but not identity between the work of art and the living woman, is insinuated here. Later in the novel, though, it is laid out with wounding clarity. Joaquín is taking care of a very sick patient who has also been painted by Abel. The quotation is relatively long, yet in the context of the earlier portrait in *Niebla* of great explanatory value. It is presented in quotation marks in the novel because it supposedly is a fragment of a diary written by Joaquín:

> Ocurrióme un caso que me sacudió las entrañas. Asistía a una pobre señora, enferma de algún riesgo, pero no caso desesperado, a la que él había hecho un retrato, un retrato magnífico, uno de sus mejores retratos, de los que han quedado como definitivos de entre los que ha pintado, y aquel retrato era lo primero que se me venía a los ojos y al odio así que entraba en la casa de la enferma. Estaba viva en el retrato, más viva que en el lecho la de carne y hueso sufrientes. Y el retrato parecía decirme: "Mira, él me ha dado vida para siempre; a ver si tú me alargas esta otra de aquí abajo." Y junto a la pobre enferma, auscultándola, tomándole el pulso, no veía sino a la otra, a la retratada. Estuve torpe, torpísimo, y la pobre enferma se me murió; la dejé morir más bien, por mi torpeza, por mi criminal distracción. Sentí horror de mí mismo, de mi miseria.
>
> A los pocos días de muerta la señora aquella, tuve que ir a su casa, a ver allí otro enfermo, y entré dispuesto a no mirar al retrato. Pero era inútil, porque era él, el retrato el que me miraba aunque yo no le mirase y me atraía la mirada. Al despedirme me acompañó hasta la puerta el viudo. Nos detuvimos al pie del retrato, y yo, como empujado por una fuerza irresistible y fatal, exclamé:

"¡Magnífico retrato! ¡Es de lo mejor que ha hecho Abel!"
"Sí," me contestó el viudo, "es el mayor consuelo que me queda.
Me paso largas horas contemplándola. Parece como que me habla."
"¡Sí, sí," añadí, "este Abel es un artista estupendo!"
Y al salir me decía: "¡Yo la dejé morir y él la resucita!" (81–82)

This disparity between the life of art and bodily existence is what the
Greek physician Hippocrates captured in his aphorism, Ὁ βίος βραχύς, ἡ
δὲ τέχνη μακρή (Life is short, art long), which became the Latin *ars longa,
vita brevis.* The order of the compared elements does matter; for a doctor,
such as Joaquín, life takes precedence, but for an artist, such as Abel, what
matters is the long-range existence of the work of art. Augusto, by
comparing the oil portrait and the living model, in a flash realizes suddenly
Unamuno's mortality and, after confronting him, departs with the
following rebellious and prophetic words:

> Pues bien, mi señor creador don Miguel, ¡también usted se morirá,
> también usted, y se volverá a la nada de que salió … ! ¡Dios dejará
> de soñarle! ¡Se morirá usted, sí, se morirá, aunque no lo quiera; se
> morirá usted y se morirán todos los que lean mi historia, todos, todos,
> todos sin quedar uno! ¡Entes de ficción como yo; lo mismo que yo!
> Se morirán todos, todos, todos. Os lo digo yo, Augusto Pérez, ente
> ficticio como vosotros, nivolesco lo mismo que vosotros. (*Niebla*
> 284)

This is very close in spirit to Calderón's conception of life as a dream,
with the difference that for Calderón there was the belief in an otherwise
eternal life beyond the simulacrum of art, and therefore portraits held less
of a bitter reminder of mortality than they do for Wilde and Unamuno.
Their mute testimony, so insightfully described by ter Horst, was intensely
felt by Unamuno, and, therefore, it is no accident that portraits play such
a decisive role in *Niebla* and *Abel Sánchez.* He had several portraits made
of himself, so a letter he wrote to a painter, Ramón de Zubiaurre (1882–
1969), who was deaf-mute from birth, is a good text with which to end this
essay about *los idiomas del silencio.* The letter is reproduced by the editor
of the volume in which it is published, Laureano Robles, with Unamuno's
own peculiar unbalanced exclamation and question marks:

> Sabía mi querido amigo, lo de la venta del retrato que usted me hizo
> a ese señor norteamericano. Y me parece la cosa muy bien. No que
> yo no hubiese estado satisfechísimo de poseerlo—y mucho!—sino
> que por una parte me considero del público y encuentro natural que

mis retratos circulen como mis escritos y hasta es un reclamo. Si yo mismo apenas me pertenezco, porqué mis retratos? Y por otra parte usted vive, en algo al menos, de su pincel, como yo vivo de mi pluma, y si fuésemos escritores y pintores a escribir unos para los que pintan y pintar los otros para los que escriben pelecharíamos mal. Unos y otros, hermanados, tenemos que vivir de la fiera, que es el público. Sobre todo si es pagano; quiero decir, si paga. Y ese Mr. Deering pertenece al mejor público. Además mi retrato será más visto y admirado en la Villa Marycell, de Sitges, que lo sería en mi casa y así le servirá a usted mejor de reclamo. Obras así deberían estar en Museos públicos más bien que en casas particulares. Quién sabe si algún día—cuando usted y yo seamos polvo y huesos—vendrá a esta Universidad de Salamanca o irá al Museo de Bilbao o a otro sitio público de mi villa natal? Ya ve que no peco de modesto. (*Epistolario inédito* 37–38)

No one, of course, ever accused Unamuno of being modest, but Augusto perceived well that, for Unamuno, the portrait contained the defiant threat of surviving when the model was just *polvo y huesos*. There is much more left behind than bones and dust, obviously: the texts themselves and the portraits that circulate around and within them, plus the critics who, at least for now, wonder at them and admire their still intense life.

Notes

[1] Not that there is an abundance of Calderón biographies. The most recent major biography in English is by Don William Cruickshank, *Don Pedro Calderón*, but it deals only with Calderón's first fifty years and focuses on the secular work. José María Ruano de la Haza's excellent review of Cruickshank's book warns about the dangers of making easy connections between life and work.
[2] The song was retitled in the singular, "The Sound of Silence," beginning with its rerelease on the 1972 compilation album *Simon and Garfunkel's Greatest Hits*.
[3] Some caution is necessary when applying scientific knowledge to literary analysis and daily life, as proven by the unfortunate experience of the very talented Jonah Lehrer, whose 2009 *How We Decide / The Decisive Moment* was retired from sales by the publisher after fact checking revealed problems with the text. (One wonders why the fact

checking was not done before publication …) Probably significant was the review in *Nature* by Adam Kepecs that castigates the author for presenting "a caricature view of brain processing" and indulging in "neurobabble." Lehrer's 2007 *Proust Was a Neuroscientist*, in which he studies Whitman, George Eliot, Auguste Escoffier, Proust, Cézanne, Stravinsky, Gertrude Stein, and Woolf is still available, even if I would not recommend his bombastic affirmations about these authors and artists having "discovered truths about the human mind—real, tangible truths—that science is only now rediscovering. Their imaginations foretold the facts of the future" (ix). Calderón and Unamuno were not neuroscientists.

[4] A consideration of how the portraits and sculptures in Calderón are gendered would surely be fruitful, but for a different essay.

[5] Nelson R. Orringer, in "Unamuno's Conversion into Segismundo," traces in detail the varied interpretations Unamuno provided for *La vida es sueño*, significantly noting that "[d]etermined to attain immortality, Unamuno tends in succeeding works to identify with fictional characters rather than with the author" (97). Orringer concludes that "[t]he mere posing of the problem of immortality in many suggestive ways forms the solution of an Unamuno determined to immortalize himself" (102). Alas, an insufficient solution.

Works Cited

Cruickshank, Don William. *Don Pedro Calderón*. Cambridge: Cambridge UP, 2009.

Dreyfus, Hubert, and Charles Taylor. *Retrieving Realism*. Cambridge: Harvard UP, 2015. http://dx.doi.org/10.4159/9780674287136

Gatens, Moira. *Imaginary Bodies: Ethics, Power and Corporeality*. London: Routledge, 1996.

Grosz, Elizabeth. *Volatile Bodies: Toward a Corporeal Feminism*. Bloomington: Indiana UP, 1994.

Kepecs, Adam. "Decisions, decisions …" *Nature* 458 (April 16, 2009): 835. http://dx.doi.org/10.1038/458835a

Lakoff, George, and Mark Johnson. *Philosophy in the Flesh: The Embodied Mind and Its Challenge to Western Thought*. New York: Basic Books, 1999.

Lehrer, Jonah. *Proust Was a Neuroscientist*. Boston: Houghton Mifflin Harcourt, 2007.

Merleau-Ponty, Maurice. *Phenomenology of Perception*. Trans. Donald A. Landes. London: Routledge, 2012.

———. *The Primacy of Perception*. Ed. James M. Edie. Evanston: Northwestern UP, 1964.

Orringer, Nelson R. "Unamuno's Conversion into Segismundo." *Pedro Calderón de la Barca's* La vida es sueño: *Philosophical Crossroads*. Ed. Andrés Lema-Hincapié and Conxita Domenech. Newark, DE: Juan de la Cuesta, 2014. 83–103.

Ruano de la Haza, José María. "Entre Don Pedro Calderón y Don William Cruickshank." *Bulletin of Spanish Studies* 90 (2013): 461–72. http://dx.doi.org/10.1080/14753820.2013.802561

Ter Horst, Robert. "The Second Self: Painting and Sculpture in the Plays of Calderón." *Calderón de la Barca at the Tercentenary: Comparative Views*. Ed. Wendell M. Aycock and Sydney P. Cravens. Lubbock: Texas Tech UP, 1982. 175–92.

Unamuno, Miguel de. *Abel Sánchez: Una historia de pasión*. Ed. José Luis Abellán. Madrid: Castalia, 1985.

———. "En torno al casticismo." *La España Moderna*, April 1895: 27–58.

———. *Epistolario inédito 2 (1915–1936)*. Ed. Laureano Robles. Madrid: Espasa Calpe, 1991.

———. *Niebla*. Ed. Mario J. Valdés. 7th ed. Madrid: Cátedra, 1988.

Wilde, Oscar. *The Picture of Dorian Gray*. Ed. Isobel Murray. Oxford: Oxford UP, 1981.

8

The Conjugations of Don Juan

Eleanor ter Horst

University of South Alabama

In his article "Epic Descent: The Filiations of Don Juan," Robert ter Horst uncovers the competitive relationships that characterize the two most famous Spanish versions of the Don Juan legend: the seventeenth-century drama, *El burlador de Sevilla y convivado de piedra*, most often attributed to Tirso de Molina,[1] and José Zorrilla's nineteenth-century version, *Don Juan Tenorio*. Positing an equality between the two versions, Robert ter Horst differentiates between the types of relationships privileged in each, stressing the competitive relationship between father and son in *El burlador*, and between Don Juan and his male peers in *Tenorio*. The similarities between the two texts—their structuring element of male competition—as well as the different relationships predominating in each, establish a rivalry that is suggestive of the father-son relationship: "In attempting to decipher the sense of how this one play relates to the other, the binary opposition of father to son seems to me to be more productive, although at the same time elusive of a final determination" (ter Horst 272). The shifting balances of power between father and son, as well as between male equals, provide a way to think about the relationships between these two texts.

This idea of an interplay between similarity and difference is also applicable to another work within the same tradition, E. T. A. Hoffmann's novella, *Don Juan* (1813), situated in time between *El burlador* and *Tenorio* but drawing most directly on Mozart's opera *Don Giovanni*. Hoffmann draws out similarities among literary and musical versions of Don Juan by linking male protagonists, authors, composers, and critics as indistinguishable equals, thus calling into question the idea of a "master" or single source of knowledge. At the same time, Hoffmann's text draws on other literary sources outside of Don Juan, such as Goethe's *Faust*, whose protagonist it joins with Don Juan, thus welding Faust's pursuit of knowledge with Juan's pursuit of sexual conquests. Within the text itself, Hoffmann's novella establishes binary structures, which, in turn, elicit a duality of interpretations and bring out the indeterminacy of perception and understanding. Hoffmann's novella explores both the drive to know and define sexuality, and the ultimate failure of this attempt: the object of inquiry, sexual relationships between men and women, is shown to be elusive of understanding and, in the end, unknowable. Expanding on the elusive quality that Robert ter Horst recognizes in the father-son relationship, this essay focuses on the indeterminacy of relationships between texts, between music and language, between various spoken languages, between men, as well as between men and women. The result is a text that, while structured by competition, undermines the conditions that enable competition, namely stable identities for the competitors and a clear sense of what might constitute dominance or mastery.

In focusing on the drive to know what is unknowable, Hoffmann is drawing on a tradition that extends back to *El burlador de Sevilla*, which opens with a conflict between a woman who seeks to uncover the identity of her seducer and a man who wishes to hide his identity. At first, the audience and the character Isabela are equally unenlightened about the identity of the man who has just seduced her, and whom she calls "Octavio," the name of her fiancé. When he refuses to let her bring a light, she asks, "¿Quién eres, hombre?" (Who are you, man?), and he replies "¿Quién soy? Un hombre sin nombre"(Who am I? A man without a name) (1: 14–15).[2] Later, the audience learns that the seducer is Don Juan, a descendant of the noble family of Tenorio and a master of deception.

In another episode, Don Juan adds to his list of victims by assuming the identity of his friend, the Marquis de la Mota, in order to seduce the Marquis's cousin and love interest, Doña Ana. What happens between Juan and Ana remains a mystery to the viewers, who in fact do not see Ana at all until the final act. Her voice off-stage is heard declaring Don Juan to be "homicida de mi honor" (assassin of my honor) (2: 520); however, the manner in which her honor is compromised remains unspecified—the presence of a strange man in her room at night could give rise to speculation and ruin her reputation, even if no sexual activity takes place between them. Further details are not forthcoming until Don Juan's final scene with the statue of Don Gonzalo, Ana's father, whom Don Juan had killed. Juan declares, "A tu hija no ofendí, / que vió mis engaños antes" (I did not cause offense to your daughter, who foresaw my deception) (3: 964–65). The audience might hesitate to believe Don Juan's declaration, since at the time he makes this pronouncement his hand is being gripped by the statue's burning hand, and he is trying to save himself from death. The confession does not in any case save him; Don Gonzalo is not concerned so much with the result of the seduction as with the seducer's intent: "No importa, que ya pusiste / tu intento" (It doesn't matter, you had already shown your intent) (3: 965–66). The father is not interested in discovering what happened between Don Juan and his daughter; rather, he is concerned with the result, which in any case is the loss of his daughter's honor because she was discovered to be alone with a man at night, and this man intended to seduce her, whether or not he completed the act. Unlike Don Gonzalo, the Marquis de la Mota, Ana's cousin and suitor whose identity Don Juan assumed, is delighted to hear the seducer's assurance, relayed through his servant, Catalinón, that Don Juan did not complete the seduction: "Por las nuevas / mil albricias pienso darte" (Many thanks for the news) (3: 1065–66). Although Juan's claim that Ana successfully resisted his advances is not called into question by any character or incident in the drama, the varying reactions of Don Gonzalo and the Marquis de la Mota do suggest two different interpretations of the claim, one attributing no importance to it, the other valuing it highly. These competing interpretations are not crucial to the plot of *El burlador*, while, in the opera *Don Giovanni*, there is a closer focus on the events taking place between Anna and Giovanni.

Mozart's opera *Don Giovanni*, with libretto by Lorenzo Da Ponte, opens similarly to *El burlador* with a struggle between Donna Anna, who wants to discover the identity of her attacker, and Don Giovanni, who is trying to escape:

> DONNA ANNA: Non sperar, se non m'uccidi, ch'io ti lasci fuggir mai!
> DON GIOVANNI: Donna folle, indarno gridi: chi son io tu non saprai.
>
> DONNA ANNA: Do not hope that I will ever let you escape, unless you kill me.
> DON GIOVANNI: Crazy woman, your screams are useless: you will never know who I am. (4)

Like the scene between Isabela and Juan in *El burlador*, this scene between Anna and Giovanni begins after their encounter, so the spectators cannot know what exactly happened between them, although Anna later tells her fiancé, Ottavio, what happened on that night. She describes how she was alone in her rooms, late at night, when someone entered who she thought at first was Ottavio, but who was in reality Giovanni. She then goes on to describe a physical struggle between herself and Giovanni, which still leaves some doubt as to whether the attack included a sexual act: "Con una mano cerca d'impedire la voce, e coll'altra m'afferra stretta così, che già micredo vinta" (With one hand he tried to silence my voice, and with the other he grasped me so tightly that I thought I was already overcome). Don Ottavio urges her to continue her narration, and she proceeds: "Alfine il duol, l'orrore dell'infame attentato accrebbe sì la lena mia, che a forza di svincolarmi, torcermi e piegarmi, da lui mi sciolsi!" (Finally the pain, the horror of the attack gave me enough strength that I was able to free myself from him by bending and twisting) (37). Ottavio's response to this narration, like the Marquis de la Mota's in *El burlador*, is relief— "Respiro" (I can breathe)—but the text itself does not necessarily warrant the interpretation that Anna was able to resist being raped. Indeed, the narrator of Hoffmann's *Don Juan* advances the opposite view, and Mozart scholars still debate this theory, first advanced in Hoffmann's novella, which is viewed by some as important to the interpretation of the opera.[3] Hoffmann's narrator insists that Donna Anna's "ruin" ("Verderben") (94) was carried out by Don Giovanni, and that this violation leads to Giovanni's ruin also. However, the manner in which the narrator's interpretation is presented, as embedded in a number of binary structures that present contradictory views of reality, leaves some doubt as to the authority of the narrator and the validity of his perceptions.

   The structure of Hoffmann's *Don Juan* echoes the binary structures that Robert ter Horst discerns in *El burlador* and *Tenorio*. The first part of the novella concerns a description of a performance of Mozart's *Don Giovanni*, attended by an unnamed "reisender Enthusiast" (traveling music aficionado). Between the two acts of the opera, the "Enthusiast" has a conversation with the singer playing Donna Anna, who had seemingly and contrary to all logic entered his private box during the first act, while she was still performing on stage. In the second half of the novella, the Enthusiast returns to the box after the performance and proceeds to write an interpretation of the opera, which, like the first part, is addressed to his friend, Theodor, and which reveals the hidden motivations of the characters, Anna and Giovanni. These two sections are framed by episodes taking place in the hotel adjacent to the theater where the opera is being performed. At the beginning of the novella, the narrator (the Enthusiast) is awakened in his hotel room by the sound a voice shouting "Das Theater fängt an" (The performance is beginning) (83) and of musical instruments tuning up. He is confused about where he is: "Sollte der allezeit geschäftige Satan mich im Rausche – ? Nein! ich befinde mich in dem Zimmer des Hotels, wo ich gestern abend halb gerädert abgestiegen." (Might the ever-industrious Satan have taken me, inebriated – ? No! I'm in the room of the hotel where I stopped last night, exhausted) (83). Having introduced and then rejected the possibility that Satan has gained control of him, the narrator nonetheless leaves some doubt as to whether he is still under the influence of some mind-altering substance, such as the champagne that he remembers drinking at lunch. This uncertainty about his mental state casts doubt on the subsequent narration, a doubt that is also introduced by the binary structure of the text itself, with its two sections (narration of experiences during performance, written evaluation of opera), each of which is framed by episodes taking place in the hotel.

At the beginning of the novella, as we have seen, the narrator awakens in the hotel room. Then, after attending the performance of *Don Giovanni*, he returns to dine at the hotel with other guests, who are discussing the performance. Their experience of the opera is at variance with his.[4] The narrator remarks "daß wohl keiner die tiefere Bedeutung der Oper aller Opern auch nur ahnte" (that nobody had the least idea about the deeper meaning of the opera of all operas) (90). They criticize the very aspects of the performance that the narrator finds moving or meaningful: "Don Ottavio hatte sehr gefallen. Donna Anna war einem zu leidenschaftlich gewesen. Man müsse, meinte er, auf dem Theater sich hübsch mäßigen und das zu sehr Angreifende vermeiden. Die Erzählung des Überfalls habe ihn ordentlich konsterniert" (They were pleased by Don Ottavio. Donna Anna was too passionate for one of them. He thought that, in the theater, knowing how to exercise artistic restraint and avoid offensive excess was important; the narration of the attack had upset him greatly) (90). The Enthusiast, by contrast, comments dismissively on the role of Ottavio without analyzing the specifics of the singer's performance: "ein zierliches, geputztes, gelecktes Männlein von einundzwanzig Jahren höchstens" (A delicate, preening, immaculate little man who was at most twenty-one) (85). On the other hand, he is carried away by the passion of Anna's acting and singing. The other theatergoer's reaction to the "narration of the attack," surely Juan's attack on Anna, as she narrates it to Ottavio, is not echoed by the Enthusiast's description of the performance—he does not mention this scene at all—but in the second part of the novella he advances the theory that Juan did succeed in raping Anna, and makes this idea the key to his understanding of the "ruin" of both characters. The effect of this discussion in the hotel dining room is, then, to provide a counterpoint to the narrator's experience of the opera while at the same time raising an issue that becomes crucial to the second, interpretive section of the novella.

This second section, entitled "In der Fremdenloge Nro. 23" (In the Visitors' Box Number 23), begins in the narrator's hotel room after he leaves the dining room. He is uncomfortable in his room and moves instead into the theater box where he had viewed the performance, in order to write to his friend Theodor about his interpretation of *Don Giovanni*. The theater is of course empty, but at 2:00 a.m., while he is writing, he feels the presence of the singer playing Anna: "Ein warmer elektrischer Hauch gleitet über mich her – ich empfinde den leisen Geruch feinen italienischen Parfüms, der gestern zuerst mir die Nachbarin vermuten ließ;

mich umfängt ein seliges Gefühl, das ich nur in Tönen aussprechen zu können glaube" (A warm, electric breath glides over me – the light scent of a fine Italian perfume that my companion had brought with her yesterday; a blessed feeling surrounds me, which I think I am only capable of expressing in music) (96). He then thinks he hears her singing, and dreams of being transported to an unknown realm of spirits ("unbekanntes Geisterreich") (96). The narrator's experience combines sensuality with mysticism and yet emphasizes the indefinite, unknowable quality of what he has experienced. As a contrast, the final section of the novella, directly following this scene and titled "Gespräch des Mittags an der Table d'Hôte, als Nachtrag" (Conversation at Noon at the *table d'hôte*, as Postscript), relates the guests' discussion about the fate of the singer playing Donna Anna. The information that they provide again stands in opposition to the experience of the narrator. The "kluger Mann" (clever man) (97) announces that she died at 2:00 a.m., precisely the moment at which the narrator experienced her presence in the theater. Further, another guest reports that the singer was unconscious during the entire intermission and that she suffered from "Nervenzufälle" (a nervous attack) (97) during the second act. Again, the remarks of the other guests provide a counterpoint to the experiences of the Enthusiast, who reports that he spoke with the singer in his theater box during the intermission and who experienced a kind of musical-erotic union with her during the second act, similar to his experience while writing the interpretation of the opera in the empty theater after the performance. The contradictions between the narrator's experiences in the theater and the accounts of the hotel guests are impossible to resolve, and the reader is left in a state of profound uncertainty, brought about by the binary structure of the narrative and its competing realities.[5]

These antagonistic ways of knowing and interpreting are anchored in two specific locales, the visitors' box and the hotel, as well as in two different modes of expression, music and words. The connections between the physical spaces as well as the interactions between musical and verbal expression are key to understanding the contradictions that structure the narration. We will begin with the physical spaces and explore how they are designated in the text. In the opening scene of the novella, when the Enthusiast awakens in his hotel room, he summons a waiter, who explains to him the layout of the spaces:

"Ew. Exzellenz wissen vielleicht noch nicht, daß dieses Hotel mit dem Theater verbunden ist. Diese Tapetentür führt auf einen kleinen Korridor, von dem Sie unmittelbar in Nro. 23 treten: das ist die Fremdenloge."

"Was? – Theater? – Fremdenloge?"

"Ja, die kleine Fremdenloge zu zwei, höchstens drei Personen – nur so für vornehme Herren, ganz grün tapeziert, mit Gitterfenstern, dicht beim Theater."

"Your Excellency perhaps does not yet know that this hotel is connected to the theater. This hidden door leads to a small corridor, from which you can enter number 23 directly; that is the visitors' box."

"What? – Theater? – Visitors' box?"

"Yes, the small visitors' box for two, at most three people – only for distinguished gentlemen, with walls covered in green tapestry, with barred windows, right by the stage." (83)

It turns out that access to the theater is not as direct as the sounds emanating from it had led the narrator to believe. A hidden door leads into a corridor, which leads into the visitors' box, which provides a view of the stage, but from behind a barred window. The visitors' box is designated by the word "Fremdenloge," literally a "theater box for strangers," for travelers visiting from outside the immediate area.[6] The word *fremd* in German designates what is unknown, unfamiliar, or strange, so the Fremdenloge could be seen as both providing access to the unknown and preserving the mystery of the unknown. It provides a view of the stage and a link, however indirect and hidden, between the hotel and the theater, but at the same time it is partially separated from the rest of the theater and the stage by the barred window. One of the functions of the Fremdenloge appears to be to limit access: the space accommodates only two or three people, and it is designated for "vornehme Herren," men who are set apart from others by their social status. The layout of the Fremdenloge reflects the narrator's ability to know and understand the opera. He claims to have superior insight into the hidden meanings of the opera, just as he has access to the hidden Fremdenloge; yet his point of view is also limited and is called into question by the reactions and reports of the other guests congregating in the hotel dining room.

The novella alternates between a demonstration of the narrator's desire to understand certain truths about the opera as well as to present these truths as insight that remains hidden to most people, and the realization that certain things are essentially unknowable. This contradiction between the desire to know and the realization of the limits of human knowledge is not made explicit in earlier versions of Don Juan, in *El burlador*, or in versions by Molière and Mozart, for example, but is of course the major preoccupation of Goethe's *Faust*, whose part 1 was published in 1808, just five years before the first publication of Hoffmann's *Don Juan*. The novella contains many echoes of *Faust*, for example when the narrator observes that the singer playing Don Giovanni has "etwas vom Mephistopheles in die Physiognomie" (something of Mephistopheles in his physiognomy) (85). In the second half of the novella, the narrator develops these parallels between the characters of Don Juan and Faust:

> In Don Juans Gemüt kam durch des Erbfeindes List der Gedanke, daß durch die Liebe, durch den Genuß des Weibes schon auf Erden das erfüllt werden könne, was bloß als himmlische Verheißung in unserer Brust wohnt und eben jene unendliche Sehnsucht ist, die uns mit dem Überirdischen in unmittelbaren Rapport setzt. ... Jeder Genuß des Weibes war nun nicht mehr Befriedigung seiner Sinnlichkeit, sondern frevelnder Hohn gegen die Natur und den Schöpfer.

> Through the cunning of the archenemy, the idea entered Don Juan's head that through love, through enjoyment of women, what only exists for us as heavenly promise, the eternal longing that puts us into direct contact with the divine, could be fulfilled on earth. ... Every moment of pleasure with women was not only the satisfaction of his sensual desire, but also sinful mockery of nature and the creator. (93)

Don Juan, as seen by the narrator, is not just a sensualist who seeks immediate satisfaction of his desires, but rather a character who, like Faust, suffers from the limitations of earthly existence and seeks knowledge that is hidden from others, to the extent that he is willing to subvert both natural and divine order. For him, sexual pleasure is not simply an end in itself; it is a means of attaining spiritual knowledge while at the same time rebelling against the divine. There is some evidence even in the opening paragraph of the novella, with its reference to Satan, that the narrator, like Don Juan, is under demonic influence, and that his struggles are similar to those of the character whom he describes.

The interpretation of Don Juan provided in the analytical section of the novella is echoed in the narrator's analysis of the music of *Don Giovanni*, in particular of the overture, which for the narrator sets up the conflicts that reemerge in the plot of the opera. When describing the experience of listening to the overture of *Don Giovanni*, the narrator emphasizes the presence of the satanic in the music and the conflicts that it expresses:

> In dem Andante ergriffen mich die Schauer des furchtbaren, unterirdischen regno all pianto; grausenerregende Ahnungen des Entsetzlichen erfüllten mein Gemüt. Wie ein jauchzender Frevel

klang mir die jubelnde Fanfare im siebenten Takte des Allegro: ich sah aus tiefer Nacht feurige Dämonen ihre glühende Krallen ausstrecken – nach dem Leben froher Menschen, die auf des bodenlosen Abgrunds dünner Decke lustig tanzten. Der Konflikt der menschlichen Natur mit den unbekannten, gräßlichen Mächten, die ihn, sein Verderben erlauernd, umfangen, trat klar vor meines Geistes Augen.

In the Andante the terror of the infernal *regno all pianto* gripped me; dreadful premonitions of horror filled my soul. The joyous fanfare in the seventh bar of the Allegro sounded like a cheerful sacrilege: from the deep night I saw fiery demons stretching out their claws – toward the lives of happy people, who were dancing merrily on the thin covering of the bottomless abyss. The conflict of human nature with the unknown, horrifying powers that surround it, awaiting its ruin, appeared clearly before my soul's eyes. (84)

The narrator describes the overture in terms of conflicting dualities. Like the novella, *Don Juan*, the overture consists of two parts, the Andante or slower section, and the Allegro or faster section. The Andante begins with a series of chords that, as the narrator suggests, may very well be related to the demonic, since they are repeated in the second act, when the statue of the dead Commendatore visits Don Giovanni. The presence of the demonic in the Andante is indicated in the narrator's description with the Italian phrase "regno all pianto," or "kingdom of lamentation," which picks up on language used in the libretto of *Don Giovanni* to express the suffering of characters including Elvira, Anna, Ottavio, and even Juan (during a seduction attempt), all of whom use the word "pianto" to express their sorrow.[7] The Allegro section of the overture contrasts with the Andante in mood and tempo, and contains some lighter, less portentous passages; nonetheless, some music critics, like Hoffmann's narrator, have discerned a duality within the Allegro section, pointing out the presence of heavier, more foreboding music followed by lighter passages.[8] Hoffmann's narrator refers to fanfare in the seventh—actually the eighth—measure of the allegro (Mozart, *Paritura* 5), which he interprets as joy built on an illusion, unawareness of the demonic. The narrator interprets the musical contrasts between the Andante and the Allegro, and within the Allegro itself, as a conflict between the human and the demonic. For him, the demonic is hidden or unknown ("unbekannt") to most; he thus establishes a contrast between the limited knowledge of most human beings and the clarity of the interpreter's understanding. He succeeds in establishing a congruency, which he undermines in the novella's second section, between his description of Don Juan's character and the musical meaning of the opera. The narrator does not stop at providing a new interpretation of Don Juan that melds the seducer's characteristics with those of Faust; he also creates a link between his own desire to understand the hidden meaning of the opera and the quests of both Don Juan and Faust to transcend human limitations.

The narrator's melding of Don Juan with Faust involves a combination of opposites: the young man's sexual energy and lack of concern for the future contrast with the older scholar's pursuit of knowledge to the exclusion of other gratification, and his skepticism about the value of sensual pleasures. The narrator himself reveals a dual attitude toward older males, sometimes adopting a combative stance, sometimes reverential. These contrasting perspectives are most apparent in the narrator's treatment of the father figure of *Don Giovanni*, the Commendatore. In his description of the performance of the opera, the narrator first displays a somewhat condescending attitude toward the Commendatore: "Der alte Papa hat seine Torheit, im Finstern den kräftigen Gegner anzufallen, mit dem Leben gebüßt" (The old dad paid with his life for the foolishness of attacking his powerful opponent in the dark) (85). In contrast to the strong and youthful Don Giovanni, the Commendatore is described as weak and lacking in judgment. In the description of the second act, these characteristics are reversed: "Endlich das gewaltige Pochen. Elvira, die Mädchen entfliehen, und unter den entsetzlichen Akkorden der unterirdischen Geisterwelt tritt der gewaltige Marmorkoloß, gegen den Don Juan pygmäisch dasteht, ein" (Finally the heavy knocking. Elvira and the girls flee, and the powerful marble colossus, next to whom Don Juan stands looking like a pygmy, enters accompanied by the horrifying chords of the demonic realm) (89). In the second act, the statue of the Commendatore has acquired the power that his living counterpart lacked, while the formerly dominant younger man is overshadowed by the older man's authority. The contrasting characteristics of the Commendatore as described by the narrator reflect the relationship of the author, Hoffmann, to another father figure, Mozart. The famous composer was born in 1756, twenty years before Hoffmann, and was of an age to qualify as a paternal figure to the writer and composer, although he was dead by the time Hoffmann wrote *Don Juan*. Indeed, the narrator refers to Mozart as "der große Meister" (the great master) (84), a term showing the reverence and respect that he feels for his predecessor. The narrator tries to claim for himself some of the authority invested in Mozart by claiming a unique understanding of his opera, and at the same time he strives to show himself the equal of the "master" by establishing himself as a particularly insightful interpreter of Mozart's music. In this respect, he resembles

Faust, who combines the authority of the older scholar with the energy and ambition of a younger man following his pact with Mephistopheles.

The narrator's Faustian ambitions are revealed in his description of physical space. At the beginning of the novella's second section, the narrator describes his hotel room in a manner that is reminiscent of certain locations in Goethe's *Faust*: the title character's study and Gretchen's room:

> Es war mir so eng, so schwül in dem dumpfen Gemach! – Um Mitternacht glaubte ich deine Stimme zu hören, mein Theodor! Du sprachst deutlich meinen Namen aus, und es schien an der Tapetentür zu rauschen. Was hält mich ab, den Ort meines wunderbaren Abenteuers noch einmal zu betreten? – Vielleicht sehe ich dich und sie, die mein ganzes Wesen erfüllt!

> It seemed so narrow, so damp in the musty room! – At midnight I thought I heard your voice, Theodor! You spoke my name clearly, and I heard a rustling at the hidden door. What prevents me from entering the place of my marvelous adventure again? – Maybe I will see you and her, the one who fills my entire being! (91)

This scene recalls the opening scene of Goethe's *Faust*, part 1, "Nacht" (Night), which takes place in Faust's study, "in einem hochgewölbten, engen gothischen Zimmer" (in a high-arched, narrow Gothic room) (20). Faust describes the limitations of his scholarly existence by referring to the physical confines of his study: "Weh! Steck ich in dem Kerker noch? / Verfluchtes dumpfes Mauerloch" (Alas! Am I still imprisoned in the dungeon? Cursed, musty hole in the wall) (398–99). This sense of being imprisoned is shared by Hoffmann's narrator, who moves the locus of his scholarly activity from the hotel room to the theater by carrying a table, lights, and writing material into the visitors' box. Like Faust, he does not abandon his pursuit of knowledge but, when confronted with limitations, seeks inspiration from unorthodox circumstances and locations. He then proceeds to write his interpretation of *Don Giovanni*, in which he draws out the connections between Don Juan and Faust, two figures with whom he himself identifies.

At the same time he identifies with Faust, the narrator also develops parallels between his situation and that of Margarete/Gretchen, the young woman seduced and abandoned by Faust. In Goethe's drama, Faust, aided by Mephistopheles, enters Gretchen's room and leaves a box filled with rare jewelry. The two escape just before Gretchen returns and remarks, "Es ist so schwül, so dumpfig hie" (It is so damp, so musty here) (2753), an indication that she has sensed the presence of evil (Mephistopheles). Hoffmann's narrator, in the passage quoted above, uses similar language ("damp," "musty room") to express the confining nature of his hotel room and the constricting quality of the judgments, expressed by the hotel guests whom he encounters in the hotel dining room. The parallels between Hoffmann's narrator, imprisoned in a reality that he wishes to escape, and Gretchen's physical imprisonment at the end of *Faust*, part 1, is also expressed linguistically. In the "Kerker" (Dungeon) scene of Goethe's *Faust*, Faust tries to free Gretchen from prison, but her senses are too distorted by the trauma that she has endured, and she is too fearful of Mephistopheles, to follow him. She hears his voice but does not see him, just as Hoffmann's narrator hears the voice of his friend, Theodor, and goes into the theater in hopes of finding him. Just as Gretchen responds to the promise of her lover's voice, which is associated with musical qualities, "den liebenden Ton" (the loving tone) (4469), so Hoffmann's narrator responds to the disembodied voice of his friend, Theodor, whom he never locates in the theater but to whom he addresses a letter containing an interpretation of the opera. His entrance into the theater is motivated by the call of Theodor, who, like Faust, seeks to free his friend from the "dungeon," and, equally, by his desire to see again the singer playing Donna Anna, whom he had encountered in the visitors' box during the performance. This double motivation implies a flexibility in sexual identity on the part of the narrator, who is capable of identifying with both male and female roles.

The narrator's encounter with the singer playing Donna Anna reinforces his identification with Margarete/Gretchen and can be seen as a reversal of the encounter between Anna and Giovanni in Mozart's opera. In the opera, Giovanni enters Anna's room at night in order to conceal his identity from her. In Hoffmann's *Don Juan*, the narrator, during the performance of the opera's first act, becomes aware that a woman has entered the visitors' box:

Schon oft glaubte ich dicht hinter mir einen zarten, warmen Hauch gefühlt, das Knistern eines seidenen Gewandes gehört zu haben: das ließ mich wohl die Gegenwart eines Frauenzimmers ahnen, aber ganz versunken in die poetische Welt, die mir die Oper aufschloß, achtete ich nicht darauf.

Often I thought that I felt a gentle, warm breath directly behind me, that I heard the rustling of a silk dress: that led me to think that a woman was present, but I paid no attention, absorbed in the world of poetry that the opera opened up to me. (87)

Unlike Anna in Mozart's opera, Hoffmann's narrator experiences the presence of another person in his space as a distraction but not as a threat. During the intermission, however, when he recognizes the singer, whom he identifies simply as "Donna Anna," he experiences a fear that parallels Anna's on encountering an unknown man in her room: "Ich fühlte die Notwendigkeit, sie anzureden, und konnte doch die durch das Erstaunen, ja ich möchte sagen, die durch den Schreck gelähmte Zunge nicht bewegen" (I felt the necessity of speaking to her, but could not move my tongue, which was paralyzed by astonishment, I should say by fear) (87). Just as Anna is gripped tightly by Giovanni and prevented from moving or speaking, so the narrator is paralyzed by the presence of Donna Anna and is at first unable to speak.

While the narrator establishes parallels between himself and Don Juan as well as Faust through his quest to understand the opera and his claim to intimate knowledge of its deeper meaning, he is also shown in the role of female victims of seduction, such as Gretchen and Anna. The Enthusiast attempts to establish himself as an authority, someone knowledgeable about music, who is himself a composer of operas, but he is also subject to the trickery or deceit of others. The struggle depicted in many versions of Don Juan between the trickster ("burlador") and his victims, who seek to gain knowledge about the one who tricked them, is concentrated in one character of Hoffmann's *Don Juan*, the narrator, who establishes his role as musician, writer, and interpreter but whose authority is cast into doubt from the start by the suggestion that he has fallen prey to Satan's deceit. As we have seen, his views are called into question by the binary structure of the text, which opposes his observations to those of the other hotel guests. Further, his identity is destabilized by his identification with both male seducer and female victim of seduction (Anna and Gretchen). He is both deceiver and deceived.

The struggle between oppositional elements (male and female, seducer and seduced) occurs in parallel to the dissolution of boundaries between these opposites. This process is reflected in the encounter of the narrator with the "Signora," more specifically in the contrast drawn by the narrator between the Italian and the German languages. The singer speaks to the narrator "im reinsten Toskanisch" (in the purest Tuscan) (87), while the narrator, in transcribing their conversation for the benefit of his friend, Theodor, uses German:

> Wie gern setze ich dir, mein Theodor, jedes Wort des merkwürdigen Gesprächs her, das nun zwischen der Signora und mir begann; allein, indem ich das, was sie sagte, deutsch hinschreiben will, finde ich

jedes Wort steif und matt, jede Phrase ungelenk, das auszudrücken, was sie leicht und mit Anmut toskanisch sagte.

Dear Theodor, how glad I am to write down for you each word of the strange conversation that began between the Signora and me; only when I translate what she said into German, I find every word to be awkward and inadequate, every phrase clumsy, although she spoke so easily and gracefully in Tuscan.(88)

The narrator makes reference to an original language in which the conversation was conducted, and to which only he has access: Tuscan, a dialect of Italian (and the basis for standard Italian), the language in which the libretto of *Don Giovanni* was written. The narrator privileges Italian as a language that provides direct access to Mozart's creative process. When he hears the opening scene of *Don Giovanni* sung in Italian, he remarks, "Also italienisch? – Hier am deutschen Orte italienisch? Ah che piacere! ich werde alle Rezitative, alles so hören, wie es der große Meister in seinem Gemüt empfing und dachte" (Italian? – Here in this German town, Italian? Ah *che piacere*! I will hear all the recitative, everything, just as the great master conceived and thought it out) (84). The narrator suggests a single language of origin and a single creator associated with that language, even though the informed reader would know that Mozart, whose first language was German, collaborated with an Italian, Da Ponte, on an Italian libretto. The blending of languages associated with the opera's creation is, however, reflected in the communication of Hoffmann's narrator with both the Italian-speaking Signora and his German reader, Theodor. It would seem that the narrator's bilingualism would provide him with a deeper understanding of the opera, and a way to connect his German audience with the German-speaking composer of *Don Giovanni* via an Italian libretto. This is what he affirms, although his acknowledged inability to communicate effortlessly, as the singer supposedly does in her native language, undermines his claim to superior insight.

The narrator's suggestion that Italian provides access to hidden reality, while German hinders understanding, itself hides the reality that neither language can reveal the truth. The continued inaccessibility of the opera to understanding is reflected in the shifting identities of all characters involved in this episode: the narrator, the singer, and Theodor. Indeed the confusion of identities extends further. The name of the addressee, Theodor, is also the second name of the author of *Don Juan*, Ernst Theodor Amadeus Hoffmann, who changed his third name to match Mozart's middle name, Amadeus. This confusion of the identities of composer

(Mozart), author and composer (Hoffmann), narrator of *Don Juan* (traveling music aficionado, also a writer and composer), and addressee of the novella (Theodor) would seem to suggest an affinity and ease of understanding among artists. At the same time, the lack of distinction between creator and fictional creation, as well as the implied competition among creators both actual and fictional (Mozart, Hoffmann, the narrator of *Don Juan*, and possibly Theodor), undermines the idea of one "große Meister" whose artistic message can be decoded.

This collapse of distinctions between roles extends to the relationship between the narrator/composer and the singer playing Donna Anna. As we have seen, the references to *Faust* suggest a role reversal in which "Donna Anna" takes on the role of seducer, while the narrator is tricked or seduced. The narrator suggests a hidden connection between himself and the singer, which she then reveals to him during their conversation:

> "Ging nicht der zauberische Wahnsinn ewig sehnender Liebe in der Rolle der *** in deiner neuesten Oper aus deinem Innern hervor? Ich habe dich verstanden: dein Gemüt hat sich im Gesange mir aufgeschlossen! – Ja" (hier nannte sie meinen Vornamen), "ich habe dich gesungen, so wie deine Melodien ich sind."

> "Did not the magical madness of love's longing in the role of *** in your latest opera emerge from your innermost soul? I understood you: your mind revealed itself to me in song! Yes" (here she spoke my first name), "I sang you, just as I am your melodies." (88–89)

The singer reveals that the narrator is a composer of operas—a detail that he had not mentioned—and that she has sung a role in one of his compositions; however, the narrator suppresses his own first name while revealing that the singer knows it, just as he keeps her name concealed, referring to her as "Donna Anna," the name of the role she plays, or "die Signora." It seems that the identities of the narrator and the singer are connected through music, a medium that allows each to create and reflect the other but that reveals nothing significant about either. This is a relationship of mutual definition and creation; yet it is completely opaque to outsiders, who have no access to the knowledge that is shared between composer and singer. Furthermore, if Theodor, as his name suggests, is related to the narrator, to Hoffmann, or to Mozart himself without being identical to any of them, we can conclude that his identity is equally opaque. All characters are essentially "sin nombre," like Don Juan of *El burlador*. Consequently, what happens between Hoffmann's narrator and the Signora is essentially unknowable, just as what occurs between Don Giovanni and Donna Anna in Mozart's opera remains a mystery.

While the narrator finds that language is an imperfect medium for the revelation of deeper truths, he claims that music grants him insight into the opera. In the second section of the novella, the interpretive section addressed to Theodor, he emphasizes the conflict between Anna and Giovanni following his "ruin" ("Verderben") of her, which leads to his own demise and damnation, according to the narrator.

> Gewiß ist es dir, mein Theodor, aufgefallen, daß ich von Annas Verführung gesprochen; und so gut ich es in dieser Stunde, wo tief aus dem Gemüt hervorgehende Gedanken und Ideen die Worte überflügeln, vermag, sage ich dir mit wenigen Worten, wie mir in der Musik, ohne alle Rücksicht auf den Text das ganze Verhältnis der beiden im Kampf begriffenen Naturen (Don Juan und Donna Anna) erscheint.

> You must have noticed, dear Theodor, that I spoke of Anna's seduction; and as far as I am able at this time, when the thoughts and ideas emanating from my mind outpace the words, I will tell you in few words, without reference to the text, my impressions of the relationship between the two opposing natures (Don Juan and Donna Anna). (94–95)

The language of this passage conceals more than it reveals. The narrator mentions Anna's seduction ("Verführung"), whereas before he had used the word ruin ("Verderben") (94), which has a different connotation, "seduction" implying some emotional involvement on the part of Anna. This shift in connotation is itself a kind of deceit or seduction of the reader, who may be led from seeing the male protagonist as a violent deceiver to viewing him as a skillful lover. Interestingly, the narrator refers to Don Giovanni (the name given him in Da Ponte's libretto) as Don Juan, the character's Spanish name. Similarly, the waiter, in the opening passage of the novella, refers to the opera being performed as "den *Don Juan* von dem berühmten Herrn Mozart aus Wien" (the *Don Juan* by the famous Mr. Mozart from Vienna) (83). The waiter's translation of the opera's title was the one commonly used in Germany, but the narrator's substitution of "Don Juan" for "Don Giovanni," when he otherwise privileges the use of the Italian language, underscores the tenuous quality of national, linguistic, and personal identity. The shift from "Don Giovanni" to "Don Juan" also suggests that there is another language, Spanish, concealed by the narrator's focus on Italian and German, and associated with *El burlador*, the first literary version of Don Juan. This language and its associated tradition is never referenced in Hoffmann's text, but the conflicts described by the narrator, which he perceives in Mozart's opera, suggest a continuity among the Spanish, Italian, and German versions of Don Juan. While linguistic distinctions seem to recede along with the stable identities of characters in Hoffmann's novella, the narrator claims that music grants him privileged insight into the opera, without reference to the text. Since he does not explain what in the music leads him to this insight, his claim cannot be examined or challenged, but remains opaque, much like his relationship with the Signora, or Anna's with Giovanni. The only instance of musical analysis on the part of the narrator occurs during his description of the opera's overture, in which he discerns the conflict between the human and the demonic, which structures his subsequent analysis of the opera. When discussing his insight about the relationship between Anna and Giovanni, however, he claims that the knowledge he gains from the music is not to be gleaned from the text.

Conflict and competition, as Robert ter Horst suggests, arise because of a combination of similarity and difference, such that the son seeks to differentiate himself from the father whom he resembles, or a young man wishes to distinguish himself from his peers. Hoffmann's *Don Juan* also explores the interplay between similarity and difference in male-male relationships, such as the chain of shifting identifications and rivalries that the text establishes among Mozart, E. T. A. Hoffmann, the narrator of the novella, the character of Don Juan as presented in the opera and described by the narrator, and Goethe's Faust. In Hoffmann's version of *Don Juan*, male-female relationships such as that between Giovanni and Anna or between the narrator and the Signora are characterized by a reversal of characteristics that destabilize established roles, and also establish alternate identities for the characters, so that the narrator is linked to both Faust and Gretchen, for example. The role reversals that are characteristic of male-female relationships in the novella, and the interplay between identification and difference linked with the male-male relationships, are associated with the more abstract qualities through which Hoffmann's narrator analyzes the opera, such as language and music, the human and the demonic, masculinity and femininity. When the differences between these seemingly opposite qualities collapse through reversal and identification, the result is that the object of analysis, the work of art, is shown to be unknowable. What is at the center of all the versions of Don Juan is the sexual relationship between men and women. In *El burlador* and *Don Giovanni*, this relationship is at least partially hidden, while in Hoffmann it is "sin nombre," eluding definition entirely. Hoffmann's merging of Faust with Don Juan presents a new interpretation of this tradition and thus suggests a rivalry with previous versions. At the same time, the novella's undermining of the idea of mastery, including a "master" work from which others derive, emphasizes the interactions among works from various linguistic heritages and genres, which struggle for dominance without allowing one to predominate. Pleasure and knowledge (Don Juan and Faust) are to be found in observing the interactions among the variety of contributions, which compete with and enrich each other.

Notes

[1] Daniel Rogers summarizes the uncertainty surrounding the authorship of *El burlador* and describes the two versions of the text (11–16).
[2] All translations from German are mine. I would like to thank Robert ter Horst for his assistance with the translations from Spanish and Italian.
[3] Hoffmann's views have influenced Mozart scholarship, inspiring a debate about what happened between Anna and Giovanni. Alfred Einstein dismisses Hoffmann's claim that Anna is in love with Giovanni, but argues that Giovanni did complete the sexual act with Anna, based on her behavior toward Ottavio (439). Aloys Greither agrees with Einstein's assessment of what occurred in Anna's room, and uses both textual and musical evidence to support the claim that Anna desires Giovanni but feels guilt surrounding her desire (117–18). Robert Moberly also follows this interpretation of events, based on an examination of temporal indications, Anna's account, and musical evidence (161–68). William Mann, however, dismisses this claim, based on an assessment of Anna's character (468), as does Alfons Rosenberg, who examines the libretto and evaluates Giovanni's character to arrive at this conclusion (270–71).
[4] Critics have noted the differences between the performance as described by the traveling enthusiast and the opera's libretto and score. Francien Markx, noting that the novella was first published in the *Allgemeine Musikalische Zeitung*, a journal of music criticism, sees Hoffmann as commenting on performance practices of his time (369). Ricarda Schmidt also sees the novella as a critique of contemporary performance practice, and in particular of the German translation of the libretto of *Don Giovanni* by Friedrich Rochlitz, the editor of the *Allgemeine Muskalische Zeitung* (68–77).

[5] Scholars are divided about the aesthetic theory suggested in the novella. Alexander Klüglich acknowledges the contradictions in the text but suggests that the novella shows the artist transcending these contradictions through the inspiration provided by Mozart's music (36). Albert Meier, on the other hand, sees the contradictions as crucial to the aesthetic theories of romanticism, in that they oblige the reader to take an active role in interpreting the text (531). Birgit Röder, focusing on the contradictions between the real and the ideal in romantic aesthetic theory, interprets the novella as illustrating the connections between artistic practice and everyday life (12). Hideki Tanabe sees *Don Juan* as a turning point in Hoffmann's own artistic production from composer of musical works to writer of fiction (35). David Wellbery reads the novella as a critique of romantic hermeneutics in that it foregrounds the conflict between representation and the nonrepresentable. He interprets the rape of Donna Anna as illustrating the artistic violation involved in representing, or making physically present, the ideal (468–73).

[6] *Fremdenlogen* were common in German theaters through the nineteenth century and still exist in some halls, for example in the Musikverein in Vienna.

[7] Elvira accuses Juan: "lasci in preda al rimorso ed al pianto" (You left me prey to remorse and sorrow) (16–17). Ottavio, in his aria, "Dalla sua pace," sings of Anna, "è mia quell'ira, quel pianto è mio" (her anger is mine, her sorrow mine) (38–39). Don Juan serenades Elvira's maid: "Deh vieni alla finestra, o mio tesoro, deh vieni a consolar il pianto mio" (Come to the window, my treasure, come console my sorrow) (74). Finally, Anna, expressing to Ottavio her grief at her father's death, sings: "sol la morte, o mio tesoro, il mio pianto può finir" (only death, my treasure, can put an end to my sorrow) (81).

[8] William Mann points out the musical contrasts between the Adagio and the Allegro sections, as well as within the Allegro itself (461–62).

Works Cited

Einstein, Alfred. *Mozart: His Character, His Work*. Trans. Arthur Mendel and Nathan Broder. London: Oxford UP, 1945.

Goethe, Johann Wolfgang von. *Faust: Eine Tragödie; Goethes Werke*. Ed. Erich Trunz. Vol. 3. Munich: Beck, 1986.

Greither, Aloys. *Die sieben großen Opern Mozarts: Versuche über das Verhältnis der Texte zur Musik*. Heidelberg: Schneider, 1977.

Hoffmann, E. T. A. *Fantasiestücke in Callots Manier: Werke 1814*. Ed. Hartmut Steinecke et al. Vol. 2/1 (1993) of *Sämtliche Werke*.

———. *Sämtliche Werke*. Ed. Hartmut Steinecke and Wulf Segebrecht. Frankfurt: Deutscher Klassiker Verlag, 1985–2004.

Klüglich, Alexander. "Aufstieg zu vollendetem Künstlertum: Ein Beitrag zur Kunstauffassung in E. T. A. Hoffmanns Erzählung *Don Juan*." *E. T. A. Hoffmann–Jahrbuch* 8 (2000): 13–36.

Mann, William. *The Operas of Mozart*. New York: Oxford UP, 1977.

Markx, Francien. "E. T. A. Hoffmann's Don Juan: Views of an Eccentric Enthusiast?" *Seminar* 41:4 (November 2005): 367–79. http://dx.doi.org/10.3138/sem.v41.4.367

Meier, Albert. "Fremdenloge und Wirtstafel: Zur poetischen Funktion des Realitätsschocks in E. T. A. Hoffmanns Fantasiestück *Don Juan*." *Zeitschrift für deutsche Philologie* 111.4 (1992): 516–31.

Moberly, Robert. *Three Mozart Operas: Figaro, Don Giovanni, The Magic Flute*. New York: Dodd, Mead and Company, 1968.

Molina, Tirso de. *The Trickster of Seville and the Stone Guest* (*El burlador de Sevilla y el convivado de piedra*). Trans. and ed. Gwynne Edwards. Oxford: Aris & Phillips, 1986.

Mozart, Wolfgang Amadeus. *Don Giovanni: Oper in 2 Akten, Partitura*. Budapest: Könemann, 1995.

———. *Mozart's Don Giovanni*. Ed. and trans. Ellen Bleiler. New York: Dover, 1985.

Röder, Birgit. "'*Ich sah aus tiefer Nacht feurige Dämonen ihre glühenden Krallen ausstrecken*': The Problem of the Romantic Ideal in E. T. A. Hoffmann's *Don Juan*." *Colloquia Germanica* 34.1 (2001): 1–14.

Rogers, Daniel. *Critical Guides to Spanish Texts: Tirso de Molina, El burlador de Sevilla*. London: Grant and Cutler, 1977.

Rosenberg, Alfons. *Don Giovanni: Mozarts Oper und Don Juans Gestalt*. Munich: Prestel, 1968.

Schmidt, Ricarda. "How to Get Past Your Editor: E. T. A. Hoffmann's *Don Juan* as a Palimpsest." *Textual Intersections: Literature, History and the Arts in Nineteenth-Century Europe.* Ed. Rachel Langford. Amsterdam: Rodopi, 2009. 63–78.

Tanabe, Hideki."Zwei Literarische Konfrontationen mit dem 'Don Juan'-Erlebnis: E. T. A. Hoffmanns *Don Juan* und E. Morikes Mozartnovelle." *Hitotsubashi Journal of Arts and Sciences* 22.1 (1981): 31–41.

Ter Horst, Robert. "Epic Descent: The Filiations of Don Juan." *MLN* 111.2 (1996): 255–74. http://dx.doi.org/10.1353/mln.1996.0029

Wellbery, David. "E. T. A. Hoffmann and Romantic Hermeneutics: An Interpretation of Hoffmann's *Don Juan.*" *Studies in Romanticism* 19.4 (1980): 455–73.

9

Aspects of Symbolism in *La Celestina*

Florence Byham Weinberg

Emerita, Trinity University (San Antonio)

La Celestina, often considered a work of Spanish realism, contains symbolic dimensions hitherto inadequately explored.[1] In this essay, I shall examine the symbolism of a number of places, objects, and Celestina herself, the "prime mover" in Fernando de Rojas's drama. In adopting Erwin Panofsky's definition of "symbol," I shall modify his distinctions to fit literature rather than the visual arts. A symbol is an object, locus, or person intended to convey more to the reader than the "primary or natural subject matter": that Celestina is an old woman, and that Melibea's belt, a cord, is merely a part of her costume. The Renaissance author doubtless assumed that his reader would understand the "secondary or conventional subject matter," that Celestina is a procuress and a witch, with all the culturally determined implications of the words, and that Melibea's belt stands for her chastity (Panofsky 6–7). Finally, a symbol is intended to convey an "intrinsic meaning or content," in which the subject matter, together with its traditional associations and the way in which it is handled by its author, is sifted for hints as to the author's purpose in composing his work, and his relation to prevailing traditions (Panofsky 7–17). This third task is the most difficult and requires a cautious accomplishment of the second step by the modern interpreter: the discovery of those traditional conventions.

Rojas's symbolism reveals, as sources of "secondary, conventional subject matter," the Judeo-Christian tradition and Neoplatonism, present throughout the Middle Ages and revived by the Florentine circle around Marsilio Ficino; the topoi of classical antiquity; "courtly love"; contemporary literature; and compendia of *loci communes*, learned and vulgar. Rojas appears to have been steeped in the culture of the time and to have held moral and religious attitudes in keeping with his erudite background and his period.[2]

Topoi in *La Celestina:* The Hawk, the Wall, the Garden

The first *argumento* informs the reader how Calisto enters the garden of Melibea: "Entrando Calisto en una huerta empos de un falcon suyo, hallo ay a Melibea, de cuyo amor preso, commençole de hablar; de la qual rigurosamente despedido, fue para su casa muy angustiado (1.21.1–6). His escaped falcon serves as an excuse to break with the severe restrictions of fifteenth-century Spain, to enter a lady's garden unannounced and unexpected. He loses no time in trying to woo the fair occupant, Melibea, who harshly repels him. Much later, in her first conversation with Celestina, Melibea reveals his method of entry and his habits in a pair of choice epithets: "saltaparedes" and "fantasma de noche" (4.93.30), which characterize his actions throughout the work.

The initial scene provides some clues to the meaning of the *tragicomedia*: led by (1) his falcon, a youth surmounts (2) a vertical barrier to enter (3) a forbidden paradise. The first clue is the falcon, a traditional symbol for rapine, appetite, and destruction.[3] When it comes to hand, it is considered a "good" bird, its aggressive hunting prowess tamed, controlled by its master's will. Calisto's falcon, however, escapes control. From the outset, the hawk out of control foreshadows the ultimate destruction of all the protagonists, victims of blind sexual passion that ignores reason and good counsel. (Calisto will disregard the deaths of his servants in order to return to Melibea's garden the very night after their fatal fall.) The falcon further stands for Celestina, incarnation of rapine and lust, who preys upon young people, in particular the unsullied virgins of the town.

In its uncontrolled rapine and appetite, Calisto's falcon breaches two loci: the wall and the garden.[4] The Renaissance reader would have recognized the secondary connotations from the beginning of the play. Melibea, when later described by Calisto, epitomizes "courtly" beauty. A traditional figure, her initial behavior is likewise stereotyped. Upon first hearing Calisto's lustful compliments, she violently casts him out of "paradise"; her garden wall with its locked door closes about her like a fortress. Calisto will use the most dishonorable means to breach the wall of Melibea's resistance; he employs the most notorious procuress in town to achieve his goal.

The fortress, the garden wall, and the locked door represent Melibea's personal integrity and chastity, her honor, her class, and her body as an illusory paradise, in a symbolic complex reminiscent of the *Roman de la rose*. The flower garden is a widespread euphemism for the female sexual organs. The little, unspoiled Eden in which Melibea is first seen has overtones of the "little garden of Mary," the pure, unsullied womb of the Virgin.[5] Melibea's garden does not remain long unsullied. Overcome by desire, she allows Calisto to enter "paradise" once more, illegitimately, not through the unlocked door of marriage but once again over the wall. She will live increasingly in and for her now-nocturnal "garden" with its illicit delights, until she destroys herself because of what took place there. The lyricism of Melibea and Lucrecia, singing in anticipation of the love tryst in Act 19, expresses their longing for that negative "noche oscura del alma" in which all the characters have come to live (Bataillon 125).

Calisto's Home

Ejected from the garden a first time, Calisto hurries home and angrily orders Sempronio to close the window of his bedroom: "¡Anda, anda malvado, abre la camara y adereça la cama! ... Cierra la ventana, y dexa la tiniebla acompañar al triste, y al desdechado la ceguedad. Mis pensamientos tristes no son dignos de luz" (1.24.24–26). Calisto's words, heavy with the traditional hyperbole of amorous lament, provide the key to his behavior. "Dexa la tiniebla acompañar al triste ... la ceguedad" evokes the equation darkness = evil (here, unbridled passion).[6] Calisto remains in spiritual blindness until the end, subservient to blind Cupid, who, according to Christian iconography, represents profane love (*loco amor*) as opposed to *caritas*. Rojas's contemporary, Leo Hebraeus, describes Cupid, "Por ser al amor después que ha nacido, *privado de toda razón, le pinta ciego sin ojos*" (57; emphasis mine).[7]

Calisto dies in blackest night, literally and spiritually, since he dies unconfessed. His inner darkness affects his mode of living. Rojas's audience never sees more than Calisto's bedroom, where he vegetates upon or near his bed, shutting out all light, because his "sad thoughts are not *worthy* of light." Suggestive light/dark symbolism is exploited here as in Racine's *Phèdre*: the character possessed by *loco amor* flees the light in order to hide his (or her) unworthy thoughts in a darkened bedroom, the very sanctuary of lust. Calisto, "fantasma de noche," now really *lives* only during the dark hours. He leaves his darkened bedroom merely to while away the time in a gloomy church sanctuary, praying, in essence, not to God but to the Devil, that Melibea might be delivered up to his lust. Later, after her surrender, he goes out only for midnight trysts in her moonlit garden.

Melibea's capitulation to lust, and her confession, not to a priest but to diabolical old Celestina, take place in her bedroom. She, too, will live thenceforth in darkness, in that negative "noche oscura" that represents the death of reason, a night only dimly lit by the sultry glow of sensual ardor (Bataillon 125). The lovers surrender their will and reason to the lower, appetitive souls: they begin to live on a subhuman, an animal, even a vegetable level (Hebraeus 28).[8] Like the inhabitants of Plato's cave, they content themselves with the shadows of reality, far from the bright light of reason, responsibility, morality, and truth.

Celestina's Hovel

Celestina's quarters are filled with the tools and helpers associated with her three trades: repairer of maidenheads, procuress, and witch. The chaotic jumble of viper's tongues, donkey's brains, eyeballs of a she-wolf, and the like; the prostitutes, procurers, and their clientele; and the stench that had surrounded her hut when it still was located on the riverbank near the tanneries: all these attributes make her hovel a negative symbol, one of *luxuria*. Her hovel mirrors Celestina herself, center of that contagion that will destroy all the principal personae in the drama.

The idyllic antithesis to the hovel, *la huerta de Melibea*, is bathed in moonlight, filled with the perfume of flowers, the rustle of foliage, and the tinkle of the crystalline fountain. As Melibea's symbolic mirror, the *huerta* represents the beauty and attraction, the lure, of *luxuria*. These two sharply contrasted aspects of lust are portrayed in a similar manner by Francesco Colonna, an Italian contemporary of Rojas. Colonna's hero, Poliphile, is allowed through a locked door to visit the sanctuary of Mater Amoris, Venus. He is delighted by the lovely hostess, who greets him, surrounded by her ladies in waiting, but his guide and counselor, Logistica, warns him: "Ha Poliphile, la baulté de ceste cy est feinct, faulse et fardée; et si tu avois veu la derriere de ses espaules tu serois contrainct de vomir: tu congnoistrois la trahison, et sentirois une charogne puante oultre mesure" (Ah, Poliphile, the beauty of this one is deceptive, false, and cosmetic: and if you had seen her back, you would be obliged to vomit; you would recognize treason and would smell a corpse, stinking beyond measure) (48). Rojas, like his contemporaries, underscores the horrors of lust, for in giving in to the appetites, man turns away from eternal light and life to wallow in darkness, prefiguring damnation in the stench of mortal decay.

Further Symbols: The Lute, the Ladder, the Tower, and the Fall

The symbolic impact of the hawk, emblem for the entire work, is intensified by other objects that serve as guideposts. Calisto, expressing his delirious love in courtly terms, demands his lute:

CALISTO: Dame aca el laúd.
SEMPRONIO: Señor, veslo aquí.
CALISTO: ¿Qual dolor puede ser talque se yguale con mi mal?
SEMPRONIO: Destemplado esta ese laud.

CALISTO: ¿Cómo templara el destemplado? ¿Cómo sentirá el armonía aquel que consigo esta tan discorde; aquel en quien lavoluntad a la razón no obedece … ? (1.16.19–26)

Normally, the lute connotes harmony, the individual in tune with himself. But the *laud destemplado* further develops the symbolism of the falcon. If the fugitive hawk represents uncontrolled appetites, the lute, when out of tune, stands for the disharmony of soul into which uncontrolled lust forces Calisto: "aquel en quien la voluntad a la razon no obedece." Leo Hebraeus summarizes this concept in two sentences: "Cuando la razón en alguna manera resiste al vicio [de lujuria], aunque de él sea vencida, entonces los tales viciososse llaman incontinentes [Melibea]" (10). "Pero los que dejan la razón del todo, sin procurar contradecir en parte alguna al hábito vicioso, se llaman *destemplados* [Calisto; más tarde, Melibea]" (25; emphasis mine).

The ladder, necessary for scaling garden walls, also betokens Calisto's breach of the "besieged fortress," Melibea's chastity. A sexual symbol, it also stresses the lovers' difference in social station. Literally and figuratively, the ladder represents a progression from one level to another. In Western literature, ladders often evoke Jacob's ladder. Calisto's ladder leads him to a deceptive "heaven," just as Celestina, the "heavenly one," opens the "celestial" path to success with Melibea. The irony of these allusions warns of a "snare and a delusion": this paradise is actually an antechamber to hell.[9]

The theme of the fall is dominant from the initial acrostic poem to Melibea's suicide. In the poem, an ant, normally allegorizing prudence and hard work, grows wings that will lead her, like Icarus, to perdition: she becomes lost in the alien element, air, to which she has so foolishly aspired, and is devoured by an "ave de rapiña," just as Calisto's falcon leads him to his fall and ignoble death. Although the author compares the ant's daring to his own in completing *La Celestina*, the insect prefigures the behavior of all characters who venture into the dangerous realm of immoral behavior: they all fall, morally and literally.

Celestina had fallen morally years before the opening of the work. She again falls, in a figurative sense, from her position as invulnerable queen of ruse and deception. In a way, all characters are devoured like the ant, preyed upon by lust or by greed. Most importantly, all the characters fall from a state of grace as Christians in good standing, a fall symbolized by their deaths without confession, deprived of priestly absolution from their sins.

Melibea's tower awakens associations with the courtly tradition, where towers symbolize chastity or enforced marital fidelity. Her lofty abode duplicates the symbolism of the garden surrounded by a high wall. The religious tradition, one probable source of courtly commonplaces, parallels the courtly use of the tower. Like the enclosed garden, it is emblematic of the Virgin Mary (Cirlot 326–27). Rojas thus repeats his implicit comparison between Melibea's original purity and that of Mary, the "candida flor," paragon of all feminine virtues. The violated garden and the ultimate leap from the tower twice portray, in graphic figurative language, Melibea's precipitate departure from chastity, honor, and social status.[10] Rojas uses the courtly tradition, reversing its values. He considers illicit love to be *luxuria* and hence does not applaud it as "true" love; the ladder and the hawk likewise become negative emblems. The tower does not represent (as in Marie de France) "legitimate" libido: it is a symbol of the positive virtue and chastity from which Melibea casts herself down as early as Act 10. On a spiritual plane, her behavior prefigures her suicidal leap.

The Thread, the Cord, the Chain

Celestina is widely known as a peddler of odds and ends for sewing and as a cosmetician or herbalist—legitimate activities that cover for her more sinister traffic (4.83.11–15). Melibea's mother, Alicia, who so imprudently allows the old woman into her house, is told immediately a likely reason for Celestina's visit: "Me sobrevino mengua de dinero; no supe mejor remedio que vender un poco de hilado, que para unas toquillas tenia allegado" (4.84.13–15). This same thread has just been invested with awesome diabolical power:

> Yo, Celestina tu mas conoscida clientula, te [al triste Pluton] conjuro por la virtud y fuerça destas bermejas letras; porla sangre de aquella nocturna ave con que estan escriptas; ... por la aspera ponçoña de las bivoras de que este azeyte fue hecho, con el cual unto este hilado: vengas sin tardança obedecer mi voluntad; y en ello te enbuelvas, y con ello estes sin un momento te partir, fasta que Melibea ... lo compre; y con ello de tal manera te quede enredada que, quanto mas lo mirare, tanto mas su coraçon se ablande a conceder mi petición. (3.78.7–19)

Whether or not the reader feels that diabolical intervention spoils the "realism" of the work, it is undeniable that Celestina's conjuring focuses attention on the thread that is to ensnare an unwary victim. The opposite of Ariadne's thread, Celestina's *hilado* will lead astray and lose its victim in the labyrinth of passion.

   Celestina, having gained entrance to Pleberio's house, is left alone with her prey, and, after a general conversation about the pains of old age and upon receiving payment for the fatal thread, she introduces the subject of Calisto. Melibea rages and will not be pacified until Celestina finds an excuse for interceding on Calisto's behalf. She asks Melibea for a prayer: "Una oracion, señora, que le dixeron que sabias de Santa Apolonia para el dolor de las muelas. Assimismo tu cordon, que es fama que ha tocado las reliquias que ay en Roma y Jerusalem" (4.95.1–4). Now that she has a good excuse for doing so, Melibea changes her behavior entirely.[11] She gives Celestina her corded belt:

> MELIBEA: En pago de tu buen suffrimiento, quiero cumplir tu demanda y darte luego mi cordon. Y porque para escrevir la oración no aura tiempo sin que venga mi madre, si esto no bastare ven mañana por ella muy secretamente.
> LUCRECIA: ¡Ya, ya perdida es mi ama! ¡Fraude ay! ¡Mas le querra dar que lo dicho! (4.99.2–9)[12]

Celestina carries away the cord in triumph, threatening Melibea as she had done before with the thread: "¡Ay, cordon, cordon! ¡Yo te hare traer por fuerça, si bivo, a la que no quiso darme su buena habla de grado!" (5.195.507). She finds Calisto and, after extracting a promise of a new cloak and gown, she gives him the cord:

> CELESTINA: Toma este cordon, que si yo no me muero yo te dare su ama.
> CALISTO: ¡O nuevo huésped! ¡O bienaventurado cordon, que tanto poder y merescimiento toviste de ceñir aquel cuerpo que yo no soy digno de servir! ¡O ñudos de mi passion, vosotros enlazastes mis deseos! (6.122.16–21)

Calisto's ranting informs the reader that, for him, the cord symbolizes his lustful desires that, like the cord, embrace the body of Melibea. Seconds later, Calisto, addressing the cord, echoes the words Celestina had used to "hex" the thread: "Conjurote me respondas, por la virtud del gran poder que aquella señora sobre mi tiene" (6.123.22–23). (Compare "Te conjuro por la virtud y fuerza destas bermejas letras, por la sangre" [3.78.8–9]). The parallel wording strengthens the link between thread and cord, underscoring the dark forces at work in whose power Calisto has lived since he first withdrew into his darkened bedroom. Even Celestina cannot stomach the wild raging of Calisto's love-madness. His reason, imprisoned in the "ñudos de ... passion" of the cord, gives way to fetishism. He treats the belt as though it were inhabited by a personal power. Celestina begs: "Cessa ya, señor, esse devanear, que me tienes cansada de escucharte y al cordon roto de tratarlo" (6.123.24–26).

The magic power of the cord upon Melibea is even stronger. When she at last confesses her *loco amor* for Calisto, she cries out to Celestina, "¡En mi cordon llevaste embuelta la possession de mi libertad!" (10.190.20–22).[13] Celestina quickly arranges a meeting. Upon leaving Pleberio's house, she sees Sempronio and Pármeno, Calisto's two servants, who lead her to Calisto. Before she has finished her story, Calisto rewards her: "En lugar de manto y saya, porque no se de parte a officiales, toma esta cadenilla, ponla al cuello, y procede en tu razon y mi alegria" (11.197.26–29).

The last link in the fatal chain is now forged. The diabolical bonds that tie all the protagonists together have gradually increased from the merest thread to the cord, to the indivisible, unbreakable chain, which now will drag each one down to death. The traditional dance of death is implicit: all the characters, high or low, tumble from their positions on the "wheel of fortune" to the same level: death without confession.[14] Celestina, closest to her dark lord, Satan, dies first, then her two fellow conspirators Sempronio and Pármeno, then Calisto, and, after him, Melibea, are inexorably pulled down. Melibea, conscious of the horror of her action and of the misery she will bring upon her parents, cannot but hurl herself off the tower to join her lover: "Porque quando el coraçon esta embargado de passion, estan cerrados los oydos al consejo, y en tal tiempo las frutuosas palabras, en lugar de amansar, acrescientan la saña (20.290.1–4).

The infernal bonds that cause the death of all the protagonists are the chains of passion (greed or lust) for which each character gives up his reason, his moral sense, and his will. The Devil, who has been considered a superfluous flourish on the part of Rojas and a concession to the "taste of his time," allegorizes powerfully the whole "underworld" of human weaknesses.

Loveable Old Celestina

However tempted one might be to sympathize with Celestina for her misfortunes and to attribute her wrongdoings to the extenuating circumstances of her "slum environment," Rojas meant her to be a symbol for the power of evil. The very sympathy she arouses assures us of her threat, since evil traditionally attracts as much as it repels. Her attraction is manifest throughout the text: servants (Sempronio and Pármeno) are seduced by a combined appeal to sensuality and greed. Lucrecia listens enthralled to the tale of prosperous times when Celestina was the madam of a profitable whorehouse. Calisto kneels down before the "reverenda persona," hoping that she will procure Melibea for him. Many, like Alicia, are lulled by the "honest" trades she exercises and amused by a creature whose activities surely could *never* touch anyone on a higher social level. All are delighted by Celestina's sharp wit, worldly wisdom, homespun philosophy, and stock of old saws. In her expert use of *loci communes* and her marshaling of arguments, she employs the gamut of the rhetorical tradition. She gains sympathy by her accuracy in describing the effects of love, old age, and poverty, or the value of friendship. She is obviously right, but Celestina tells only half the story. When she discusses love, she tells Melibea: "Cada dia ay hombres penados por mugeres y mugeres por hombres, y esto obra la natura, y la natura ordenola Dios; y Dios no hizo cosa mala" (4.100.27–29).

All this sounds true enough: yet mere physical attraction never sufficed, in the Judeo-Christian tradition, to justify the union of two *human* beings. Celestina further underscores that there are no sublime aspects to the "love" she sells:

> Es forçoso el hombre amar la muger y la muger al hombre … que por el hazedor de las cosas fue puesto, porque al linaje de los hombres [se] perpetuasse … no solo en la humana specie, mas en los peces, en las bestias, en las aves, en las reptilias; y, en lo vegetativo, algunas plantas han este respecto … en que ay determinación de herbolario … ser machos y hembras. (1.48.28–29; 49.1–10)

These examples from the animal and vegetable kingdoms make it abundantly clear that love, for Celestina, resides on a subhuman level.[15] In Christian thought, God created sexual desire, yet he gave man will and reason to control the appetites. Celestina's arguments do, however, appear convincing, and perhaps all the more appealing to the modern reader, since the Neoplatonic distinction between "higher" and "lower" souls has been forgotten except by the specialist.

Celestina: *Magna Mater*/Terrible Mother

Celestina exercises far greater power over her fellow citizens than did Juan Ruiz's Trotaconventos. Her hegemony is manifest in the ravages she brings about. The reader glimpses her vast, shadowy power when, despite

Pármeno's lengthy warnings, Calisto loses no time in falling down to worship her:

> CALISTO: ¡O Parmeno! ¡Ya la veo! ¡Sano soy, bivo soy! ¡Mira que reverenda persona. ... Por la filosomia es conocida la virtud interior ...! ¡O salud de mi passion, reparo de mi tormento, regeneración mia, vivificación de mi vida, resurrección de mi muerte! ... aquí adoro la tierra que huellas y en tu reverencia la beso.
>
> PARMENO: ¡O Calisto desventurado, abatido, ciego! ¡Y en tierra esta adorando a la mas antigua puta tierra, que fregaron sus espaldas en todos los burdeles! Deshecho es, vencido es, caydo es. No es capaz de ninguna redención ni consejo ni esfuerço. (1.47.7–27; 48.1–3).

Pármeno clearly sees the connection between Celestina, archwhore, and that greatest whore of all, Mother Earth, who provides a tolerant bed for all the coupling creatures within the universal "brothel." The indifferently productive earth has archetypally been identified as the *Magna Mater* (*mater*/matter).[16] In her positive aspects, the Great Mother represented the mysteries of birth, fruition, rebirth, and (cyclical) immortality, as did Demeter. Also, spiritual transformation, wisdom (Sophia), vision, inspiration, and ecstasy (Muse). These primitive feminine virtues still survive in the medieval Virgin Mary, but, unlike Mary, the Great Mother always has her dark side. Negative counterparts of inspiration and ecstasy are drunkenness, madness, and stupor. Just as birth and fruition are regular, seasonal occurrences, so are decline, decay, and death. As negative counterparts of Demeter, Sophia, and Muse, we find, among others, the Sirens, Circe and Aphrodite (young witches, as Erich Neumann describes them), the hideous, devouring Gorgon, and the archetypal old witch Hecate.[17] In patriarchal Jewish and in Neoplatonic Christian thought, where the "fanaticism of the male spiritual principle" early became dominant, the positive aspects of the Great Mother have been largely suppressed and the productive/reproductive earth devalued as "mere" whoring matter. The Great Mother survived the Christian onslaught but was transformed into a witch or demon (Neumann 333). Preoccupation with the life force, reproduction, and increase in this world came to be considered, by the "male principle" of Platonizing Christianity, as a "snare and a delusion," luring the faithful away from higher considerations of law and from the eternal contemplation of forms, the rational and intellectual "light" of the male godhead (Neumann 233, 333).

At the dinner table in Act 9, Celestina discusses her experiences of life, love, and fate. Thanks to the needy males in her city, she reached the top of the wheel of fortune, only to fall: "Mundo es, passe, ande su rueda. ...

Ley es de fortuna que ninguna cosa en un ser mucho tiempo permanesce.
… Mi honrra llego a la cumbre, según quien yo era; de necesidad es que
desmengue y se abaxe. … sobi para descender, floresci para secarme"
(9.175.16–29). As latter-day Great Mother (called "madre"—sometimes
ironically—by all who know her), Celestina never considers an
otherworldly existence. Since her essence and "honrra" are material, she
is strictly bound by the laws of nature. She is, however, cyclically
immortal, like plants and animals: although she flowers only to wither and
die, her place will never be long vacant.

In Christian terms, Celestina's religion of *amor*, since it excludes
caritas, is wholly evil. Having practiced the venereal arts as a young witch
and representative of Aphrodite, Celestina now, as an old whore and witch
(Hecate), preaches a religion of love that leads its practitioners to
diminution, but a tempting one. She describes love's power in great detail,
portraying it as both natural law and supernatural force:

> Mucha fuerça tiene el amor: no solo la tierra, mas aun las mares
> traspassa segun su poder. Ygual mando tiene en todo genero de
> hombres, todas las dificultades quiebra. Anziosa cosa es, temerosa y
> solicita; todas las cosas mira en derredor. Assi que, si vosotros buenos
> enamorados aveys sido, juzgareys yo decir verdad. (9.171.18–24)

Her account of *amor* parodies Saint Paul on *caritas*:

> Love is patient, love is kind. It is not jealous, is not pompous, it is not
> inflated, it is not rude, it does not seek its own interests, it is not quick-
> tempered, it does not brood over injury, it does not rejoice over
> wrongdoing but rejoices with the truth. It bears all things, believes all
> things, hopes all things, endures all things. (1 Cor. 13.4–7)

Priestess of a religion that rivals and reverses the "true faith," Celestina
performs her services in the hearts of those who believe themselves
perfectly Christian. Calisto rejects the label "Cristiano" in favor of
"Melibeo";[18] Melibea, agonizing in her bedroom, apostrophizes the absent
Lucrecia: "¡O si ya vinieses con aquella medianera de mi salud!"
(10.182.15–16). Upon her arrival, Celestina at once grasps her role and
urges Melibea: "Por ende, cumple que al medico, como al confessor, se
fable toda verdad abiertamente" (10.185. 6–7). Both Calisto and Melibea
use the medico-religious vocabulary of Christian ritual in praising
Celestina. It is Celestina, not Christ, who has become the "resurrection and
the life" for Calisto (1.47.7–27), and it is she, too, who is "medianera de
la salud" (salud = salvation) for Melibea.

Celestina, Spinner/Spider

The *hilado* that plays such an important symbolic role in Rojas's work is the dominant attribute of Celestina, the spinner and vendor of threads. In both her positive and negative aspects, the Great Mother is traditionally portrayed as a spinner who "weaves the web of life and spins the threads of fate" (Neumann 227).[19] The most obvious negative symbol for the spinner is the spider, together with other wielders of net and noose.[20] The image of Celestina as the spider at the center of her web is close to the surface of Rojas's text. As Sempronio discusses the potential profits of the Calisto-Melibea affair with the bawd, she explains her expertise: "Pocas virgines, a Dios gracias, has tu visto en esta ciudad que ayan abierto tienda a vender, de quien yo no aya sido corredera de su primer hilado. En nasciendo la mochacha, la hago escrevir en mi registro, y esto para que yo sepa quantas se me salen de la red" (3.72.13–18).

Almost immediately after praising her own prudence, she explains the device that will afford her entry into Pleberio's home, and that transforms the *hilado* from metaphor to reality: "Aqui llevo un poco de hilado en esta mi faltriquera, con otros aparejos que comigo siempre traygo, para tener causa de entrar" (3.75.25–27). The *hilado*, besides indicating the "wares" of both the neophyte businesswoman and the veteran, tells us that *all* virgins "que ayan abierto tienda a vender" are potential ensnarers. The image of the thread is combined with and completed by that of the net, a composite of many threads, which archetypally as well as in Rojas's text stands for a trap, either air or water borne, in which innocent victims struggle.[21] Celestina's filaments afford her entry into all the homes in town where ripening virgins await their doom like so many innocent "flies." Once caught, they are either devoured like Melibea, or they join the devourers, like Elicia and Areusa, to prey on the animal instincts of the male clientele. Rojas's work permits us to see a partial picture of Celestina's web and those caught in it, providing an occasional glimpse of other, more extensive involvements, such as Celestina's service to the religious community of her city.

Rojas's explicit teaching in *La Celestina*, "compuesta en reprehension de los locos enamorados … vencidos en su desordenado apetito" (18.4–5), is equally strong on the literal level and on the symbolic plane. Here, every figure enhances the power of a Judeo-Christian morality that rejects "darkness" (blindness) and recommends the "light" (vision), refuses the passions in favor of reason, demonstrates the fate of those who give themselves up to the illusory pleasure of the garden of *luxuria*, and shows the monstrosity of one who has dedicated her being to the service of *amor*, a Great Mother transformed and demonized by the Christian distinction between caritas and *amor*. Celestina, powerfully representing man's archetypal preoccupation with this material existence, perpetually threatens to usurp the place of the abstract, rational Christian godhead. Demonstrating the perils of *amor-luxuria*, Rojas, thoroughly—even blatantly—representative of the orthodox attitudes of his time, employs *all* the rhetorical means at his disposal.[22] They include local color and all those elements that formed a common cultural bond for men of the Renaissance: the Bible and the Christian tradition, the commonplace tradition, classical themes and motives, and a renewed interest in Neoplatonic values. With these weapons of persuasion at his command, Rojas tries to convince his readers to reject ensnaring "animal" passion and keep to the "upper path" of rational behavior and intellection, guided by free will.

Notes

[1] This essay, newly edited and updated, first appeared in *MLN* 86.2 (1971): 136–53. Exceptions to my first statement are Raymond E. Barbera, who explores the symbolism of the hawk, the garden with its wall, and the ladder, and Vicenta Blay Manzanera, on the metaphor of the serpent as symbol of *cupiditas*.
[2] When the earlier version of this essay was published, a scholarly debate was raging between Marcel Bataillon, who maintained that Rojas had more in mind than a portrayal of the stark realism of the late medieval/early Renaissance period in Spain, and Stephen Gilman and María Rosa Lida de Malkiel, who maintained that Rojas's main aim was to bring before his readers a hard-hitting, realistic portrayal of his time. I sided—and still side—with Bataillon. Among later authors, Kevin S. Larsen explores Rojas's psychological insight, while Ricardo Castells sees in Rojas various aspects of the "Renaissance Vision."
[3] See McCrary 172; Cirlot relates that, in the *Mirach*, Mohammed in heaven sees the Tree of Life surrounded by many other trees, filled with colorful songbirds. These are souls of the faithful, while souls of evildoers are reincarnated in birds of prey (27).
[4] Bataillon recognizes later in the play (14.243.29–30) the correspondence between Calisto's lyrical longing for Melibea's nocturnal garden and his longing for her flesh (194–95).
[5] Gonzalo de Berceo furnishes an example:

En esta romería avemos un buen prado,
en qui trova repaire tot romeo cansado,
La Virgin Gloriosa, madre del buen criado,
del qual otro ninguno egual non fue trovado.
Esti prado fue siempre verde en honestat,

ca nunca ovo macula la su virginidat,
Post partum et in partu fue Virgin de verdat,
Illesa, in corrupta en su entegredat. (19–20)

The "garden of Mary" transcends national and linguistic barriers:

Wir cellen dich einem garten
giceichneten unt bisparten
da der boum inne wûhs,
von dem uns des hungers war buz.

(We consider thee a garden,
chosen and barricaded,
in which the Tree grew,
which stills our hunger.) (Heinrichs Litanei, ca. 1150)

This verse (De Boor 1.39.61–64) is only one of a wealth of similar texts in Helmut de Boor's *Mittelalter: Texte und Zeugnisse.*

[6] This equation of darkness = sin, light = virtue, the good, may be seen already in Plato's Myth of the Cave. It remains a commonplace in the Middle Ages that by "blind man" is meant "the sinner," as in Petrus Berchorius, s.v. "Cecus, Cecitas": "[N]ota quod cecitas est privatio visus, unde cecitas dicit mihi proprie aliquid negativum et nihil positivum. ... Nota igitur generaliter per cecum intelligitur peccator." *Dictionarii seu repertorii moralis ... pars prima-tertia* (Venice, 1583; qtd. in Panofsky 190n47).

[7] The emphasis here falls on the opposition between *razón* and *amor*. Panofsky, in his essay "Blind Cupid" (95–128), remarks that, in the iconography of the late Middle Ages and Renaissance, Cupid gropes in blind company with Night, Synagogue, Infidelity, Death, and Fortune. Three of these personifications, Night, Fortune, and Death, apply to Calisto, since, in giving up his reason for Amor, he has placed himself in their power. His fate will be determined by blind Chance. Panofsky later cites Marsilio Ficino's assertion that the lower souls are strictly determined by fate (136).

[8] Leo Hebraeus clearly distinguishes between "proper" and "improper" love: "Amar y desear las cosas honestas es lo que hace el hombre verdaderamente ilustre, porque los tales amores y deseos hacen excelente la parte más principal del hombre, por la cual es hombre, o la que está más alejada de la material y de la obscuridad y más propincua a la divina claridad, que es el ánima intelectiva" (28). John England underscores Calisto's degradation from the upper souls to the lower, especially during his second nocturnal visit to Melibea.

[9] For a discussion of the ladder as symbol, see Cirlot (297–99).

[10] Striking parallels with Rojas's symbols may be seen in fairy tales, e.g., Rapunzel, in which the fair maiden lets down her long braids to her lover. On this "ladder," he may climb the tower to woo her. In Marie de France's *Lais*, "Yonec," too, shows parallels to *La Celestina*: An old bachelor decides to marry in order to have an heir. Fearful that his bride might deceive him, he shuts her

away in a tower, where for seven years she sees no one but her husband and her maid. One day, a large hawk flies into her window and is transformed into a handsome knight. The hawk-lover and his lady enjoy repeated trysts in the tower, but the sly and suspicious husband discovers the pair and spears the hawk as it flies, one night, through the lady's window (82–90). I spare the reader references to similar situations in plays, from Molière's *L'École des femmes* to Beaumarchais's *Le Barbier de Séville*.

[11] María Rosa Lida de Malkiel condemns a number of German critics (Bülow, Wolf, Klein, Petriconi, Rauhut, Eherwein, Küchler, Pabst, and Kruse) for believing that magic plays a vital role in *La Celestina*. Lida de Malkiel points out that Melibea's change is easily explicable in realistic psychological terms. She agrees with Bohigas and Castro "en reconocer a la magia de Celestina valor ornamental y no dramático." Azorín supposes that Melibea is lovestruck on first seeing Calisto, and her passion "incuba oscuramente en el fondo del alma hasta que toma posesión del alma entera, y, en consecuencia, las artes mágicas de Celestina ... resultan un desdoblamiento ocioso" ("Los valores literarios," qtd. in Lida de Malkiel, 221–22). Lida de Malkiel, like the critics she favors, does not recognize that Renaissance works take place on at least two levels, literal and symbolic, and that "winsome old Celestina" represents demonic forces. William McCrary, in the chapter "*Alcahuetería* and brujería" (51–82), demonstrates that Rojas's contemporaries took their witchcraft very seriously. Fray Juan de Pineda cites two *auctores* who link prostitution and witchcraft: "Ciceron escribe (*ad Herenn.* 4) que los Romanos reputaban por hechizeras a las mugeres deshonestas, presumiendo dellas que procurarían la muerte de aquellos que oviessen de ser temidos dellas, y lo mesmo tiene Seneca: (*Controversia* 4, C, *de reputatione,* etc.) y es presunción jurídica" (4.32). Melibea is not *forced* by witchcraft to give in; Celestina's rhetoric and her magic represent on two levels the powerful temptation to which Melibea yields voluntarily. She chooses freely to give up free will and ultimately her life.

[12] For a treatment of Lucrecia's role in the *tragicomedia,* see Okamura.

[13] Fray Juan de Pineda also explains the significance of the belt, using the example of Hercules and the "cinta" of the Amazonian queen: "Todo el punto de la emblema depende de haber ganado Hércules por su diligencia y trabajo la cinta de la reina, porque por la cinta de la mujer, que la ciñe el vientre, se significa su castidad, y la tal cinta se llama entre latinos *cestus.* ... De esta raíz sale decir los latinos que alguno desciñió o desató el *cestus* y cinta de la mujer cuando la conosció carnalmente" (7.162.125a).

[14] Stephen Gilman sees no such significance in the deaths of the characters: "Death in *La Celestina* seems to have lost much of the significance seen for it by Salinas. It appears to have been reduced almost to a mere termination of life. ... One of the most convincing signs of this change is Rojas's disinterest in the traditional thesis of the *Danza de la muerte*. He fails consistently and it would seem purposefully to underline the so-called democratic death of his time—to notice Death's unrelenting equalization for rich and poor, fair and plain, proud and humble, foolish and wise" (132).

[15] Gilman believes that Celestina's examples from the animal kingdom fall outside the classical tradition: "All along La Celestina's continuing argument, precedents are chosen not just from antiquity but also from the world of animals. … The significance of these excursions outside the world of men resides in Rojas's treatment of animals as animals—as sharing certain traits of human life in their own way" (135–36). On the contrary, the classical tradition always treated "animals as animals," i.e., as having two souls only: the vegetative and the animal. Man has always "shared certain traits" with the animal, i.e., the lower souls. Celestina, however, wishes her victims to forsake their higher nature, the rational and intellective, and her animal comparisons are deliberate attempts to corrupt and degrade.

[16] Beside earth, three other elements are evoked in *La Celestina*, and just as negatively. Fire represents the flames of passion, air bears up the hunting falcon, and water flows past Celestina's hovel and the tannery: an association with death and destruction rather than with baptism and life. Celestina speaks of her net; Pleberio wonders why he built ships. The net that floats in the water is a hunting device that traps the innocent, and Pleberio's ships are at best an evocation of the futility of worldly activity. (See notes 20 and 21 below for the dual connotations of Celestina's net.)

[17] This brief summary is drawn from Erich Neumann, *The Great Mother* (75–83). For a fuller treatment of Celestina and the power of her witchcraft, see Severin ("Celestina and the Magic Empowerment of Women"; and "Witchcraft in Celestina") and Herrero.

[18] "Melibeo," worshipper of Melibea, also may refer to Meliboeus, an exiled shepherd in Virgil's *Eclogue* 1. Rojas twice underscores Calisto's reversion to paganism.

[19] "In line with its archetypal character, weaving has its positive as well as its negative significance, and all the Great Mothers—Neith, Netet, and Isis, Eileithyia or Athena … and even the witch in the fairy tales—are spinners of destiny" (Neumann 228).

[20] "We encounter again a negative aspect, for the spider is also a symbol of the Terrible Mother. Similarly net and noose are typical weapons of the feminine's terrible power to bind and fetter, and the knot [cf. the *ñudos de passion* of Melibea's belt, 6.122.16–21] is a dire instrument of the enchantress" (Neumann 233).

[21] "The function of ensnaring implies an aggressive tendency, which, like the symbolism of captivity, belongs to the witch-character of the negative Mother. Net and noose, spider, and the octopus with its ensnaring arms are here the appropriate symbols" (Neumann 65–66).

[22] On the theme that the *converso*, Rojas, doth protest too much, see Deyermond.

Works Cited

Barbera, Raymond E. "Medieval Iconography in the *Celestina*." *Romanic Review* 61 (1970): 5–13.

Bataillon, Marcel. *La Celestine selon Fernando de Rojas*. Paris: Librairie Marcel Didier, 1961.

Berceo, Gonzalo de. *Milagros de Nuestra Señora*. Madrid: Espasa Calpe, 1964.

Blay Manzanera, Vicenta. "Más datos sobre la metáfora de la serpiente-*cupiditas* en *Celestina*." *Celestinesca* 20.1–2 (1996): 129–54.

Castells, Ricardo. *Fernando de Rojas and the Renaissance Vision, Phantasm, Melancholy, and Didacticism in* Celestina. University Park: Penn State UP, 2000.

Cirlot, J. E. *A Dictionary of Symbols*. New York: Philosophical Library, 1962.

Colonna, Francesco. *Hypnerotomachie, ou discours du songe de Poliphile* (1546). Paris: Club des Libraires de France, 1963.

De Boor, Helmut. *Mittelalter: Texte und Zeugnisse*. Munich: Beck, 1956.

Deyermond, Alan. "Fernando de Rojas from 1499 to 1502: Born-Again Christian." *Celestinesca* 25.1–2 (2001): 3–20.

England, John. "Testigos de mi Gloria: Calisto's bestial behavior." *La Corónica* 28.2 (2000): 81–90.

Gilman, Stephen. *The Art of "La Celestina."* Madison: U of Wisconsin P, 1956.

Hebraeus, Leo. *Diálogos de amor*. Trans. Inca Garcilaso de la Vega. Buenos Aires: Gleizer, 1944.

Herrero, Ana Vián. "El pensamiento mágico en *Celestina*." *Celestinesca* 15.1 (1991): 41–91.

Larsen, Kevin S. "Calisto on the Couch: An Aspect of Fernando de Rojas's 'Modern' Psychological Insight." *Neuphilologische Mitteilungen* 101.4 (2000): 505–17.

Lida de Malkiel, María Rosa. *La originalidad artística de "La Celestina."* Buenos Aires: Editorial Universitaria de Buenos Aires, 1962.

Marie de France. *Lais*. Ed. Alfred Ewart. Oxford: Blackwell, 1958.

McCrary, William C. *The Goldfinch and the Hawk: A Study of Lope de Vega's Tragedy, "El caballero de Olmedo."* Chapel Hill: U of North Carolina P, 1966.

Neumann, Erich. *The Great Mother: An Analysis of the Archetype*. Trans. Ralph Manheim. Princeton: Princeton UP, 1970.

Okamura, Hajime. "Lucrecia en el esquema de *Celestina*." *Celestinesca* 14.2 (1990): 53–62.

Panofsky, Erwin. *Studies in Iconology*. New York: Harper Torchbooks, 1962.

Pineda, Juan de (O.F.M.). *Diálogos Familiares de la Agricultura Cristiana.* Salamanca: En casa de Pedro de Adurça y Diego López, 1589, Dial. 4.32.107. Biblioteca Virtual Andalucía. Consejería de Cultura, Jaén. Acc. 2.4.2016.

Rojas, Fernando de. *Tragicomedia de Calixto y Melibea.* Ed. M. Criado de Val and G. D. Trotter. Madrid: Consejo Superior de Investigaciones Científicas, 1958.

Severin, Dorothy Sherman. "Celestina and the Magic Empowerment of Women." *Celestinesca* 17.2 (1993): 9–28.

———. "Witchcraft in Celestina." *Papers of the Medieval Hispanic Research Seminar*, 1. London: Department of Hispanic Studies, U of London, 1997: 1–58.

10

The Translator's Translator:
On Englishing a Portuguese Cleric's Spanish Captivity Chronicle

Diana de Armas Wilson

University of Denver

As a post-9/11 translator of Antonio de Sosa's chronicle of captivity in Muslim Algiers during the late 1570s—the same years that Miguel de Cervantes languished there as a slave—I wish to clarify both my role and my labors. The initial aim of this NEH-funded English translation of Dr. Sosa's *Topographia* was to bring Anglo-American readers a more complex understanding of Muslim societies after centuries of either massive indifference or intense hostility. But did my translation render any of these complexities? How faithful is it to the original? Does it have "soul"? An American designer of wedding gowns attacked a copycat version of her design being made in China at a fraction of the cost: "There's no soul" in that kind of gown, she lamented. "It has all the weird faults of translation. You get the literal words but not the poetry" (Solie 22).[*]

Used to debase the handiwork of "copycats," these remarks are an unwitting attack on the literalist school of translation. Its most famous spokesman was perhaps Vladimir Nabokov, who regarded "free translation" as a "knavish" enterprise (71). As a proponent of the literalist school that assumes the sanctity of the source text—doubtless a legacy of biblical translations since Jerome—Nabokov recommended absolute fidelity to the original.

A sly correction to this servile portrait of the translator arose in the 1970s, when Jorge Luis Borges—the so called "guru" of translation theory—came to the rescue of translators, giving them primacy over their sources. Declaring originals to be unfaithful to their translations, Borges praised translators for their "happy and creative infidelity" (45). Buoyed up by Borges, translators were made to feel empowered. But not for long.

---

[*] I am happy to contribute to this volume in honor of Robert ter Horst. It has been a pleasure to work with him over the years.

A generation later, Nabokov's demeaning notion of translators was reenergized by the *cervantista* Michel Moner, who pictured the translator as "una figura invisible, tardía, o secundaria" (an invisible, belated, or secondary figure) (513–24). Moner's ideal translator was an invisible figure, not unlike the position advocated by Nabokov. Invisibility, however, may be preferable to treachery. Claiming, with some justice, that "all translators rewrite and rectify," a Cambridge University teacher of translation chose to title his article "The Treachery of Translators" (Martin).

The above series of judgments on translation—viewing it as "apoetic" or unfaithful, as servile or treacherous—was far from my mind when I began translating Dr. Sosa's sixteenth-century chronicle from its 1612 edition, for centuries attributed to Diego de Haedo (Garcés, "Introduction" 51–52). I did remember, however, Cervantes's portrait of Transila, a female translator in his last novel, *Persiles y Sigismunda*. Her function was—as Robert ter Horst memorably wrote of a similarly learned Tirso heroine—to provide both "a deed of translation and a theory of translation" (287).

My own deed of translation began by learning more about Dr. Sosa's life and times. I knew that, during their shared captivity in Algiers, Dr. Sosa became a friend of Cervantes, an eyewitness to his sufferings, and his first biographer. In Relato 25 of his *Diálogo de los mártires de Argel*, Dr. Sosa left a vivid account, titled "La cueva de Cervantes," of one of Cervantes's four unsuccessful escape attempts, doubtless the most harrowing. Dr. Sosa was also the privileged witness of the *Información de Argel*, a notarized document of 1580 to which he contributed, from his prison, a valuable testimonial for Cervantes.

For many of the circumstances of Dr. Sosa's personal, political, and sexual life—including the scandals that framed his captivity—archival details may be found in María Antonia Garcés's monumental introduction to *An Early Modern Dialogue with Islam*. Captured while on a galley en route to Malta in 1577—while traveling with his so-called sister and a "nephew"—Dr. Sosa would eventually become the victim of Philip II's "ira regia": the king's fury was moved not only by the discovery that the cleric may have been traveling with his *barragana* or lover but also by the fact that he had left the Augustinian order and "lied about his status as a lay priest" (Garcés, "Introduction" 70–71).

Dr. Sosa's galley was captured by the Greek renegade Dalí Mamí, the very same corsair who, two years earlier, had captured Cervantes off the coast of Cadaqués in his homecoming galley, the *Sol*. Cervantes had become the property of this corsair, who set his ransom at 25,000 escudos, based on letters found on his person from Don Juan de Austria and the

Duke of Sessa. Dr. Sosa, however, was carried to Algiers to become the official slave of a renegade Jew called Muhammad. But whereas Cervantes managed to write very little during his captivity—perhaps only a clutch of poems in praise of Christ and the Virgin Mary (McCrory 78)—Dr. Sosa completed an enormous three-volume chronicle while in prison. Thanks to his insatiable curiosity, he was intensely attentive to the Algerian world, the customs and pastimes of all its inhabitants, their virtues as well as their vices. He was also immersed in the various languages of Barbary.

Our chosen title for the first book of Dr. Sosa's captivity chronicle, *An Early Modern Dialogue with Islam*, is meant to signal the cleric's dialogue with his Muslim captors. In the introduction to a new English version of *War and Peace*, Richard Pevear describes translation as "a dialogue between two languages" (qtd. in Wood 163). My translation of Dr. Sosa's dialogue with Islam, however, may be described as more of a "trialogue" among various languages. The official language of the Algerian regency was Osmanli Turkish, a fusion of Turkish, Arabic, and Persian words. Dr. Sosa uses all the above languages, as well as the odd Hebrew term (e.g., *geniza*), for his descriptions of the political, religious, and cultural life in Muslim Algiers. That is, Dr. Sosa often uses what he *thinks* he hears: he offers readers his own *transliterations* into Castilian of these words. Such a practice constitutes for the translator the problem of double or triple translation. Dr. Sosa was having a Spanish dialogue with multiple languages in the Islamic world, whereas I was trying to move that dialogue into English. Early in my labors, I began to think of myself as a kind of "translator's translator."

Only after the translation was published did I find a name for what I was doing. And it came *from* a translation: from Umberto Eco's *Decir casi lo mismo*, a text originally written in Italian. After inquiring into the meaning of translation, Eco argues that to translate is to say *almost* the same—*casi lo mismo* (14). Notions of fidelity are for him obsolete. There is, for starters, the problem with *dichos*, which Eco exemplifies with the impossibility of translating *llueve a cántaros*, best translated into English as "it's raining cats and dogs" (14). I would add to Eco's example the proverb *la sangre llama*, ritually Englished as "blood is thicker than water." Translating the many proverbial sayings encountered in Dr. Sosa's text presented a problem. For instance, he uses a phrase for Algerian gift givers who greedily expect much greater gifts in return, "dar aguja por sacar reja," whose literal translation would be "to give a needle while expecting a ploughshare." Reflecting on the rarity of gifting ploughshares in idiomatic English, I decided to translate this into "give them an inch and they'll take a yard" (Sosa, *An Early Modern Dialogue* 224)—which is *casi* but not quite *lo mismo*.

Umberto Eco sees translation as a procedure that may be inscribed "bajo el epígrafe de negociación" (under the epigraph of negotiation) (15). Negotiation is, of course, a process of give and take: "para obtener una cosa se reununcia a otra" (to obtain one thing you must renounce another) (Eco 25). But the process itself allows the translator to emerge "con una sensación de razonable y recíproca satisfacción a la luz del principio áureo por el que no es posible tenerlo todo" (with a sense of reasonable and reciprocal satisfaction in light of the golden rule that one cannot have it all) (Eco 25). The section that follows will explain some of the problems that I encountered in translating Dr. Sosa's chronicle, not only in his own translations and transliterations but also in his stylistic tics.

Negotiating the Source Text

Even as early as chapter 1, "The Founding of Algiers"—in which Dr. Sosa himself struggles to clarify Strabo's distinctions between the Mauritanian kings Juba I and Juba II—I could foresee a need to negotiate with the Spanish prose at every stage of the project. My translation was scarcely going to be a simple transfer of meaning from Spanish to English. After Sosa's text moved beyond the ramparts, gates, and fortifications of Algiers to introduce readers to its diverse inhabitants, numerous words appeared that could not be found even after exhaustive searches in the *Encyclopedia of Islam*. It was often necessary to divine the term that Dr. Sosa had aimed to translate from the Turkish or Arabic, to reach it either by approximations or with help from Arabic or Ottoman scholars. A trio of examples may serve.

When sixteenth-century Turks celebrate the ritual of circumcision, as Dr. Sosa explains, "dan una comida a que llaman *sosfia*" (they give a dinner that they call *sosfia*). The celebrated Ottoman scholar Virginia Aksan intuited that Dr. Sosa was trying to translate the word *sofra* (Arabic and Turkish), which means a round platter used for serving food, a word that may or may not extend to a banquet. But then an Algerian student we met in Oran insisted that Dr. Sosa had derived the term *sosfia* from the Arabic *sefa* or *sfifa*—a plate of *kuskusu* made with sugar, eggs, and cinnamon. Like many other words in Dr. Sosa's text, the term lacks any connotation for a Spanish, let alone an Anglo-American, audience. The solution was to keep Dr. Sosa's original, and drop the above two definitions into a footnote. We may never know the culinary truth about that circumcision party.

Moving in and out of the kitchen for my second example, I was stunned by Dr. Sosa's catalogue of fishes eaten in Algiers, including some strange and unfamiliar species: "Tómase mucha sardina, lazca, pachón, lija, pargo, doradas, salmonetes, otrillas, cazón , raya ... paselas o lapas, amoja, rizos [*sic*; erizos] ... caracoles de la mar ... y mucho hinojo marino." Dr. Sosa's French translators confined themselves to citing fewer than half of the above species—"la dorade, la bonite, le saulmon, la sardine, etc."—and oddly identifying the seaweed as a type of "maritime fennel" (Sosa, *Topographie*, 226). Despite my own limited ichthyological vocabulary, I took this as a challenge to negotiate all of Dr. Sosa's sea world for English readers: "sardines, bream, dogfish, red snapper, dolphin, red mullet, sting rays, mackerel shark, limpets, sea urchins, snails, and much edible seaweed" (Sosa, *An Early Modern Dialogue* 264). Despite the excess of nourishing fish oils in this catalogue, readers may be startled to learn that many of the Christian captives in Algiers were surviving on seaweed.

Moving from the kitchen to the mosque for my third example, we might glance at Dr. Sosa's mysterious translation of the *h* or profession of Islamic faith. According to his text, faithful Muslims loudly shout out, "*Yla Yla Ala Mahamed hera curra Ala*, etc." This transliteration from the Arabic is erroneous, as is Dr. Sosa's Spanish translation for it: "Dios es, y Dios será, y Mahamed es su mensajero" (God is, and God will be, and Muhammad is his messenger). The correct English translation from the Arabic is well known: "There is only one God, and Muhammad is his prophet." One has to choose in this situation to remain faithful either to Dr. Sosa or to Islam. During this particular negotiation, I kept thinking of a great line attributed to the British novelist Hilary Mantel—that "God is beyond translation."

Apart from countless other transliterations from the Arabic or Turkish in Dr. Sosa's text, I should note his frequent use of the lingua franca of Barbary, which he describes as "el hablar franco de Argel, casi una jerigonza o a lo menos, un hablar de negro boçal traído a España de nuevo" (the lingua franca of Algiers, a veritable mumbo-jumbo or, at least, a speech of the muzzled black slave recently brought to Spain) (*An Early Modern Dialogue* 185). Translating "jerigonza" or "gibberish," needless to say, is challenging work, especially when the suggested comparison to the speech of black slaves has racist overtones.

Occasionally the only available translation in English was virtually obsolete, as occurred with Dr. Sosa's use of the term *levante*. This word appeared to signal a type of marine musketeer whose services were contracted by the day. After hours of scouring through a number of dictionaries with the help of my editor, we finally hit upon the English term *lewend*. Because readers without a British seagoing background might not recognize this kind of historical musketeer, we opted to stay with the Spanish term in italics: *levante*.

Of the various stylistic tics that I had to negotiate, perhaps the most pronounced was Dr. Sosa's repetition of adjectives, a trait that, despite my reservations, I chose to keep. Added to this, his Spanish prose at times vies with that of Henry James in the length of its sentences, often packed with one prepositional phrase after another. These I would often break up with little or no loss of meaning. But Dr. Sosa's pronouns would often refer to a distant entity, which took time to unscramble. Despite these challenges—or because of them—I learned a great deal about Ottoman Algiers and the Islamic Maghreb beyond it. Europeans and Americans often use the negative term "Barbary" for the Maghreb—a word derived from the Arabic *al-maghrib*, which signifies "the west" or "the sunset." From the Greek *Barbaroi*, Barbary was the toponym used by sixteenth-century Europeans to refer to this region. The stereotypical notions that underlie the geography of Barbary bring me to the third and final part of my essay, the ideological part.

Islamophobia

The reduced size and increased volatility of our world today are making it easier to circulate new stereotypes of Islam—those warped sound bites of Islamophobia in the Western imaginary. The ideological question that most concerned me was that, given present-day fears of terrorism, a translation of Dr. Sosa might encourage or reinforce religious stereotyping. In my translator's note, I wrote that Dr. Sosa's occasional "crusading moments may astonish readers unaware of the mutual demonizing between Christians and Muslims during the sixteenth century" (Sosa, *An Early Modern Dialogue* iv). I did not "screen" Dr. Sosa's anti-Islamic moments, trusting readers to understand the limitations of his subject position as a Christian captive, a candidate for what he called "barbaric cruelty." Dr. Sosa's demonization of certain Muslim practices, his disapproval of women's pastimes, and even his tone deafness to Algerian music (which he compares to "the howling of wolves") reflect the attitudes of countless sixteenth-century European Christians or *Franj*, the colloquial Arabic word used to designate the enemy. When Dr. Sosa writes that the Algerians give themselves over "to licentiousness and lechery, and particularly to the heinous and revolting act of sodomy" (*An Early Modern Dialogue* 148), he is parroting the demonization of Orientals for an act that had a long and vexed history in Spain itself. We know that sodomy was an act for which the *Siete Partidas*, compiled in the thirteenth century by Alfonso X of Castile, required the death penalty.

But although Dr. Sosa displays the heightened Islamophobia in vogue in sixteenth-century Spain, he tries to be fair about customs of the enemy that he admires. He notes that the Algerian Muslims never, ever blaspheme or gamble the way Christians do. And if and when they fall to fighting among themselves, a rare occurrence, Algerians never reach for their swords. As soon as these fighting men are pacified, he adds, "they embrace and kiss each other in the French manner" (Sosa, *An Early Modern Dialogue* 149). Dr. Sosa's view of the Muslim world is, in short, a curious mix of disdain and admiration. His references to Turks and Moors are always more instructive—and often more negative—than those of Cervantes. It bears recalling that Dr. Sosa, unlike Cervantes, was a cleric in captivity. Steven Hutchinson rightly notes that treatises written by early modern clerics about sites holding Christian captives tend to be saturated "with religious difference and moral judgment and all that this implies" (534). One thing this implied for Dr. Sosa was a particular loathing for renegades.

Googling the term *renegade* today brings up a dozen rock bands, a cluster of video games, or the infamous *Time* magazine cover story on Sarah Palin. The present-day notion of a renegade is largely that of a person who rejects conventional behavior. In sixteenth-century Spain, however, the term *renegado* was specifically applied to a Christian who had converted to Islam. Elizabethans borrowed the Spanish term, which first shows up in 1583 as the English *renegade* and whose Latin etymology means "to deny." Renegades—often called men who "took the Turban"— were also called "Christians for Allah," a conversion as radical as our present-day "Jews for Jesus." The act of conversion itself was also known as "turning Turk." Shakespeare's Othello, a Christian Moor fighting Muslims on behalf of Venice, turns the phrase into a shaming question: "Are we turned Turks, and to ourselves do that / Which heaven hath forbid the Ottomites?" (*Othello* II.3). Such a religious turn in that period could be either a voluntary or a forced affair. Dr. Sosa calls voluntary converts to Islam "turcos de profesión" (Turks by profession) (*An Early Modern Dialogue* 125).

Shifts of religious allegiance are notoriously hard to chart, and many renegades could be found negotiating and renegotiating their allegiance to Islam. The French research team of the Bennassars calculates that over three hundred thousand Christians turned Turk during the early modern period, because "one could live with more abundance" in Barbary (419). From our present-day point of view, when the migratory traffic is going the other way, the levels of Christian assimilation into Muslim society during the sixteenth century seem astonishing. But even Spanish garrisons were "decimated by epidemics of desertion," and a 1564 memo annotated by Spain's Philip II complains, "It is *raining* Christians in Algiers" (Braudel 882). Roughly half of that city's population had voluntarily converted to Islam. According to Dr. Sosa, would-be renegades from some fifty different nations had converged on Algiers:

> These renegades and their children outnumber all their neighbors in Algiers—Muslims, Turks, and Jews—because there is no Christian nation on earth that has not produced renegades in this city. Beginning with the remote provinces of Europe, the following renegades may be found in Algiers: Muscovites, Russians, Ukrainians, Valacos, Bulgarians, Poles, Hungarians, Bohemians, Germans, Danish and Norwegians, Scotsmen, Englishmen, Irishmen, Flemish, Burgundians, Frenchmen, Navarrese, Basques, Castilians, Galicians, Portuguese, Andalusians, Valencians, Aragonese, Catalonians, Majorcans, Sardinians, Corsicans, Sicilians, Calabrese, Neapolitans, Romans, Tuscans, Genoese, Savoyans, Piedmontese, Lombards, Venetians, Slavs, Bosnians, Albanians, Greeks, Cretans, Cypriots, Syrians, Egyptians, and even Abyssinians of Prester John, as well as Indians from the Portuguese Indies [India], from Brazil, and from New Spain [Mexico]. (*An Early Modern Dialogue* 125)

Although renegades poured into Algiers from all over the known world, it is a historical fact that no comparable flow came out of there into Europe. Muslims back then did *not* choose to live in Christian countries, the more common phenomenon today, as witnessed by the massive, often death-defying African immigration across the Mediterranean into Europe.

So why did these early modern Christians choose to "turn Turk"? How come their religious commitments were so negotiable? Archives of the Spanish Inquisition are filled with documents judging the heresy ("la herejía") of these converts if they returned to Spain, when they would normally be tried as repentant renegades wanting to be reconciled to the Church. So why did they convert? Most renegades came to Algiers and Constantinople for jobs. Many conversions were essentially strategies for survival. All the heavy work in these cities was done either by renegades or slaves. Slavery in the late sixteenth-century Mediterranean may be understood, from an economic perspective, as a response to a demand for workers in a specific area or region. The Grand Turk had jobs for everyone, both at home and in his Turkish-Algerian regency: he needed artisans, weavers, shipbuilders, bronze workers, ironmongers, and so on.

"Men flocked from Christendom to Islam, which tempted them with visions of adventure and profit—and paid them to stay" (Braudel 799). Christians for Allah were seeking a better life, and the Sultan promised them upward mobility. The strong socioeconomic motives for conversion ranged from prison release to lucrative positions of power and privilege in the Turkish meritocracy. Many renegades enjoyed a meteoric ascent as corsairs (also known as privateers), captains, admirals, and even as kings or governors of provinces (*beylerbeys*). Muslim masters would give these fresh converts money, "credit cards," and even slaves of their own. The converts themselves were regarded in their new communities as *mujtadíes*—"los que han encontrado el camino recto" (those who have found the straight path) (Sola 339).

Upward mobility of this kind was virtually unknown in the rigid hierarchies of Europe, where oligarchies were decided by blood and birth. The Ottomans were far more culturally inclusive than Europeans, whose attitude was partly class conscious: they scorned renegades not merely because they were the Muslim enemy but also because they were of low birth, often the sons of fishermen or boatmen (Garcés, "Grande amigo mío"). Dr. Sosa, however, oddly excoriates renegades for their "fainthearted refusal to take on the work of slavery" (*An Early Modern Dialogue* 125). He considered them not only the chief enemies of Christianity but also a population holding all the power, dominion, and riches of Algiers. There is no question that a great part of the Ottoman Empire was administered and policed by these Christian converts to Islam, by men whose identity had been reconstructed, either willingly or forcibly.

Thanks to the first book of Dr. Sosa's captivity chronicle, we have an amazing portrait of a rich outpost of that empire and an early modern dialogue with its Muslim inhabitants. Our edition and translation of Dr. Sosa's second volume, *Epítome de los reyes de Argel*, is now finished and awaiting publication under the title *Of Caliphs and Corsairs: A History of Sixteenth-Century Algiers*. This volume seems even more timely, now that the dogmas and pieties of the Christian West are on the defensive again, with added fears of an "ISIL caliphate" abroad and "creeping Sharia" on the home front. Compared with recent Western cartoons of Muhammad or jeremiads against the so-called Green Menace of Islam, Dr. Sosa's occasional negative portraits of Muslim culture may seem tame. In recent portraits of the old clash between believers and infidels, we hear that Christian and Muslim value systems cannot coexist, that there is an implacable conflict between Islam and secular humanism, that there can be little prospect for peace as long as religion shapes civil societies in both the Islamic world and the West.

In many areas of Western culture, however, we have begun to understand the idea that fixed identities are mutable, that one *can* overcome differences of birth and culture and turn to another faith. Such an idea was considered a serious heresy by the Spanish Inquisition, which saw only one path to salvation. The idea that "all can be saved"—the title of a recent study by Stuart B. Schwartz—was punishable by death in the sixteenth century. Speaking before the Inquisition in Cuenca before being burned at the stake, Beltrán Campana made this prescient claim:

> [L]a religión de los calvinistas, de los romanos, de los luteranos, todas son buenas ... y que cada hombre puede salvarse en su ley, como el moro, el turco en su ley, el hebreo en la suya, el inglés en la suya y el español en la suya, y todos los demás en el mundo en su propia ley. Lo que importa es la libertad de consciencia.
> (The religion of the Calvinists, of the Romans, of the Lutherans, is all good ... and that each man could be saved in his own faith, like the Moor, the Turk in his faith, the Hebrew in his, the Englishman in his, the Spaniard in his and all others in the world in their own faith. Freedom of conscience is what matters). (qtd. in García-Arenal 917)

Although a theologian such as Dr. Sosa would scarcely have endorsed this kind of "freedom of conscience," his ethnographic writings help readers understand what the above Christian "heretic" meant by the salvation of "the Turk in his faith." Dr. Sosa's massive captivity chronicle may even provide a step toward a dialogue, even a trialogue, of religions. By showing us how early modern Algerians lived and loved, reared their children, and buried their dead, his treatise enriches our understanding of the Islamic world. To serve as his English translator in these turbulent times has been both a challenge and a privilege.

Fin

Works Cited

Bennassar, Bartolomé, and Lucille Bennassar. *Los cristianos de Alá: La fascinante aventura de los renegados*. Trans. José Luis Gil Aristu. Madrid: Nerea, 1989.

Borges, Jorge Luis. "The Translators of the Thousand and One Nights." *Translation Studies Reader*. Ed. Lawrence Venuti. London: Routledge, 1999. 34–48.

Braudel, Fernand. *The Mediterranean and the Mediterranean World in the Age of Philip II*. Trans. Siân Reynolds. Vol. 2. New York: Harper and Row, 1973.

Cervantes, Miguel de. *Información de Argel: Información de Miguel de Cervantes de lo que ha servido a S. M. y de lo que ha hecho estando captivo en Argel ... (Documentos)*. Ed. Pedro Torres Lanzas. Madrid: El Árbol, 1981. 45–166.

Eco, Umberto. *Decir casi lo mismo*. Trans. Helena Lozana Miralles. Barcelona: Lumen, 2008.

Garcés, María Antonia. *Cervantes in Algiers: A Captive's Tale*. Nashville: Vanderbilt UP, 2002.

———. "'Grande amigo mío': Cervantes y los renegados." *USA Cervantes: 39 Cervantistas en Estados Unidos*. Ed. Georgina Dopico Black and Francisco Layna Ranz. Madrid: Consejo Superior de Investigaciones Científicas; Ediciones Polifemo, 2008. 545–95.

———. Introduction to *An Early Modern Dialogue with Islam: Antonio de Sosa's* Topography of Algiers *(1612)*, by Antonio de Sosa. Notre Dame: U of Notre Dame P, 2011. 1–78.

García-Arenal, Mercedes. "Religious Dissent and Minorities in the Morisco Age." *Journal of Modern History* 81 (December 2009): 888–920. http://dx.doi.org/10.1086/605489

Haedo, Diego de. *Topographia, e historia general de Argel, repartida en cinco tratados do se verán casos extraños, muertes espantosas y tormentos exquisitos que conviene se entiendan en la Cristiandad ...* Valladolid: Diego Fernández de Córdoba y Oviedo, 1612.

Hutchinson, Steven. "*Renegadas* in Early Modern Spanish Literature." *Perspectives on Early Modern Women in Iberia and the Americas. Studies in Law, Society, Art and Literature in Honor of Anne J. Cruz*. Ed. Adrienne L. Martín and María Cristina Quintero. New York: Escribana Books, 2015. 528–48.

Martin, Andy. "The Treachery of Translators." *New York Times*, January 28, 2013.

McCrory, Donald P. *No Ordinary Man: The Life and Times of Miguel de Cervantes*. New York: Dover, 2006.

Moner, Michel. "Cervantes y la traducción." *Nueva Revista de Filología Hispánica* 38.2 (1990): 513–24.

Nabokov, Vladimir. "Problems of Translation: Onegin in English." *Translation Studies Reader*. Ed. Lawrence Venuti. London: Routledge, 1999. 71–83.

Pevear, Richard, and Larissa Volokhonsky, trans. *War and Peace*, by Leo Tolstoy. Introduction by Richard Pevear. New York: Vintage Classics, 2008.

Schwartz, Stuart B. *All Can Be Saved: Religious Tolerance and Salvation in the Iberian Atlantic World*. New Haven: Yale UP, 2008.

Sola, Emilio. "Historias de la frontera y oralidad: Una cautiva que llega a Gran Sultana." *Las Relaciones de Sucesos en España (1500–1750)*. Alcalá de Henares: Publicaciones de la Universidad de Alcalá; Publications de la Sorbonne. 339–48.

Solie, Stacey. Field Notes in "Vows." *New York Times*, March 3, 2013: 22.

Sosa, Antonio de. "La cueva de Cervantes." *Diálogo de los mártires de Argel*, Relato 25. Ed. Emilio Sola and José María Parreño. Madrid: Hiperión, 1990. 178–81.

———. *An Early Modern Dialogue with Islam: Antonio de Sosa's Topography of Algiers (1612)*. Ed. María Antonia Garcés. Trans. Diana de Armas Wilson. Notre Dame: U of Notre Dame P, 2011.

———. *Topographie et Histoire générale d'Alger*. Trans. Dr. Monnereau and Adrien Berbrugger. Saint-Denis, France: Bouchène, 1998.

Ter Horst, Robert. "Aspects of Love and Learning in *El amor médico*." *Revista Canadiense de Estudios Hispánicos* 10.2 (Winter 1986): 270–98.

Wood, James. "Moveable Types: How War and Peace Works." *New Yorker*, November 26, 2007. At http://www.newyorker.com/magazine/2007/11/26/movable-types.

11

The Futuristic Arc of Early American Literature

Ali Shehzad Zaidi

State University of New York at Canton

After independence, the United States was torn by internal conflicts over land, debt, taxes, and slavery. The first US census, taken in 1790, counted less than four million, almost wholly rural, inhabitants (roughly the same number as in Shakespeare's England). The two largest cities, Philadelphia and New York, had barely forty-two thousand and thirty-three thousand inhabitants, respectively (Nevins and Commager 114). The United States remained vulnerable to invasion until the War of 1812. The literature of the early American republic conveys not only the insecurity of a fragile social order but also the expectancy of a new nation bent on self-definition.

Both the Declaration of the Independence (1776) and the US Constitution (1787) use language that is designed to create an artificial consensus among the loose confederation of states that had seceded from Great Britain. Neither document uses the word "nation" to describe that consensus (Winik 55, 67). As James Roger Sharp observes, scholars tend to stress the continuity of institutions from the colonial to national periods while minimizing their dissonance (5–6). During the first decades of the new republic, farmers and tradesmen fiercely resisted federal taxation. In 1794, President George Washington had to send militiamen to quell a rebellion in western Pennsylvania against an excise tax on distilleries that had been enacted by Congress three years earlier (Morison 61–62). It took several decades for the federal government to consolidate its power and for national identity to be forged. Even as late as 1838, Nathaniel Hawthorne commented: "I wonder that we Americans love our country at all, having no limits and no oneness; and when you try to make it a matter of heart, everything falls away except one's native State" (qtd. in Ziff 125).

The founding document of the United States stabilized and defined the new country. The Declaration of Independence is an anticipatory text that refracts the future in light of the past. It recalls the abuses of King George III in order to affirm the right of a people to dissolve a government that no longer obeys its will. In foreseeing new forms of tyranny, the Declaration suggests that the United States would never assume a finished form but must exemplify a continual process of yearning and striving. The United States would remain an ideal to be sought but never attained; its meaning would evolve in succeeding generations. This dynamic conception of political and social existence is reflected in the futuristic bent of early American literature. The awareness of the inevitability of change in the new nation contributed to greater civic inclusion with regard to religion, ethnicity, and gender.

The US Constitution, in its commitment "to form a more perfect union," foresaw that this founding document would continue to be written by citizens through eternity. Religious freedom in the United States was first codified in the First Amendment to the Constitution, ratified in 1791, which states that "Congress shall make no law respecting an establishment of religion, or prohibiting the free exercise thereof" (*Declaration* 33). Thomas Paine's writings shaped the future of the United States, although it would be several decades after they were written before the United States became a more tolerant and pluralistic polity. In *The Age of Reason* (1794), Paine characterizes human language as inherently unstable and perishable. Thus the meaning of religious texts, like that of the nation's founding documents, remains uncertain and contested. It is only in nature that one finds divine signs and an enduring universal language. Although many conservative American clergy condemned it as a polemical anti-Christian tract, *The Age of Reason* broadens our sense of the scope of the sacred and envisions a future in which reason, science, and the love of nature inform religious belief.

Although Paine and others advocated democratic rights for women, the new republic refused to grant them. As Rosemarie Zagarri observes, the expansion of democratic rights for white men in the early years was paradoxically accompanied by the restriction of political rights for women (2). After briefly gaining the right to vote in certain counties of New Jersey, women were entirely excluded from the electoral process. Although many citizens of the new republic believed that national independence had permanently secured their rights, the grammarian Noah Webster warned in 1789: "A fundamental mistake of the Americans has been that they considered the revolution as completed when it was just begun" (qtd. in Wilentz 10). Women would not secure the right to vote until the ratification of the Nineteenth Amendment to the US Constitution in 1920.

Significantly, one of the first major fictional works by an American concerns the rights of women. Charles Brockden Brown's *Alcuin* (1798) consists of a series of extended dialogues between a pedantic young schoolteacher and a widowed socialite. The first two dialogues of *Alcuin* appeared in a heavily edited form at a time of conservative backlash against women's rights. In the third and final dialogue, which was not published in Brown's lifetime and which gauges the hidden depths of a seemingly enlightened man, the pedagogue enthuses about a future society in which women are ostensibly liberated and have become the equals of men. This futuristic vision is intended to impress the woman and gain her trust.

The first two parts of *Alcuin* were published in the year in which the new Federalist government began a crackdown against dissent. The Alien Act of 1798, which remained in effect for two years, allowed the US president to expel foreigners deemed subversive and dangerous. The Sedition Act of 1798 made anyone who wrote or spoke against the president or Congress subject to fine and imprisonment. Several editors were fined and jailed as a result of the Sedition Act, which violated the First Amendment right to freedom of speech (Morison 77–78). The resulting climate of fear explains the self-censorship on the part of Brown's editors, who feared that the ideas regarding female emancipation contained in *Alcuin* might be too volatile for their readership (Arner 291).

Brown was once considered a minor novelist, in part because of the misconception that the United States did not achieve a national culture until after the War of 1812 (see, for instance, Nevins and Commager 148). Larzer Ziff, for example, identifies Poe, Emerson, Hawthorne, Thoreau, Whitman, and Melville as the writers who established the literary independence of the United States (xi). This assertion overlooks the importance of Brown's novels, and especially that of *Arthur Mervyn* (1799–1800), which reveals the nightmares that underlie our national mythology and imaginary.

The Philadelphia of *Arthur Mervyn* has a haunting, oneiric quality. It is a city of murky schemes and frenetic speculation, panic stricken in the midst of a yellow fever epidemic. The novel opens with the first-person narration of Dr. Stevens, who describes how he found young Arthur Mervyn, delirious from yellow fever, and proceeded to nurse him back to recovery. The kind doctor trusts Mervyn, who tells various stories in which he refashions himself in light of an imagined prosperous future. However, the narratives of other characters undercut Mervyn's veracity. We come to suspect that Mervyn projects his own monstrosity onto others in ways that both conceal and reveal his identity. Such is the case during the yellow fever epidemic when Mervyn sneaks into a house. Mervyn describes how a Negro looter, whom he glimpses momentarily in a mirror, knocked him unconscious. The flash of recognition in the mirror is ambiguous. It may have been Mervyn, not the slave, who was the looter.

The motif of darkness pervades the novel; the unspeakable can only be glimpsed obliquely. At one point in the narrative Mervyn alludes to an unspecified object hidden in an attic, suggesting a hidden condition of the mind (McNutt 60). At the end of the novel, Mervyn is set to marry a rich widow. Although his future appears bright and prosperous, Mervyn relates a nightmare that undercuts his rosy prospects and that perhaps helps us foresee the widow's murder. Mervyn is about the same age as the United States at the time of the novel, and he seems to personify the country's capacity for fabulation and self-delusion. Mervyn's bright future, like that of the young American republic, brings into sharp relief a disturbing and opaque present. Brown anticipates the intuition, expressed by Ariel Dorfman among others, of the United States as the domain of innocence whose people see themselves as good and well meaning notwithstanding their country's crimes (201).

Venture Smith's slave narrative (1798) evokes the future with regard to past losses and griefs. At the end of his oral narrative, Smith reflects on what might have been had his sons followed his life path. One son, Solomon, died of scurvy after Smith leased him to a master for a whaling voyage. As he shares his grief, Smith recalls the seventy-five-pound monetary loss that resulted from his son's death. Although he seemingly internalizes the diseased logic of slavery, Smith in fact subverts that institution by exposing the commodification of human beings in the only way possible, which is to say, obliquely.

The themes of innocence and amnesia pervade the stories of Washington Irving, whose protagonists are bewildered by a future that is refracted through the past. Irving's "The Mutability of Literature," which first appeared in a collection titled *The Sketch Book of Geoffrey Crayon, Gent.* (1819), evokes the future, like *The Age of Reason*, through a meditation on the evanescence of language. In this whimsical short tale, the archive emerges both as a place for the diffusion of knowledge and as a place to dream.

Irving's tale concerns the surreal experience of a scholar who discovers a manuscript that had been moldering for the past couple of centuries in the library archives of Westminster Abbey. As the scholar becomes lost in reflection, the dusty quarto rather humorously stirs to life and assumes a human voice. Speaking in an asthmatic wheeze and the quaintly archaic lexicon of a bygone age, the quarto questions the startled scholar about what had transpired since the date of its creation, which was when young Shakespeare was about to become a sensation. Like Robert Greene, the benighted critic who famously called Shakespeare an "upstart crow" and "Shake-scene," the quarto had failed to grasp the young playwright's significance. The quarto is astonished to learn from the scholar that

Shakespeare had become the preeminent writer of all time and had lifted his own age out of obscurity.

The image of dust assumes rich symbolic significance in "The Mutability of Literature." Carolyn Steedman identifies the image of dust as a metaphor for the circularity and eternal return of the archive, the exploration of which unsettles the dreams of the dead, stirring up and rearranging the dust of memories in new configurations that continually alter our sense of the past (164, 167). For the present day reader, the equidistance of Irving's time from that of the quarto's creation and from our own time creates a rich interplay between past and future. In privileging the archive as a site of the imagination, Irving anticipates an American republic that was, like young Shakespeare, on the verge of greatness and about to assume mythic proportions. His tale undermines the authoritative weight of tradition to reinforce the new forward-looking national imaginary then being created.

In "Rip Van Winkle," perhaps the most famous short story in *The Sketch Book*, Irving employs the narrative device of a found document, namely the papers of an elderly gentleman named Diedrich Knickerbocker, who, like Irving himself, was steeped in the Dutch lore of New York. In the tale's preface, Irving uses a fictional alter ego to anticipate his own legacy in a commodified age, telling us that Knickerbocker, though deceased, is still held in high esteem "by certain biscuit makers who have gone so far as to imprint his likeness on their new-year cakes, and have thus given him a chance for immortality" (29). Knickerbocker has undergone a transmutation from a historical figure into a character of imaginative literature.

Rip Van Winkle is an indolent villager who encounters a disconcerting future after a twenty-year slumber. He lives amid a spiritualized landscape whose summits in the setting sun "glow and light up like a crown of glory" (29), but he needs to escape the company of a scolding wife. As he descends into a mountain glen, he hears his name called, and meets some bearded Dutchmen dressed in ancient costumes and playing ninepins. They invite him to drink with them, and Rip soon falls into a deep sleep. He returns to his village to find it transformed.

At the Dutch inn where Rip used to engage in somewhat somnolent discussions with elders, Rip hears a man haranguing people about elections, liberty, and the heroes of seventy-six. It is all gibberish to Rip, who does not understand that the likeness of King George on the sign of the inn has become that of George Washington. A crowd soon gathers around Rip, and men begin to quiz him as to where his political sympathies lie. Rip is bewildered and declares himself a loyal subject of the king. In a moment of paranoia and hysteria, the crowd mistakes him for a British spy. When they finally establish his identity, Rip rejoins his community and tells his story to the delight of all. Sarah Wyman points out that, in this tale, storytelling restores social cohesion (219). In creating a future course for American literature, Irving pays homage to imaginative memory through a literary past rooted in Europe.

Irving was in Europe when he wrote *The Sketch Book*. His extended absence from the United States would last seventeen years, nearly as long as Rip's absence from his village. The Industrial Revolution, which had transformed the Hudson Valley in the four decades prior to the publication of "Rip Van Winkle," provides another subtext of this tale. *The Sketch Book* was published in 1819, the year that the Erie Canal opened, allowing barges to replace wagons for transportation. Within five years of the opening of the canal, the cost to transport a ton of goods from New York City to Buffalo dropped from $100 to $9, which greatly reduced the prices of goods (Cowan 105). "Rip Van Winkle" hints at the destruction caused by blind progress that, like the headless horseman in another famous Irving tale, "The Legend of Sleepy Hollow," hurtles toward the future without memory or direction. Both stories evoke the effects of displacement and rupture from the past.

In "Traits of Indian Character," another piece from *The Sketch Book*, Irving considers the plight of Native Americans: "The rights of the savage have seldom been properly appreciated or respected by the white man. In peace he has too often been the dupe of artful traffic; in war he has been regarded as a ferocious animal whose life or death was a question of mere precaution or convenience" (225). As James Fenimore Cooper did in the five novels that make up *The Leatherstocking Tales*, Irving portrays Native Americans as noble savages doomed to perish: "They will vanish like a vapour from the face of the earth; their very history will be lost in forgetfulness" (233). Colin G. Calloway notes that, during the early American republic, artistic representations of Native Americans showed them exiting from history as they retreated westward toward the setting sun (32). Native Americans were missing from the imaginary future of the United States. Although many became extinct, other indigenous tribes and languages survived and continued to contribute dynamically to the shaping of the American nation.

Paul Johnson argues that the US Constitution pointedly ignores Native Americans other than to say that Congress has the power to regulate commerce with Indian tribes. While the British Crown regarded Native Americans as subjects, notes Johnson, the Americans regarded them as savages to be subdued by treaties, promises, deception, attrition, and disease (269–70). The 1783 Treaty of Paris established peace between

Great Britain and the United States but failed to mention the Indian tribes (Calloway 23). The expansion of the United States doomed the efforts of Native Americans to preserve communal cultures. As Bernard W. Sheehan observes, the civilizing efforts of early American philanthropists only hastened the demise of indigenous cultures (qtd. in Calloway 32). Native Americans only become US citizens after the Indian Citizenship Act of 1924, but citizenship was restricted to those born after the act took effect.

Despite its injustices to Native Americans, the imperial expansion of the United States left its citizens with a welcome sense of security. In his short sketch "Old Ticonderoga" (1836), Nathaniel Hawthorne synecdochically represents the emergence of the United States as a world power, not through an image of military might but through a poetic description of abandoned Fort Ticonderoga. First built by the French between 1755 and 1757, Fort Carillon, as it was then known, was designed to guard access to the southern part of Lake Champlain. The fort was captured by the British in 1759 during the French and Indian War. The renamed Fort Ticonderoga was stormed by Ethan Allen and his Green Mountain Boys in 1775 at the outset of the American Revolutionary War. The British briefly regained the fort for two months in 1777 when the fort saw its last battle.

During his first visit to Fort Ticonderoga, Hawthorne listened to the guide, a young lieutenant of engineers, dwell on the fort as a feat of tactical construction. In contrast, Hawthorne casts "a dream-like glance over pictures of the past" (387) of Fort Ticonderoga, conjuring in succession an Indian chief gliding across the lake on a canoe, a French chevalier courting an Indian woman, a French and Indian war party, a Jesuit priest, and epic battle scenes. With blurred double vision caught between past and future, Hawthorne foretells: "Banner would never wave again, nor cannon roar, nor blood be shed, nor trumpet stir up a soldier's heart, in this old fort of Ticonderoga" (389). His meditation on Fort Ticonderoga's epic past epitomizes the futuristic orientation of early American literature. Paradoxically, the fort, in its state of decrepitude and collapse, denotes the military might and financial power of the ascendant new republic. It is precisely because it is no longer needed that the fort acquires transhistorical meaning. Like other writers of the new republic, Hawthorne used his alchemic imagination to lift history out of sordidness into a dream-realm rife with promise that nonetheless recalls the brutal events that accompanied the transformation of the American colonies into the United States.

Works Cited

Arner, Robert D. "Historical Essay." *The Novels and Related Works of Charles Brockden Brown.* Vol. 6, *Alcuin: A Dialogue* and *Stephen Calvert.* Kent, OH: Kent State UP, 1987. 273–312.

Brown, Charles Brockden. *Alcuin: A Dialogue.* Ed. Cynthia A. Kierner. Albany: New College and University Press, 1995.

———. *Arthur Mervyn* [1799–1800]. Kent, OH: Kent State UP, 2002.

Calloway, Colin G. "The Continuing Revolution in Indian Country." *Native Americans and the Early Republic.* Ed. Frederick E. Hoxie, Ronald Hoffman, and Peter J. Albert. Charlottesville: UP of Virginia, 1999.

Cooper, James Fenimore. *The Last of the Mohicans.* Albany: State U of New York P, 1983.

Cowan, Ruth Schwartz. *A Social History of American Technology.* New York: Oxford UP, 1997.

The Declaration of Independence and the Constitution of the United States. Washington, DC: US Citizenship and Immigration Services, 2008.

Dorfman, Ariel. *The Empire's Old Clothes.* New York: Pantheon, 1983.

Hawthorne, Nathaniel. "Old Ticonderoga." *Tales and Sketches.* New York: Library of America, 1982. 385–89.

Irving, Washington. "The Mutability of Literature." *The Complete Works of Washington Irving.* Vol. 8, *The Sketch Book of Geoffrey Crayon, Gent.* Ed. Richard Dilworth Rust. New York: Twayne, 1978. 100–108.

———. "Rip Van Winkle." *The Complete Works of Washington Irving.* Vol. 8, *The Sketch Book of Geoffrey Crayon, Gent.* Ed. Richard Dilworth Rust. New York: Twayne, 1978. 29–42.

———. "Traits of Indian Character." *The Complete Works of Washington Irving.* Vol. 8, *The Sketch Book of Geoffrey Crayon, Gent.* Ed. Richard Dilworth Rust. New York: Twayne, 1978. 225–33.

Johnson, Paul. *A History of the American People.* New York: HarperCollins, 1999.

McNutt, Donald J. *Urban Revelations: Images of Ruin in the American City, 1790–1860.* New York: Routledge, 2006.

Morison, Samuel Eliot. *The Oxford History of the American People.* Vol. 2, *1789 through Reconstruction.* New York: Penguin Books, 1972.

Nevins, Allan, and Henry Steele Commager. *A Pocket History of the United States* [1945]. New York: Washington Square Books, 1986.

Paine, Thomas. *The Age of Reason* [1794]. San Diego: Book Tree, 2003.

Sharp, James Roger. *American Politics in the Early Republic*. New Haven: Yale UP, 1993.

Smith, Venture. "A Narrative of the Life and Adventures of Venture, a Native of Africa." *Five Black Lives*. Ed. Arna Bontemps. Middletown, CT: Wesleyan UP, 1987. 1–25.

Steedman, Carolyn. *Dust: The Archive and Cultural History*. New Brunswick: Rutgers UP, 2002.

Wilentz, Sean. *The Rise of American Democracy: Jefferson to Lincoln*. New York: W. W. Norton, 2005.

Winik, Jay. *The Great Upheaval: American and the Birth of the Modern World, 1788–1800*. New York: HarperCollins, 2007.

Wyman, Sarah. "Washington Irving's *Rip Van Winkle*: A Dangerous Critique of a New Nation." *ANQ* 23.4 (2010): 216–22. http://dx.doi.org/10.1080/0895769X.2010.517049

Zagarri, Rosemarie. *Revolutionary Backlash: Women and Politics in the Early American Republic*. Philadelphia: U of Pennsylvania P, 2007. http://dx.doi.org/10.9783/9780812205558

Ziff, Larzer. *Literary Democracy*. New York: Viking, 1981.

The Publications of Robert ter Horst

Books

Calderón: The Secular Plays. Lexington: UP of Kentucky, 1982.
Studies in Honor of Bruce W. Wardropper. Ed. Dian Fox, Harry Sieber, and Robert ter Horst. Newark, DE: Juan de la Cuesta, 1989.
The Fortunes of the Novel: A Study in the Transposition of a Genre. New York: Peter Lang, 2003.
Eclogue, Ode, Sonnet: Garcilaso de la Vega and Classical Antiquity (forthcoming).

Essays

"The Angelic Prehistory of *Sobre los ángeles*." *MLN* 81.2 (1966): 174–94.
"Time and the Tactics of Suspense in Garcilaso's *Égloga primera*." *MLN* 83.2 (1968): 294 306. http://dx.doi.org/10.2307/2908463
"The Economic Parable of Time in Calderón's *El príncipe constante*." *Romanistisches Jahrbuch* 23 (1972): 294–306.
"The *Loa* of Lisbon and the Mythical Substructure of *El burlador de Sevilla*." *Bulletin of Hispanic Studies* 50 (1973): 147–65.
"On the Character of Don Juan in *El burlador de Sevilla*." *Segismundo* 9 (1973): 1–10.
"The Meaning of Hypothesis in the *Poema de mio Cid*." *Revista Hispánica Moderna* 37 (1972–1973): 217–28.
"The Ruling Temper of Calderón's *La dama duende*." *Bulletin of the Comediantes* 27 (1975): 68–72. http://dx.doi.org/10.1353/boc.1975.0026
"Calderonian Cartesianism: The Iconography of the Mind in *La exaltación de la Cruz*." *L'Esprit Créateur* 15 (1975): 286–304.
"The True Mind of Marriage: Ironies of the Intellect in Lope's *La dama boba*." *Romanistisches Jahrbuch* 22 (1976): 347–63.
"From Comedy to Tragedy: Calderón and the New Tragedy." *MLN* 92.2 (1977): 181–201. http://dx.doi.org/10.2307/2907210
"Experienced Innocence: Tirso's *El vergonzoso en palacio*." *Kentucky Romance Quarterly* 25 (1978): 129–43. http://dx.doi.org/10.1080/03648664.1978.9932298
"Ritual Time Regained in Zorrilla's *Don Juan Tenorio*." *Romanic Review* 70 (1979): 80–93.

"Nature against Nature in *Yerma*." *The World of Nature in Poetry of García Lorca*. Ed. Joseph Zdenek. Rock Hill, SC: Winthrop College, 1980. 43–54.

"The Sacred and the Profane in the Plays of Tirso de Molina." *Bulletin of the Comediantes* 32 (1980): 99–107. http://dx.doi.org/10.1353/boc.1980.0027

"Poetry in the Drama: The Case of *Peribáñez*; A Speculation." *Folio* 12 (1980) 70–95.

"Death and Resurrection in the Quevedo Sonnet 'En crespa tempestad.'" *Journal of Hispanic Philology* 5 (1980): 43–49.

"The Poetics of Honor in Calderón's *El alcade de Zalamea*." *MLN* 96.2 (1981): 286–315. http://dx.doi.org/10.2307/2906351

"The Origin and Nature of Comedy in Calderón." *Studies in Honor of Everett Hesse*. Ed. William McCrary and José A. Madrigal. Lincoln: U of Nebraska P, 1981. 143–54.

"'Half in Love with Easeful Death:' The Comicity of Tirso's *Marta la piadosa*." *Homenaje a Tirso, Revista Estudios*. Madrid, 1981. 439–46.

"The Second Self: Painting and Sculpture in the Plays of Calderón." *Calderón de la Barca at the Tercentenary: Comparative Views*. Ed. Wendell Aycock and Sydney Cravens. Lubbock: Texas Tech UP, 1982. 175–91.

"A New Literary History of Don Pedro Calderón."*Approaches to the Theater of Calderón*. Ed. Michael McGaha. Washington, DC: University Press of America, 1982. 33–52.

"El concepto de la frontera en Cervantes y Calderón: Hacia una geopolítica de la literatura." *Neophilologus* 67.1 (1983): 71–77. http://dx.doi.org/10.1007/BF01956990

"On the Importance of Being Earnest: A Reply to Professor Cesáreo Bandera." *Cervantes* 5 (1985): 59–63.

"Une Saison en enfer: *La gitanilla*." *Cervantes* 5 (1985): 87–127.

"The Seventeenth-Century Aesthetic."*Journal of Hispanic Philology* 10 (1985): 39–50.

"The Duke and Duchess of Alba and Juan del Enzina: Courtly Sponsors of an Uncourtly Genius." *Studies in Honor of William C. McCrary*. Ed. Everett Hesse, John Keller, and José A. Madrigal. Lincoln, NE: Society of Spanish and Spanish-American Studies, 1986. 215–20.

"Aspects of Love and Learning in Tirso's *El amor médico*." *Revista Canadiense de Estudios Hispánicos* 10 (1986). 279–98.

"Poetry and Power in Garcilaso's *Égloga primera*." *Revista de Estudios Hispánicos* (1988): 1–10.

"In an Echoing Grove: *Quijote II* and a Sonnet of Garcilaso." *Studies in Honor of Bruce W. Wardropper*. Ed. Dian Fox, Harry Sieber, and Robert ter Horst. Newark, DE: Juan de la Cuesta, 1989. 334–45.

"By Love Dispossessed: Comic Pharmacology in Calderón's *Antes que todo es mi dama.*" *Bulletin of the Comediantes* 42 (1990): 53–91. http://dx.doi.org/10.1353/boc.1990.0014

"From Poem to Novel: The Syntax of the Baroque." *Indiana Journal of Hispanic Literatures* 1 (1992): 39–61.

"Pedro Calderón de la Barca." *Dictionary of the Literature of the Iberian Peninsula.* Vol. 1. Westport, CT: Greenwood Press, 1993. 265–72.

"Garcilaso and the Subject of Apostrophe." *Romance Languages Annual* 4. West Lafayette, IN: Purdue Research Foundation, 1993. 599–604.

"A Poetics of Effacement: The Tradition of Antonio Machado's 'Caminante' Poem." *Neophilologus* 78 (1994): 407–18. http://dx.doi.org/10.1007/BF01000360

"From *Lazarillo de Tormes* to Dickens's *Our Mutual Friend*: The European Topography of *La vorágine.*" *Revista de Estudios Hispánicos* 28 (1994): 25–41.

"The Spanish Etymology of the English Novel." *Indiana Journal of Hispanic Literatures* 5 (1994): 291–305.

"Cervantes and the Paternity of the English Novel." *Cultural Authority in Golden Age Spain.* Ed. Marina Brownlee and Hans Ulrich Gumbrecht. Baltimore: Johns Hopkins UP, 1995. 165–77.

"Poetics and Economics in the 'Vida retirada' of Fray Luis de León." *Hispanic Review* 64 (1996): 149–69. http://dx.doi.org/10.2307/474645

"Epic Descent: The Filiations of Don Juan." *MLN* 111.2 (1996): 255–74. http://dx.doi.org/10.1353/mln.1996.0029

"The Sexual Economy of Miguel de Cervantes." *Bodies and Biases: Sexualities in Hispanic Cultures and Literatures.* Ed. David William Foster et al. Minneapolis: U of Minnesota P, 1996. 1–23.

"*Ut Pictura Poesis*: Self-Portrayal in the Plays of Juan del Enzina." *Brave New Words: Studies in Spanish Golden-Age Literature.* Ed. Edward H. Friedman and Catherine Larson. New Orleans: UP of the South, 1996. 1–18.

"The Antipodal Góngora: Sor Juana in *El sueño.*" *Homenaje a Don Luis Monguió.* Newark, DE: Juan de la Cuesta, 1997. 247–67.

"Sex and the Chain Gang." *Don Quijote.* Ed. Diana de Armas Wilson. New York: W. W. Norton, 1998. 805–10.

"Juan del Encina." *Encyclopedia of the Renaissance.* Vol. 2. New York: Charles Scribner's Sons, 1999. 269–70.

"Was Miguel de Cervantes a Homosexual?" *Lesbianism and Homosexuality in Early Modern Spain: Literature and Theater in Context.* Ed. Maria José Delgado and Alain Saint-Saëns. New Orleans: UP of the South, 2000. 395–417.

"Elective Affinities: Walter Scott and Miguel de Cervantes." *Cervantes for the 21st Century/Cervantes para el siglo XXI: Studies in Honor of Edward Dudley*. Ed. Francisco LaRubia-Prado. Newark, DE: Juan de la Cuesta: 2000. 199–220.

"'Error pintado': The Œdipal Emblematics of Lope de Vega's *El castigo sin venganza*." *"Never-Ending Adventure": Studies in Medieval and Early Modern Spanish Literature in Honor of Peter N. Dunn*. Ed. Edward Friedman and Harlan Sturm. Newark, DE: Juan de la Cuesta, 2002. 279–308.

"A Rhetorical and a Materialist Cervantes, Angst over the Married Female, and a Comparative Miscellany." *Renaissance Quarterly* 55.4 (2002): 1350–78.

"Francisco de Quevedo and the Poetic Matter of Patronage." *Objects of Culture in the Literature of Imperial Spain*. Ed. Mary Barnard and Frederick de Armas. Toronto: U of Toronto P, 2013. 181–202.

Book Reviews

Juan de la Cueva and the Portuguese Succession by Anthony Watson. *Romanic Review* 66 (1975): 244–45.

Studies in Tirso I: The Dramatist and His Competitors, 1620–26 by Ruth Lee Kennedy. *Revista Hispánica Moderna* 37.1–2 (1976): 62–63.

Las jarchas mozárabes y los comienzos de la lírica románica by Margit Frenk Alatorre. *Hispania* 60.2 (1977): 389.

Garcilaso de la Vega by Bernard Gicovate. *Modern Language Journal* 61.3 (1977): 152.

Tirso de Molina by Margaret Wilson and *Tirso and the Drama of the Counter Reformation* by Henry W. Sullivan. *MLN* 94.2 (1979): 428–31. http://dx.doi.org/10.2307/2906765

Cayetano Javier de Cabrera Quintero: Obras dramáticas by Claudia Parodi. *Latin American Theatre Review* 15.1 (1981): 95–97.

Four Comedies: Pedro Calderón de la Barca by Kenneth Muir. *Modern Philology* 79.4 (1982): 435.

Juan de Zabaleta: El diá de fiesta por la mañana y por la tarde by Cristóbal Cuevas García. *Hispanic Review* 53.4 (1985): 497–99. http://dx.doi.org/10.2307/473946

Pedro Calderón de la Barca: Una fiesta sacramental barroca by José María Díez Borque. *Hispanic Review* 54.2 (1986): 224.

El personaje dramático: Ponencias y debates de las VII jornadas de teatro clásico español (Almagro, 20 al 23 de septiembre, 1983) by Luciano García Lorenzo. *Hispanic Review* 55.2 (1987): 230.

The Bounds of Reason: Cervantes, Dostoevsky, Flaubert by Anthony Cascardi. *Cervantes* 7.2 (1987): 91–94.

Pedro Calderón de la Barca: Fieras afemina amor, edited by E. M. Wilson, D. W. Cruickshank, and C. C. D. Bainton. *Bulletin of Hispanic Studies* 64.1 (1987): 95–99.

The Return of Astraea: An Astral-Imperial Myth in Calderón by Frederick de Armas. *Hispanic Review* 56.2 (1988): 265.

Tirso de Molina: El vergonzoso en palacio by Enrique Rull. *Hispanic Review* 56.1 (1988): 110.

Diego Hurtado de Mendoza by David Darst. *Symposium* 44.2 (1990): 143–44.

Eléments pour une théorie du théâtre espagnol du XVIIe siècle by Marc Vitse. *MLN* 106.2 (1991): 448–50. http://dx.doi.org/10.2307/2904870

The Play of Power: Mythological Court Dramas of Calderón de la Barca by Margaret Rich Greer. *Romance Quarterly* 39.2 (1992): 255–57. http://dx.doi.org/10.1080/08831157.1992.10545002

Pedro Calderón de la Barca: The Schism in England(La cisma de Inglaterra), translated by Kenneth Muir and Ann L. MacKenzie. *Hispanic Review* 60.2 (1992): 224–25.

El mundo del teatro español en su Siglo de Oro: ensayos dedicados a John E. Varey, edited by J. M. Ruano de la Haza. *Bulletin of Hispanic Studies* 69.2 (1992): 194–95.

The Play of Allegory in the "Autos Sacramentales" of Pedro Calderón de la Barca by Barbara E. Kurtz. *Renaissance Quarterly* 46.2 (1993): 382–83. http://dx.doi.org/10.2307/3039077

The Poem on the Edge of the Word: The Limits of Language and the Uses of Silence in the Poetry of Mallarmé, Rilke, and Vallejo by Dianna C. Niebylski. *Yearbook of Comparative Literature* 42 (1993): 172–74.

Calderón y el barroco by María Alicia Amadei-Pulice. *Hispanic Review* 61.2 (1993): 282–84.

Structures from the Trivium in the Cantar de mío Cid by James Burke. *Speculum* 69.2 (1994): 439–41. http://dx.doi.org/10.2307/2865106

Don Juan and the Point of Honor by James Mandrell. *Revista Canadiense de Estudios Hispánicos* 19.1 (1994): 199–200.

The Sacred Game: The Role of the Sacred in the Genesis of Modern Literary Fiction by Cesáreo Bandera. *Cervantes* 15 (1995): 107–13.

Allegories of Kingship: Calderón and the Anti-Machiavellian Tradition by Stephen Rupp. *Hispanic Review* 65.4 (1997): 458–60. http://dx.doi.org/10.2307/474305

Garcilaso de la Vega and the Italian Renaissance by Daniel L. Heiple. *Revista de Estudios Hispánicos* 31.1 (1997): 138–39.

Irony and Theatricality in Tirso de Molina by Jane Albrecht. *Revista de Estudios Hispánicos* 31.1 (1997): 129–30.

Cervantes y/and Shakespeare: Nuevas interpretaciones y aproximaciones comparativas / New Interpretations and Comparative Approaches, edited by José Manuel González Fernández de Sevilla. *Bulletin of Spanish Studies* 87.1 (2010): 112–13.

Love Poetry in the Spanish Golden Age: Eros, Eris and Empire by Isabel Torres. *MLN* 130.2 (2015): 410–12. http://dx.doi.org/10.1353/mln.2015.0018

Radio Discussions
Soundings Project from the National Humanities Center

"Notions of the Tragic in Western Literature, Part 1 of 4." May 29, 1983.
"Notions of the Tragic in Western Literature, Part 2 of 4." June 12, 1983.
"Notions of the Tragic in Western Literature, Part 3 of 4." June 26, 1983.
"Notions of the Tragic in Western Literature, Part 4 of 4." July 24, 1983.
"The Art of Literary Biography, Part 7 of 7: Cather." March 18, 1984.
"The Gilded Age, Part 1 of 2; (2) Book Review of *History of the Idea of Progress*." April 29, 1984.
"The Gilded Age, Part 2 of 2: Henry Adams." May 6, 1984.
"Reader and Writer: French and Hispanic Literature." January 5, 1986.
"Accounting for the Novel, Part 1 of 2." December 7, 1986.
"Accounting for the Novel, Part 2 of 2." December 14, 1986.
"Crosscurrents." January 14, 1990.

Contributors' Biographies

William R. Blue is professor of Spanish at Pennsylvania State University. He has published three books and numerous essays on early modern Spanish drama. His main interests are the historical and artistic contexts of the plays and their potential impact on audiences. He recently coedited, with James A. Parr, a special issue of *Comparative Literature Studies* on *"Don Quijote" and 400 Years of World Literature*. He is a member of the editorial board of *Bulletin of the Comediantes* and is also on the board of the Association for Hispanic Classical Theater.

Edward H. Friedman is Gertrude Conaway Vanderbilt Professor of Spanish and comparative literature at Vanderbilt University, where he also serves as director of the Robert Penn Warren Center for the Humanities. His research focuses on early modern Spanish literature and contemporary narrative and drama. His books include studies of Cervantes's full-length plays, the figure of the antiheroine in literature, and the development of the novel in Spain. Among his recent publications are *Quixotic Haiku* (2014) and *Trading Up* (2015), based on Juan Ruiz de Alarcón's seventeenth-century comedy *Mudarse por mejorarse*. He has served as editor of the theater journal *Bulletin of the Comediantes* and is a past president of the Cervantes Society of America.

María Antonia Garcés is professor of Hispanic studies at Cornell University. A specialist in Cervantes and early modern Spanish literatures and cultures, her research interests focus on the encounters between the Cross and the Crescent in the sixteenth- and seventeenth-century Mediterranean. In 2003, Professor Garcés was awarded the James Russell Lowell Prize of the Modern Language Association of America for her book *Cervantes in Algiers: A Captive's Tale* (Vanderbilt University Press, 2002), a study of Cervantes's Algerian captivity (1575–1580) and its effects on his fiction. Her own revised and expanded translation of this book was published in Spain: *Cervantes en Argel: historia de un cautivo* (Gredos, 2005). Her archival research has produced another major project on the sociopolitical world of Algiers, with Professor Diana de Armas Wilson (translator): *An Early Modern Dialogue with Islam: Antonio de Sosa's Topography of Algiers (1612)* (University of Notre Dame Press, 2011).

Patricia Kenworthy, Professor Emerita of Hispanic studies at Vassar College, completed her doctorate, under the direction of Professor Robert ter Horst, at the University of Arizona. She has presented conference papers and has published articles on Cervantes and on the *Comedia*. Her most recent work has focused on recovering the staging conventions of *corral* performances.

Adrián Pérez Melgosa is associate professor of Hispanic languages and literature at Stony Brook University. His work centers on the transnational and cross-cultural dynamics that are registered in the cinema of Latin America and Spain. His articles have appeared in the journals *Social Text, Studies in Hispanic Cinemas, American Quarterly, Journal of Spanish Cultural Studies*, and *Latin American Literary Review*, among others. His book *Cinema and Inter-American Relations: Tracking Transnational Affect* appeared in 2012 (Routledge, reprinted 2014). He coedited the collection *Revisiting Jewish Spain in the Modern Era* (Routledge 2013). He is currently at work on a manuscript about the pedagogies of migrant identities and the representation of the immigrant body in the cinema of the Americas.

Kirsten F. Nigro is professor of Spanish at the University of Texas at El Paso. She has also taught at the University of Arizona, Arizona State University, Miami University of Ohio, and the University of Cincinnati. Professor Nigro has published widely in the field of Latin American and Mexican theater, women's theater, the theory of drama, and US-Mexico border themes related to performance and violence against women. She has been awarded various grants from the National Endowment for the Humanities and from the Mexican government; she also has been a Fulbright scholar twice, most recently in Tijuana, Mexico.

Randolph Pope is the Commonwealth Professor of Spanish and comparative literature at the University of Virginia, where he has served as chair of Spanish, Italian, and Portuguese (2004–2007) and director of Comparative Literature (2008–2011). He is currently director of Graduate Studies in Spanish. Born in Chile, he studied Spanish literature and classics at the Universidad Católica de Valparaíso. He received an MA and PhD in Spanish from Columbia University. His field of specialization is the peninsular novel and autobiography, but he has also written extensively on other topics such as Latin American literature, cultural studies, literature and architecture, literature and the arts, and literature and philosophy. His most recent publication is *¿Porqué España? Memoria* *personal del hispanismo estado unidense* (Galaxia Gutenberg, 2015), coedited with Anna Caballé of the University of Barcelona.

Eleanor ter Horst is associate professor and chair of the Department of Modern and Classical Languages and Literature at the University of South Alabama, where she teaches courses in French, German, and comparative literature. Her research interests include comparative literary studies and the reception of the classics in eighteenth- and nineteenth-century German and French literature. She is the author of a book, *Lessing, Goethe, Kleist and the Transformation of Gender: From Hermaphrodite to Amazon*, and numerous articles on the topics of comparative literature, gender and sexuality studies, and classical reception. She has also researched and published in the area of interdisciplinary foreign-language pedagogy.

Florence Byham Weinberg, a native of New Mexico, received her BA (1954) from Park College (now Park University), MA in Spanish literature and history from the University of British Columbia (1962), and PhD in French literature from the University of Rochester (1968). She taught at that university, at St. John Fisher College, and at Trinity University for thirty-six years, publishing four scholarly books on French Renaissance subjects and on the archetype of the cave from Homer to Ariosto. Since retirement, she has published ten historical novels and is writing the eleventh, featuring the Battle of the Alamo from a Hispanic (Tejana) woman's point of view. She was married to eminent literary scholar, comparatist, and critic, Professor Kurt Weinberg, for forty-three years until his death in 1996.

Diana de Armas Wilson, Professor Emerita in Renaissance studies at the University of Denver, now lives in Boulder, Colorado. She is an NEH translator for Antonio de Sosa's *Topografía e historia general de Argel (1612)*, with volume 1 now published as *An Early Modern Dialogue with Islam: Antonio de Sosa's* Topography of Algiers *(1612)*, and volume 2 in progress. She is the author of *Allegories of Love: Cervantes's "Persiles and Sigismunda"* (Princeton University Press, 1991) and *Cervantes, The Novel, and the New World* (Oxford University Press, 2000). She is sole editor of the Norton Critical Edition of *Don Quijote* (1999), and will be editing Norton's second edition.

Ali Shehzad Zaidi is associate professor of humanities at the State University of New York at Canton, where he teaches courses in world literature, civilization, and Spanish language. He holds a PhD and an MA in comparative literature from the University of Rochester, an MA in Spanish literature from Queens College (City University of New York), and an MA in English literature from the University of Peshawar (Pakistan). His comparative studies on the plays of Shakespeare and Calderón have appeared in publications such as *Studies in Philology* and *Hispanófila*.

Freshman-class photograph
Princeton
1947

Commissioned ensign
USNR, OCS
Newport, RI
March 1953

Robert and Eleanor M. ter Horst
Tuscan, AZ
1971

Photo to accompany article in
*Calderón de la Barca at the
Tercentenary:
Comparative Views* 1981

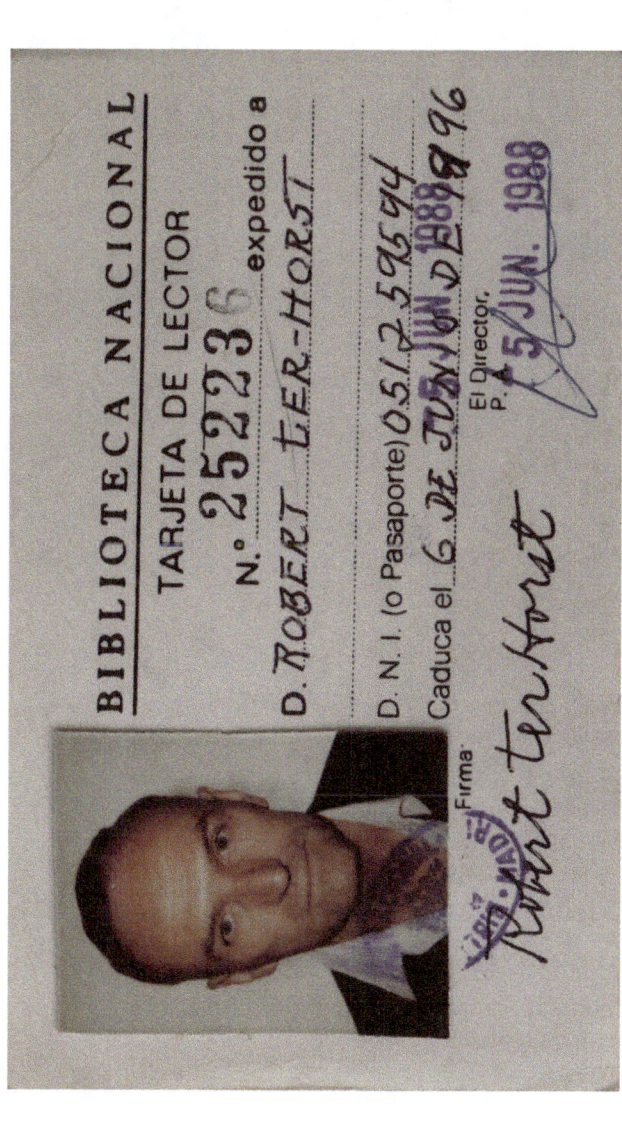

"Sometimes I wonder if Robert doesn't spend too much time with his books. I think there are times when he would benefit by forgetting them."
—Ruth B. Winters
(R's sixth-grade teacher)

Reception at University of South Alabama
with daughter Eleanor E. ter Horst
2015